IN GOVERNMENT WE TRUST

WARWICK FUNNELL is Professor of Accounting at the University of Kent and the University of Wollongong. He is also Visiting Professor of Accounting at the University of Newcastle upon Tyne, where he is a member of the Cultures, Imperialism and Accounting Practice Research Group. He has written extensively on the impact of the marketisation of the state upon the accountability of governments. His book, *Government by Fiat: The Retreat from Responsibility* was published by UNSW Press in 2000.

ROBERT JUPE, MA, PGCE, CPFA, is Senior Lecturer in Accounting at the University of Kent. He has written extensively on the origins and consequences of Britain's fundamentally flawed privatisation of the rail industry, and on how New Labour's Third Way approach to public services has led to the increased marketisation of the state.

JANE ANDREW is a Senior Lecturer in Accounting at the University of Wollongong. Her keen interest in the consequences of modern capitalism has driven her research in environmental accounting and the privatisation of prisons.

IN GOVERNMENT WE TRUST

MARKET FAILURE AND THE DELUSIONS OF PRIVATISATION

WARWICK FUNNELL
ROBERT JUPE
JANE ANDREW

PLUTO PRESS
www.plutobooks.com

First published in the UK 2009 by Pluto Press
345 Archway Road, London N6 5AA
and in Australia, New Zealand and Oceania by UNSW Press
UNSW, Sydney, New South Wales 2052 Australia
as part of the ANZSOG Program in Government, Politics and Public Management

www.plutobooks.com

British Library Cataloguing in Publication Data
A catalogue record for this book is available from the British Library

ISBN   978 0 7453 2908 6   Hardback
ISBN   978 0 7453 2907 9   Paperback

Library of Congress Cataloging in Publication Data application pending.

CONTENTS

PREFACE

Pour gouverner mieux, il faudrait gouverner moins.
[To govern better, one must govern less.]

(Marquis d'Argenson, 1751)

This book is a critique of the continuing marketisation of government. Its central thesis is that government deserves to be, and should be, recognised as a more positive economic and social participant than it has been portrayed by the neoliberal evangelists of market virtue who have refashioned much of government and society over the past three decades. Despite the magnitude and supposed success of these transformations in a number of Western democracies, experience has shown that the presumption that the market can outperform the public sector in delivering services efficiently and reliably may be far too simplistic and an unwarranted distortion of the significant, even unique, contributions of the public sector. Exploring these concerns across an international landscape, with particular reference to Britain and Australia, this book examines the social and political consequences of the retreat of government engineered by neoliberal beliefs. It highlights the disappointment with economic justifications and motivations which made the private sector and the promises of neoliberalism so attractive to many governments.

The breadth and dogmatic exclusiveness of neoliberalism has meant that it has not only transformed government but also society in Anglo-American states by imposing market values as social values to ensure a supportive, unquestioning community. A decade ago Feigenbaum and his co-writers in their book *Shrinking the State* believed that it was 'premature to determine empirically the effects of relatively recent privatisation initiatives'.[1] Since then, sufficient difficulties associated with the marketisation of the state have been exposed to refute this suggestion. Prominent market failures have confirmed the legitimate contributions of government to the well-being of a nation. They have also confirmed that there are some things only governments can and should do.

The transformation of many liberal democratic states from the 1980s according to the dictates of market principles – the process referred to here as the marketisation of the state – was propelled by the seductive inducements and promises of those who believed in the moral and practical superiority of markets. With each new proposal to shift responsibility for the provision of essential, core government services from the state to the private sector, the same motivations and justifications derived from the principles of the free market were present, irrespective of location. However, while the process of marketisation of the state in Australia and Britain bore many similarities, their different histories and political forms meant that they have often varied in the extent and nature of this replacement. In particular, the unitary form of government in Britain which centralised most authority and policy at Westminster ensured that any privatisations of public services and assets would be readily and comprehensively implemented. Thus, the dramatic refashioning of much of the British state in the image of the market provides the more extreme examples of the consequences of the market failing to fulfil the expectations advocated on its behalf by its impassioned supporters.

In contrast, the marketisation of the Australian state has been far less comprehensive. Australia is a federation of largely autonomous states with specific powers enshrined in the Australian Constitution, and which are often governed at any one time by political parties with very different political beliefs and commitment to markets. Accordingly, in Australia the process of marketisation was to be more varied and uneven in the range of services which would be relinquished by the governments. Most notably, unlike Britain and America, services relinquished by government in Australia have tended to be other than core public services. Thus, in late 2008 in New South Wales, Western Australia and Tasmania, the retail electricity companies, the generators and electricity transmission infrastructure were still state-owned. In the Australian Capital Territory the government and private partners share equally the ownership of retail electricity companies, whereas the electricity industry was fully privatised in Victoria and South Australia in the 1990s.[2] Australian states such as Victoria and New South Wales, which happened to have market-driven Liberal governments in power during the 1990s when the neoliberal transformation of states reached its peak, experienced the greatest market penetration in the provision of services which were once the exclusive domain of government.

The transformation of public services and the motivations for this have produced a vast body of research related to the unique experiences of each country.[3] No attempt is made here to replicate this research. Instead, the intention is, first, to highlight the more significant commonalities in justifications derived from market principles which have driven the reform programs of many liberal democratic states. The contributions of early liberal theorists and economists are shown in Part I to have been especially influential both in their enduring analysis of the principles upon which markets operate and in their beliefs about the legitimate functions of government. The same justifications have been used across states to compel governments to abdicate responsibility to the private sector and to the purportedly more virtuous and trustworthy workings of markets free from the distortions of political intervention. Thus, the justifications used by the New South Wales government in its privatisation proposals for the electricity industry in 2008 echoed in principle and in detail those most often used by others who had similar exalted expectations of the private sector in industries which historically have had a strong government presence. The government proclaimed that the people of New South Wales would benefit as a result of the competitive pressures of the market by a reduction in electricity prices, a higher quality service which would result from the opportunity for private firms to invest in infrastructure assets, and reduced public debt.

The universality of these justifications among those liberal democratic governments which have engaged most vigorously with the promises of market fundamentalists reflect a belief that markets have an unchanging and incorruptible nature which, with the right encouragement, can only but create great good for all. Throughout Part II of this work, however, the reasons given by governments to relinquish responsibility for both delivering and paying for core public services are shown too often to have been deceptive and self-serving. In chapters covering three areas of marketisation – transport infrastructure in Britain, the essential public utilities of electricity and water, and private prisons – the recurrent failures of privatisation have established that it is not the panacea promised. British trains are now both more costly and far less reliable than when under public control, while privatised water and electricity providers have also abused their market power, against the public interest. Utility prices have risen dramatically and the resulting profits have been diverted to shareholders, rather than invested in infrastructure – which was amongst the most compelling reasons for privatisation.

THE STATE UNDER SIEGE

> The administration of Government differs, and must necessarily differ, from the activities of the business world, both in the objects to which it is directed, in the criteria of its success, in the necessary conditions under which it is conducted, and the choice of instruments which it employs ... There are certain crucial values which must underlie public administration ... traditional standards of probity and integrity should not be relaxed in order to secure economy and efficiency.
> (House of Commons, *Report on the Civil Service*, 1994)

This study scrutinises the hopes and the extravagant promises which were made by those who championed a greater presence for private motives and disciplines in the provision of government services over the past three decades in Anglo-American states, and the consequent realities of their reforms. For Will Hutton in 1995 the 'overall judgement on the market experiment must be at best mixed, at worst negative'.[1] By 2002, Hutton was far less ambivalent, arguing that 'Any rational calculation of the overall costs and benefits of the whole ...

5

experiment must give a negative result'.[2] Indeed, throughout the liberal democracies in which the reforms have been most pronounced, there is mounting disquiet with the social and political consequences of aggressive free-market philosophies that have transformed government and society. Those individuals most affected have been left feeling vulnerable and apprehensive as their governments have seemingly abandoned them to the selfishness of the market. Concern has been increasingly expressed about 'our threadbare public transport, the casualisation of workplaces, deepening concerns about the anxious state of modern childhood, rising personal debt and an all-pervasive feeling that our lives are running out of control'.[3] Lawson, among many other social commentators, refers to the way in which the prioritisation of the market over the needs of society has diminished social cohesion, creating an anxious and isolated citizenry: 'Today we stand alone, without the bonds of solidarity and community to withstand the onslaught of global competition' and the market.[4] After a spate of particularly brutal murders in 2007 and a marked rise in anti-social behaviour, the British Conservative Party declared that 'social breakdown' was the big question facing British society.[5]

As market principles have been extended into almost every aspect of daily life in many advanced economies, there is a well recognised crisis of public trust resulting from an increasing number of particularly high-level failures in private sector services which had been previously delivered by government. These crises have confirmed the enduring contributions of governments to the well-being of their citizens, and that the state is not always the villain of the free-market advocates. Hutton now calls for the restoration of public purpose to politics.[6]

In an age of international terrorism and global internet crime, the responsibility of governments for the welfare of their citizens has assumed greater prominence and urgency. This is reflected in the ever-increasing expenditure by governments, as opposed to the reduction promoted by neoliberalism. Hibou believes that 'more than ever', especially after the September 2001 terrorist attacks in New York, there are calls for the state to champion the public interest.[7] Even the strongest supporters of the market have been reminded that governments after all may have a much more important role than simply providing the institutional skeleton necessary for markets to operate efficiently. The *State of the Future* survey conducted by the World Federation of United Nations Associations reported in September 2007 that global organised crime had become so successful that it now threatened to undermine the very foundations of democratic institutions in the wealthiest nations. According to the survey, organised crime was now amongst the greatest threats to the future of the planet with only strong, timely action by governments providing any hope of protection.

A book such as this, which highlights the virtues of government in the delivery of some services, would have faced a predominantly hostile audience in the last decades of the twentieth century – during the ascendancy and early hegemony of the neoliberal marketisation of government and society in many Western liberal democracies. Today, however, with the rising financial, social and human cost of a number of critical yet privatised services which have failed spectacularly, the mood of the public is now less ready to condemn government.[8] Indeed, the timely intervention of government which has avoided or ameliorated catastrophes originating in the private sector has seen a growing awareness of the value of the contributions of government. In the wake of September 11, formerly influential neoconservative thinker Frances Fukuyama now criticises the overly zealous neoliberal program for undermining the ability of states to carry out the essential 'residual' functions of government which ensure domestic and foreign security according to the rule of law. Milton Friedman, who had advised rich and poor countries alike to 'privatise, privatise, privatise', was sufficiently shaken by the attacks on New York and the Pentagon to concede that 'It turns out that the rule of law is probably more basic than privatisation'.[9]

In the later decades of the twentieth century, as governments succumbed to the persuasive priorities of free markets, they reduced the level of their intrusion in markets and transferred many of their functions to the private sector, most prominently through the sale of public assets – that is, privatisation. As a result, many Western governments have significantly diminished their presence in airlines,

·hospitals, employment agencies, coastline surveillance, prisons, lotter-
ies, electricity distribution, water services, aged and invalid care, telecommunications, ports, roads, public transport, court security and
railways. The international compass of this reform has been far from
homogeneous, however, especially in Europe where there has been a
sharp difference in attitude towards reform between Britain, which
has followed a model similar to Australia's, and northern European
states such as Norway and, until 2007, Sweden.

While the partial sale by the British government of British Petroleum in 1977 was one of the first significant instances of the wave
of privatisations throughout the world, privatisation is by no means
a recent phenomenon. Unlike the present ideologically driven programs of privatisation, earlier privatisations appear to have been more
random in occurrence.[10] Privatisation started very early in Australia,
for instance, when the transportation of convicts and settlers to Australia was taken out of government hands and awarded to private
contractors. There were disastrous results, and the British Government was eventually forced to resume control of the transport ships.[11]
Privatisations also occurred in Australia during the 1920s, when a
number of government war-time industries and enterprises, including
the Commonwealth Shipping Line, were sold.[12] These privatisations,
however, were but isolated occurrences and not part of a coherent
program of privatisation. They were also not consistent with the otherwise strong government presence thought necessary in a nation-
building state, at least until the 1980s.

In the early stages of recent privatisations, withdrawal of government from those activities which were most often the province of
the private sector, such as office cleaning, caused comparatively little
angst with the public. Less well received has been the withdrawal
from activities which have been accepted as core or 'sovereign' services
of government.[13] Thus, in the first wave of the extensive privatisations
in the 1980s and early 1990s in Australia, government corporations
which were already operating in a commercial environment, such as
Telecom (Telstra), the Commonwealth Bank and Qantas, were among
the first to be either partially or fully sold. Also popular at this time
with both state and federal governments in Australia was the sale of

state banks and government insurance offices. In Victoria, the Liberal Kennett government was notable as a pioneer in the privatisation of major public utilities. By 1996, Victoria's State Electricity Corporation had been divided into five separate, corporatised distribution and generation companies which were eventually sold for A$8.8 billion.[14] By the late 1990s, the proceeds of privatisation in Australia had amounted to A$61 billion, thereby placing Australia amongst the leaders of privatisation in the world.[15] For the years 1990 to 1997, Australia was second only to the United Kingdom in the value of privatisations.[16] Especially influential in legitimising the transformation of the Australian public sector over the past two decades were the recommendations of the Independent Committee of Inquiry on National Competition Policy (the 'Hilmer Report') in 1993, with the National Commission of Audit in 1996 providing further persuasive impetus.[17]

Throughout Western democracies, protests about the wisdom of the scale, content and speed of public-sector reforms – which were frequently criticised as dangerous experiments with the potential for unforeseen, even unimagined, consequences – had little effect on either the pace of change or the reach of market innovations. Critics have referred to the Thatcher reforms in Britain as being based upon theories which were really only working hypotheses, rather than proven experience and hard evidence. With recent unprecedented corporate collapses such as Enron, the failure of some critical privatised services to match expectations of cost and quality of service, and audacious terrorist attacks in Britain, the United States and Spain, governments and their citizens are no longer so inured to these complaints. Contrary to the persuasive protestations of neoliberals, and especially those who justified their opposition to state provision of services on the economic grounds of public choice theory, within a decade of the privatisation revolution in government some observers were pointing to pervasive market failures that were emerging – failures which contradicted the very reason for the marketisation of the state and which were proving to be compelling reasons for the return of the state.

The rising social and economic toll of market failures has confirmed, as demonstrated in part II of this book, the benefits of some government interventions and the dangers of unfettered markets. Consequent public anxiety has led to legislation to better regulate the freedoms of the market. Governments have also been forced to re-enter services only recently delegated to the private sector, with railways in Britain particularly noteworthy in this regard. While regulation in many guises had been a feature of the relationship between government and the private sector since the nineteenth century, the extent of regulation in the later twentieth century was unusual and refuted the extreme views of market fundamentalists that markets always worked best without any interference. However, despite the significant problems and disappointments following the privatisation of public assets and the withdrawal of government from direct responsibility for the delivery of other services, neoliberal remedies continue to be promoted without reference to the empirical realities of the changes, of which some of the more arresting are examined here.

Failures by private firms to deliver the essential services for which they assumed responsibility have confirmed that, irrespective of the financial advantages advocated for free markets, ultimate responsibility for providing high-quality essential services will always remain with government. The conclusive, irrevocable transfer of operational and financial risk to the private sector for many services – a substantive and popular reason given for privatisation – is a fictitious impossibility. According to the Victorian Public Accounts and Estimates Committee, most risks cannot be separated from the responsibilities of government.[18] Although governments promoted the values, habits and disciplines of the market as the salvation for an increasingly costly and purportedly inefficient public sector, in many instances they have been required to intercede after the market has subsequently failed to deliver.[19] This is the paradox which this study explores: that, while the market was supposed to perform better than the public sector, a growing number of private sector service providers have revealed themselves to be less proficient and less reliable than government in the delivery of core public services. The distress of Railtrack in Britain, which saw the intervention of government in 2001 to ensure that rail services were maintained (discussed in chapter 4), and the attempt in July 2007 by the public authority Transport for London to assume

responsibility for the operation of that part of the London Underground operated by the failed contractor Metronet,[20] provide prominent examples of the potentially serious consequences of the failure
of privatised bodies and confirm the ultimate obligation of government to assume responsibility for services. Similar consequences were
manifested in the late 1990s when the profit motive corroded the ability of the Australian government's corporatised Civil Aviation and
Safety Authority to ensure the highest standards of safety for airlines,
with tragic and avoidable results which saw the regulatory role of the
authority again clearly separated from any commercial responsibilities. In 2005, in another blow to the credibility of privatising governments, the New South Wales government was forced to resume
responsibility for the Port Macquarie Base Hospital from the private
firm Mayne which had operated the hospital since 1994.

Notwithstanding the criticisms levelled in this book, we do not
see the changes to the public sector resulting from the introduction
of market values to the delivery of public services as entirely without merit. On the contrary, throughout history great benefit has been
obtained from many successful relationships between the public and
private spheres. Thus, our purpose is not to denounce the private
sector and markets, irrespective of any litany of failures. Rather, we
critique some of the interventions by the private sector in government domains which subsequently have proved to be ill-considered.
The aim is to identify some significant disappointments in core public
services which indicate that marketisation has been taken too far and,
thereby, suggest whether recent highly prominent market failures have
established that there are indeed limits to the substitution of government by the private sector in modern liberal democracies, irrespective of the political complexion of government. Too often the scale of
corporate failures involving the provision of public services has also
exposed communities and governments to increased social, economic
and political instability as a result of the massive costs involved in
governments re-establishing services or seeking redress on behalf of
aggrieved citizens. The benefits once provided by government services
are not easily or economically retrieved.

This study examines those services which until recently have been generally regarded as core or 'sovereign' government responsibilities by most liberal theorists and governments, most importantly basic education, defence, policing, prisons, public health, public transport and economic infrastructure – activities that ensure a stable, productive and secure society. The intention is not to provide a global and exhaustive assessment of the successes, which are many, or of the failures. Neither will our observations primarily follow the justifications of prominent economists; rather they are informed by the fundamental roles expected of government as advanced by the political theorists who have been the most influential in driving and legitimating the marketisation of the state. This book is teleological, in that it examines government in terms of its ends, some of which have been reconfirmed as incompatible with a market culture.

The state vilified

Throughout history each age has had its villains and its miscreants, its heroes and saviours. For much of the twentieth century it was the turn of governments in liberal democratic states to increasingly assume a mantle of virtue as the provision of social welfare, and public services by governments accelerated the momentum of reform which had begun in the late nineteenth century. This was especially noticeable in Great Britain, parts of Europe, countries such as Australia and New Zealand which Britain had spawned as part of its empire, and to a much lesser extent the United States. While the roots of the welfare state lay in the late nineteenth and early twentieth centuries, its rise to maturity occurred after World War II during a period of unprecedented prosperity. It was no coincidence that after a war in which many millions died, and the remainder endured years of sacrifice and uncertainty, the citizens in the victorious states expected that their governments would recognise and reward their contributions. As increasingly affluent governments took on more responsibilities in response to these demands, expenditure grew quickly as a proportion of gross domestic product, as did the number and variety of agencies used by governments to fulfil their responsibilities. A century of expansion in the influence and compass of state responsibilities continued in liberal democracies until the 1970s when many governments abruptly and decisively changed direction, and embarked on a program of public sector reform which sought to challenge and denigrate belief in the virtue of state intervention and to force the retreat of government from the daily lives of its citizens.

The apparently unrestrained growth of the welfare state throughout the twentieth century was seen by its predominantly liberal critics as an alarming escalation of state intervention which had delivered very little at great financial and social cost. According to the state's fiercest critics, the state was incapable of doing much that would benefit its citizens apart from removing itself as much as possible from their lives and allowing the private sector to redress the imperfections and failings of the state. For Savas, whose views are representative of those who favour a minimal state, the state's 'extensive collectivization of goods … that were heretofore considered private goods … has resulted in excessive waste and … has failed to achieve reasonable expectations'.[21] Offe, in a comprehensive denunciation of state intrusion, was also critical of how:

> excessive statism often inculcates dispositions of dependency, inactivity, rent seeking, red tape, absenteeism, authoritarianism, cynicism, fiscal irresponsibility, avoidance of accountability, lack of initiative, and hostility to innovation, if not outright corruption.[22]

The inability of Keynesian economics to deal with the 'stagflation' of the 1970s – simultaneously rapid inflation and faltering economic growth – allowed competing monetarist remedies both greater credibility and the opportunity to establish themselves as the legitimate successor to demand-side economics. Although it has taken three decades to expose the hollowness of this response to Keynesianism, the coincident world credit and oil crises in 2008 have created the previously derided possibility of stagflation returning.[23] In the 1970s, strident and influential public sector critics such as Niskanen, Tullock and Buchanan argued that the allegedly selfish, utility-maximising behaviour of state bureaucrats was the source of much of the stress experienced in public services and of the distress of taxpayers and those dependent upon state services. Peters, however, found that such criticisms of the capacity of the state to act in the best interests of its citizens were 'excessively pessimistic'. He argued they are 'at best vague and tailored to meet the particular demands of the moment', as well as being used to further the interests of those with the most to gain from any marketisation initiatives.[24]

According to this view, government, contrary to what the public choice theorists would have us believe, is not overwhelmingly about self-interest. Further, even if criticisms of the extent of the self-interest of public servants were sustainable, when a major crisis occurs in practice it matters little how much politicians and bureaucrats may have been accustomed to prosecuting their own interests, fostering the well-being of the public becomes unavoidable if they are to retain their legitimacy. Thus, should a hurricane devastate large sections of heavily populated cities, as did Katrina at New Orleans in 2005, the public will insistently and unforgivingly remind their politicians and bureaucrats of their public interest obligations. There is far less tolerance for government failure than tolerance for market failure.[25] The empowerment of a select few by the majority, who then trust the elected and the appointed to behave in a manner which furthers the public's best interests, leads to widespread and ready intolerance of any perceived betrayals. In the market place it generally matters little if businesses get things wrong 10 per cent of the time. What is important are the final results, the overall outcome, the other 90 per cent. In stark contrast, in government it is the 10 per cent of the time when things go wrong which might matter most, not the 90 per cent of things that are done right.

From the 1970s, in the face of ever-mounting criticisms of the seemingly inexhaustible propensity of governments to increase their responsibilities at the expense of taxpayers, governments of most political beliefs in liberal democracies retreated from service provision. Their place was taken by private providers who were expected to be motivated in their actions by the selfish pursuit of their own interests. This was meant to be the guarantee that both directly and indirectly all would benefit: those who received the services and those who had previously paid for them. Privatisation was promoted as a powerful antidote to the economic ossification and mismanagement of moribund government administrators who were supposedly more concerned about their pensions and perquisites than the public interest. Amongst the most successful and influential supporters of privatisation and of smaller government were Osborne and Gaebler, whose book *Reinventing Government* was seized upon and popularised by neoliberals and right-leaning governments in the 1980s because it provided the apparent empirical evidence alluded to, but not provided, by public choice theorists. *Reinventing Government* was an unapologetic polemic of private virtues and public evils. Hayek's *The Road to Serfdom* was also highly influential, with British prime minister Margaret Thatcher reportedly giving each of her ministers a copy. The greater competition and contestability in public service provision enforced by the unforgiving drive of a self-interested market was praised by reformists as the means to allow citizens greater choice, lower prices and better services, in part a result of the incentives to invest which the profit motive encourages. The mantra of choice and the unique, unrivalled ability of the market to create choices, has been especially successful as a persuasive principle of neoliberal reforms, even for 'new' labour governments, despite the fact its underlying deceitfulness – that there is often no real choice, or individuals do not have the financial capability to exercise a choice – has been regularly exposed.[26]

Early in the privatisation campaign, the advocates of reform sought to construct a faultless image of the private alternative in order to dislodge faith in the state.[27] They sought to compensate for the deficiencies of the state, which were exaggerated as legion by public choice theorists (discussed in chapter 3), through the ability of the market to remedy these faults. Only an image of absolute virtue would do in these circumstances, for to do otherwise may not have been a sufficient reason to dislodge the entrenched status quo. The private sector had to be seen to promise to be everything to everyone to gain sufficient momentum for revolutionary change, for this is what was sought. This attitude was very prominent in the British government's highly controversial support in 1994 for the privatisation of air traffic control services. The Minister for Aviation and Shipping declared that experience 'has shown that even where opportunities for competition are limited, there are good reasons to believe that the transfer of ownership should *of itself* produce economic benefits ... Privatisation can also be expected to lead to more innovation and responsiveness to customer needs.'[28]

Although reformist governments may have had few concerns about contracting out or privatising essential or sensitive services, such as prisons, many others outside government have raised concerns about diminished accountability and threats to the public's safety and welfare, especially when there was the potential for the vaunted profit motive to conflict with the public interest.[29] Many critics are especially uneasy with the tendency for organisations motivated by profit to hide any problems which may have unpalatable consequences for the wider community. Somewhat pessimistically, Giddens has observed how a 'society that allows the market to infiltrate too far into other institutions will experience a failure of public life'.[30] Whitfield similarly laments the way in which:

> The concept of collective responsibility, the importance of democratic control of the state, the expression of care for others in the way we go about our lives ... were all devalued in the 1980s. Health and safety was regulated in the interests of balanced budgets and accountancy notions of efficiency ... Social needs, equality, democracy, public interest and justice has a low priority.[31]

The difficulty in determining the boundaries between the market and the state, and how far reform should proceed, was recognised by Hayek. He pointed out that 'When a conflict arises between the basic principles of a libertarian order and what appear to be unquestioned necessities of governmental policy ... we still lack adequate theoretical principles for a satisfactory solution of some of the problems which arise in this field'.[32] Similarly, Tullock noted that 'no one can say with certainty exactly what should be left to the market and what should be undertaken by government'.[33] Our exploration here of the state reformed in the image of the market does not attempt to provide any absolute answers about the relative merits of state and private provision of services, nor does it seek to judge the efficacy of the reforms other than on the basis of the results promoted by reformists, both inside government and elsewhere. That which was promised by liberal theorists and politicians will be compared with the consequences; the promises of the zealots will be the standard used to identify and judge the success of some key reforms. With no end in sight to these reforms, or even a significant diminution of reformist momentum, this book is therefore a journey and not a destination. It does present the view, however, that in the marketisation of core responsibilities of the state, in the exposure of publicly provided services to market contestability and values, the resulting limits to the market state become apparent.

The vagaries of market virtue

The conceptions of the state informing the transformation of government in Westminster democracies owe more to nineteenth-century liberal theorists and their utilitarian notions of the state than to the historical trajectory of the twentieth century. These prescriptions are best known today under the rubric neoliberalism, a convenient term which encompasses a diverse array of theoretical justifications for a minimal state that have proven over the past three decades to be extremely persuasive in influencing government reform. Neoliberal theories for good government question the extent to which the state should be made responsible for the welfare of its citizens and how best to deliver those services which are accepted as the legitimate concern of government. Freedom to pursue one's self-interest and the exercise of compulsion by outside bodies such as government are mutually exclusive for the neoliberal. While neoliberals may want market principles and discipline to be insinuated in as much of government as is possible, at the same time they know that in the last resort no government would ever let essential, core services fail completely. Prior to the onslaught of neoliberal reforms, governments took responsibility for tempering the worst excesses of the market in the public interest. Neoliberalism interprets the public interest as reducing government interventions and allowing the operation of the market to benefit as many 'consumers' as is possible.

Neoliberalism justifies its prescriptions with the need to ensure individual liberty above everything else. By releasing the restrictions which have bound individual initiative throughout the long night of the welfare state and which had been encouraged by Keynesian demand economics, individuals are allowed to use their initiative to develop their potential. For the neoliberal, it is not the place of government to set goals for individuals or to force upon its citizens the government's conception of 'the good life'.[34] Freeing individuals from the cloying interference and paternalism of government, contend Friedman and Hayek, is the only means to gain access to all the possible benefits which naturally flow from the individual's free will and the energies of their initiative.[35] The greatest strength of the private sector is seen to be its freedom from most of the stultifying organisational and decision-making restraints which afflict the public sector. However, this freedom has frequently come at a cost.

Contrary to the confident promises of neoliberals, after three decades of the marketisation of the state and society, citizens in liberal democratic states who have experienced the greatest impacts of neoliberal reforms, including in Australia, Britain and New Zealand, are far more apprehensive about the future and about the professed virtue of the market. Britain, where the pace of marketisation has been amongst the fastest and most penetrating, is criticised as a society where:

> Market rule has recoiled on the state's finances; as the polarisation of
> society has worsened, public spending on crime, health and specialised
> education has increased, and social security spending itself … has
> ballooned as poverty drives millions through the drab waiting rooms
> of the rump welfare state'.[36]

Examination of the newspapers and even a cursory acquaintance with the electronic media reveal a widespread, persistent and deepening sense of despondency and alienation amongst many sections of society. The elderly and the young have been shown to be especially vulnerable in societies where many of the long-standing social taboos have broken down and in which the temperance afforded society by the observance of basic social manners is no longer as certain. In Britain these concerns were recognised by the Blair government with its 'respect agenda' – policies designed to promote good behaviour amongst the youth in public places.

A major UNICEF study reported in early 2007 that of 21 advanced economies that it had examined, Britain ranked last on most measures of the well-being of its children. Of the states surveyed, the report identified British children as suffering the greatest physical deprivations, the worst health, the most dysfunctional relationships with adults, and as being exposed to the greatest risks from alcohol, drugs and unsafe sex.[37] Al Aynsley Green, the children's commissioner for England, believed that the study indicated that there 'is a crisis at the heart of our society'.[38] Possibly more surprising, the United States was ranked only slightly above Britain on most of these measures. The other similarity between Britain and the United States, according to the UNICEF study, is that they both embraced the neoliberal reforms of the past three decades with greatest gusto. By contrast, northern European states such as Denmark, Finland and Norway, which chose not to sacrifice their social democratic credentials to the more demanding aspects of neoliberalism, occupied the highest positions on measures of the well-being of their children.[39] Coincident with the UNICEF report, a study by the British right-wing think-tank Civitas concluded that there was a widespread perception that Britain was plagued by high levels of crime and a culture of dependency that had widened and deepened over the last three decades, the period of greatest affluence and the period in which the marketisation of the British state, and thus society, had occurred.[40]

Informed by neoliberal ideological prescriptions, each new economic alarm brings with it more job uncertainty and the deterioration of employment conditions as firms are urged to become more globally competitive by cutting their employment costs.[41] As the workforce becomes increasingly casualised, expectations of a career with a well-recognised progression of positions and long-term security as a reward for faithful, effective performance are dashed by the realisation by most new workers, and many of those currently with a full-time job, that their future will be far less predictable and more chaotic. Soon after the election in July 2007 of Nicolas Sarkozy as president of France, who promised to reform the public services by forcing greater market discipline, these concerns led to widespread strike action as workers attempted to protect their working conditions and their right to the state's benevolence.

Polly Toynbee, a prominent journalist and noted advocate of a stronger state presence, has argued that the state's acceptance of the burdens of the welfare of citizens, especially those in most need, is what makes a society civilised. In a powerful attack on the motives of the private sector in the unconvincing pursuit of the public interest, she warns that for the state to abdicate more of its responsibilities to the market, while allowing the market to operate with less regulatory intervention, would be to place everyone in jeopardy. The legal duty of firms to maximise their value to their shareholders compels them to 'poison, maim, cheat and exploit in the pursuit of profit ... [Business] hardly makes a good case for entrusting more public services to the mercies of the market when, red in tooth and claw, it demands ... low taxes and the freedom to do what [it] likes'.[42] Hutton has also called for governments to use their democratic authority on behalf of their constituents to reassert control over the markets, while Hobsbawn warns that no less than 'the fate of humanity in the new millennium [will] depend on the restoration of public authorities'.[43] Referring to the amorality of markets, Giddens, whose contributions to debates about the role of the state are mostly remembered through his advocacy of a 'third way', cautions that:

> Excessive dependence on market mechanisms has to be avoided. ...
> Markets can breed a commercialism that threatens other life values.
> Without external controls, markets have no restraining mechanisms
> ... [E]thical standards ... have to be brought from the outside – from
> a public ethics, guaranteed by law ... Nor can markets nurture
> the human capital they themselves require – government, families
> and communities have to do so ... [M]arkets aren't self-regulating.
> Their tendency to cyclical fluctuation needs to be limited by outside
> intervention, as does their tendency to create monopoly.[44]

Clark and Pitelis point out that, with almost all industrialised countries choosing to maintain a large public sector, there are indeed things that the public sector is able to do that private entrepreneurship can not and should not do.[45] Meanwhile, Jackson and Price conclude surprisingly, and controversially, that despite the freedom now afforded the market, the devotion of governments to market principles and their unwavering belief in the benefits of market provision of services, it is very difficult to identify specific improvements in efficiencies and cost savings in the public services most affected.[46] Certainly, any improvements that may be possible cannot be unambiguously identified as the consequence of the discipline of competition and the unbridled efforts of the market.

The refuge of last resort

Despite the growing pessimism about the effects of marketisation, there is little doubt that the privatisation of some services previously provided by government has produced significant benefits to many citizens in many liberal democracies. In the majority of these cases, the benefits of privatisation have been most closely associated with the transfer of services that are peripheral to the core responsibilities of government – services which John Stuart Mill referred to as 'optional'. The privatisation of cleaning services, banks, airlines, insurance companies and many other publicly owned businesses which operate in competitive markets and for a profit do not impinge on the core, elemental responsibilities expected of governments as they are services in which the private sector has had a long and successful history. If, subsequent to privatisation, these essentially commercial services are poorly delivered by private bodies, the repercussions for the well-being of citizens are unlikely to be significant since the existing competitors will ensure that dissatisfied customers can access the services that they require. When, however, governments privatise services that impinge upon core responsibilities, for example infrastructure sales where competition may be absent or limited by the status of the service as a 'natural monopoly', the consequences of service failure are far more significant. Should a private provider of services which were once regarded as public goods fail to meet their obligation to ensure a high standard of service and regular supply, their customers may not have the option of going elsewhere. When confronted with a poorly performing public monopoly, citizen-customers' ability to voice their concerns to bring about change may also be far less potent with a private monopolist than their ability to influence politicians through the ballot box.

When the privatisation of previously regarded core public responsibilities was being promoted by governments and their fellow travellers, warnings of the inability of the private sector to reliably deliver these critical services, both profitably and in the public interest without either suffering or the need for government to provide protection as the provider of last resort, were vigorously denied. To ensure that victory for radical reformists would be unimpeded, efforts were made to humiliate opponents by referring to their objections as 'hysterical' and without foundation.[47] However, particularly notorious infrastructure privatisation failures have exposed the level of residual risk which remains with government after privatisation. This risk, and the inability of government to relocate it finally and irrevocably to the private sector, recognises that government exists and derives its legitimacy by accepting responsibility for the welfare of its citizens. The foundations of government, the reasons for governments, lie in political necessity; they are not matters of economics, although a state will not be stable and enduring without a viable economy. This was highlighted when the inability of a private contractor to ensure the safety of passengers on London Underground railway stations, tragically demonstrated with a high-profile murder, saw the mayor of London, Ken Livingstone, announce late in 2006 that the public body Transport for London would resume responsibility for security on some of London's railway stations, thereby partially reversing a previous, highly contentious privatisation initiative which had seen the transfer of these responsibilities to private firms such as Silverlink.[48]

In Australia, auditors-general have been particularly critical of inconsistencies between the benefits afforded by contracting out to private providers and governments' continued financial exposure. In the case of the long-awaited Sydney Harbour Tunnel, opened in

1992 as a partnership between the New South Wales government and a joint-venture company, the state's auditor-general highlighted the inconsistencies and risks in private contracting. He found that as a result of revenue guarantees given by the government in the contract, the private contractor which built and will operate the tunnel until 2022 had been insulated from most of the associated operating risks. In these circumstances, 'the private sector, *prima facie*, ... should not be the equity participant ... [I]f the private sector wishes to claim ownership in substance as well as form, it must also take the risks that are normally borne by proprietors.' Certainly the impression should not be given that risks have been assumed by the private sector partner when this is not the case or 'the concomitant appearance that the public sector has avoided risks which it has not'.[49]

The preference of private contractors for only the most lucrative public sector services, often referred to as 'cherry picking' or 'creaming', can leave government with expensive and high-exposure responsibilities without the ameliorating revenue benefits of those more profitable services. Irrespective of the technical virtuosity of contracts, should private contractors fail to provide the essential services for which they are contracted, governments will ultimately be forced to step in to make up any deficiencies. Governments may also continue to be under a non-delegatable duty of care and to be legally accountable. In some circumstances the courts may not permit the government, as a principal to an agreement, to contract to their agent, a private firm, all responsibility for the interests of a third party. In this regard the Australian High Court has noted that:

> It has long been recognised that there are certain categories of case
> in which a duty to take reasonable care to avoid a foreseeable risk of
> injury to another will not be discharged merely by the employment of
> a qualified and ostensibly competent independent contractor.[50]

The problem all reformers have faced is determining the irreducible minimum for government which does not destroy the very conditions necessary for markets to operate. The alarming recent failures of some prominent privatised services recognise that the limits of private provision have been exceeded in these instances. They also emphasise how the purported failures of government have been traded for the failures of the market, but without the redeeming virtues permitted by public values which had restrained and directed public provision. This for Peters signifies that 'many of the critiques of the role of government in governing are too facile and appear to ignore the continuing necessity for some form of centralized direction for society'.[51]

At times of extreme crisis, such as war or a natural calamity, arguments over the role of government become irrelevant. Unlike the private sector, which is prepared to operate in the most favourable of circumstances, governments do not have the ability to accept or refuse responsibility when all others have stepped aside. Government is indeed the last resort in the most extreme circumstances of national, social or economic peril. Irrespective of the level of private sector involvement in the delivery of core services, the public reaction to crises indicates that there is a latent and strong belief that government is meant to serve the public interest, a belief which is to be found even in America where there has been a long history of antipathy to government intervention when there are viable private alternatives. September 11 has reminded the American public and its political representatives of not only the ability of governments to be neglectful in their duties but also that it is only their government which is capable of providing a measure of security. Such catastrophic events expose both the limits of the capabilities of the private sector and the fundamental, irreplaceable contributions of government. This was recognised when President Bush announced in January 2002 that government expenditure on home defence would be immediately increased, thereby confirming that government success in dealing with major political and economic crises will be that which determines the future of society.

The private sector and the self-interest of the market are not meant to deal with major crises beyond seeking to protect their own best interests and ensure their own survival. It would be both unrealistic and contrary to their responsibilities to shareholders if the public interest were to be the first consideration of business managers. To perceive crises as anything other than presenting a set of opportunities by which businesses or individuals might benefit would be to deny the intent and requirements of the market, and the source of the virtues of the market that governments want to harness. Should the interests of individual private actors in the market be threatened, the motive of self-interest and self-preservation will compel them to walk away, for ultimately those who supply the market, to function efficiently, must have no ultimate responsibility to any individual or institution other than to promote the interests of shareholders. Businesses which disappoint their owners and customers are meant to fail.

At the time of calamity the private sector will withdraw to minimise unfavourable effects, including, if necessary, dismissing as quickly as possible all employees involved. It will also, hypocritically, seek government assistance to restore order on the pretext that getting businesses operating again is first and foremost in the public interest. This was seen no more clearly than in the alacrity with which businesses and the wealthy took flight with the approach of Hurricane Katrina in 2005, and the speed during reconstruction with which large construction firms moved into the most desirable locations of New Orleans, and only these locations, which had previously had a large and impoverished black population but who now were financially unable to return. The same private sector had been conspicuous in its absence when the citizens of New Orleans were in great peril. Naomi Klein has argued that this cycle of self-preservation by the private sector in the midst of trauma followed by aggressive opportunistic behaviour has become the distinguishing feature of 'disaster capitalism'. Thus, while the fire fighters and police officers in public employment responded at the most critical and dangerous time in September 2001, too often at the cost of their lives, in the aftermath the Bush administration has created massively profitable opportunities for the private sector to profit from the tragedy. Klein mocks how:

> all of a sudden having a government whose central mission was self-immolation did not seem like a very good idea … [with] a frightened population wanting protection from a strong, solid government …
>
> For weeks after the attacks, the president went on a grand tour of the public sector … embracing and thanking civil servants for their

contributions and humble patriotism ... But far from shaking their determination to weaken the public sphere, the security failures of 9/11 reaffirmed in Bush and his inner circle their deepest ideological (and self-interested) beliefs – that only private firms possessed the intelligence and innovation to meet the new security challenge ...

The Bush team, Friedmanite to the core, quickly moved to exploit the shock that gripped the nation to push through its radical vision of a hollow government in which everything from war fighting to disaster response was a for-profit venture.[52]

Feigenbaum and others have also reminded us that the public 'often discover the appeal of government when efforts to pare the fat from the system begin to cut near the bone'.[53] This study explores this concern.

———

Irrespective of the political complexion of governments in liberal democratic states, all continue to constitute a significant market presence. In many countries they are the largest employer and by far the largest single consumer of resources. In addition to its role as a participant, the state also affects the actions of the private sector, and thereby the lives of its citizens, through its role as a regulator. By legislation and decrees, governments are able to encourage some activities and, if necessary, prohibit others according to criteria seen to constitute the public good.[54] Despite these myriad contributions to the well-being of a nation, it would be very difficult and foolish to argue with either conviction or legitimacy that government is so free from fault that it cannot benefit from a close examination of the appropriateness and benefits of existing practices. However, modifications to practices, institutions and organisations are very different from a revocation of the fundamental mission of government to promote the interests of all citizens. The constitutions of Westminster governments, for example, embody the hope of a common destiny, not a fractured, tense collective of suspicious individuals who are so concerned for their own well-being that they have no time to contribute to that of others. This was clearly in evidence when Australia, upon being granted its independence from Britain, was to be known as the *Commonwealth* of Australia, with the government responsible for the common 'weal' or good. For an increasing number of critics of marketisation of the state, it is now time to be more positive about the role which the state can play, especially in light of the alarming social problems which have become more accentuated under neoliberal policies.

There continues to be widespread public resistance to government standing apart from everyday events and making its presence felt only in the event of crisis or when the rules of the market are violated. As the restrictions on competition are taken away and more government services previously seen as essential find their way into the hands of a few, very large and powerful private sector firms, uneasy and sceptical citizens have demanded a return to the previous protections of government against the often rapacious market. Public outrage over the transfer of mad cow disease from animals to humans in Britain in the 1990s was a reaction to both the perceived health risks, of which there had been no warning, and the way in which government had been prepared, for the sake of an ideology, to surrender its protective responsibilities to the entirely self-interested private sector, for whom profit was the supreme consideration.

While it is unrealistic to envisage that competitive relationships will be, or ever should be, entirely absent in the provision of government services, private service failures have shown that it is an equally dangerous delusion to believe that competitive relationships are able to provide on their own the cohesive substance which allows communities to exist and to prosper. Recurring economic catastrophes in the twentieth century, and with intimations already in the world credit crisis of 2008 that the twenty-first century may not be very different, have shown how the necessary selfishness of the market works best only when combined with a preparedness of individuals to occasionally put the community first. When conditions have deteriorated to levels which threaten the very existence of society, let alone the market and the wealth of its participants, it has been the timely and decisive interventions of governments, not market adjustments, which have saved the day.

PART

I

BELIEFS

You can't buy dedication to public interest

Fire companies began to ascend stairwell B at approximately 9:07, laden with about 100 pounds of heavy protective clothing, self-contained breathing apparatuses, and other equipment. Firefighters found the stairways they entered intact, lit, and clear of smoke. Unbeknownst to the lobby command post, one battalion chief in the North Tower found a working elevator, which he took to the 16th floor before beginning to climb. In ascending stairwell B, firefighters were passing a steady and heavy stream of descending civilians. Many civilians were in awe of the firefighters and found their mere presence to be calming. Firefighters periodically stopped on particular floors and searched to ensure that no civilians were still on it. Climbing up the stairs with heavy protective clothing and equipment was hard work even for physically fit firefighters.

Just prior to 10:00, in the North Tower one engine company had climbed to the 54th floor, at least two other companies of firefighters had reached the sky lobby on the 44th floor, and numerous units were located between the 5th and 37th floors. In the South Tower a battalion chief and a ladder company found a working elevator to the 40th floor and from there proceeded to climb stairwell B. Another ladder company arrived soon thereafter, and began to rescue civilians trapped in an elevator between the first and second floors. The first FDNY (Fire Department of New York) fatality of the day occurred at approximately 9:30, when a civilian landed on and killed a fireman near the intersection of West and Liberty streets.

At 9:50, an FDNY ladder company encountered numerous seriously injured civilians on the 70th floor. With the assistance of a security guard, at 9:53 a group of civilians trapped in an elevator on the 78th-floor sky lobby were found by an FDNY company. They were freed from the elevator at 9:58. By that time the battalion chief had reached the 78th floor on stairwell A; he reported that it looked open to the 79th floor, well into the impact zone. He also reported numerous civilian fatalities in the area. At 9:54 an additional 20 engine and 6 ladder companies were sent to the WTC (World Trade Centre). As a result, more than one-third of all FDNY companies now had been dispatched to the WTC.

At 9:58 the South Tower collapsed in ten seconds, killing all civilians and emergency personnel inside, as well a number of individuals – both first responders and civilians – in the concourse, in the Marriott, and on neighboring streets. The building collapsed into itself, causing a ferocious windstorm and creating a massive debris cloud … The 911 calls placed from most locations in the North Tower grew increasingly desperate as time went on. As late as 10:28, people remained alive in some locations, including on the 92nd and 79th floors.

By 10:24, approximately five FDNY companies reached the bottom of stairwell B (of the North Tower) and entered the North Tower lobby. The units then proceeded to exit onto West Street. While they were doing so, the North Tower began its pancake collapse, killing some of these men. Those in the lobby were knocked down and enveloped in the darkness of a debris cloud. Some were hurt but could walk. Others were more severely injured, and some were trapped. Several firefighters came across a group of about 50 civilians who had been taking shelter in the restaurant and assisted them in evacuating. Up above, at the time of the South Tower's collapse four companies were descending the stairs single file in a line of approximately 20 men. Four survived.

After the South Tower collapsed, some firefighters on the streets neighboring the North Tower remained where they were or came closer to the North Tower. Some of these firefighters did not know that the South Tower had collapsed, but many chose despite that knowledge to remain in an attempt to save additional lives. According to one such firefighter, a chief who was preparing to mount a search-and-rescue mission in the Marriott, 'I would never think of myself as a leader of men if I had headed north on West Street after [the] South Tower collapsed' … Three of the most senior and respected members of the FDNY were involved in attempting to rescue civilians and firefighters from the Marriott.

(The 9-11 Commission Report: *Final Report of the National Commission on Terrorist Attacks Upon the United States*, US Government Printing Office, Washington DC, 2004, pp 299–309)

'THE BENEVOLENCE OF THE BUTCHER': SELF-INTEREST VS PUBLIC INTEREST

> It is not from the benevolence of the butcher, the brewer, or the baker, that we expect our dinner but from their regard to their own interest. We address ourselves not to their humanity but their self love.
>
> (Adam Smith, *The Wealth of Nations*, book 1, chapter 2)

A direct and undiminished line of intellectual ancestry and debt can be drawn between the classical liberal economists of the seventeenth and eighteenth centuries and the neoliberals of today. Adam Smith is especially remembered for his genius in describing in *An Inquiry into the Nature and Causes of the Wealth of Nations* the principles which determine the operation of markets – the foundation of modern economics. Less well known is Smith's earlier work, *A Theory of Moral Sentiments* (1759), which had much to say about the empathetic motivations of individuals and the consequences of these for their relations with others in society. While in *The Wealth of Nations* Smith established that he was a keen admirer of the benefits of competitive markets, in this and his earlier work he also made it very clear that his admiration was not unqualified. In addition to the great social and economic benefits which were made possible by competitive markets, he was also very aware of the problems that the pursuit of self-interest, upon which these benefits depended, could cause and the very restrictive conditions necessary for markets to work efficiently.

Buchan has argued that *The Wealth of Nations* was the most important book to influence political economy, and that it has defined the compass and concerns of economics, thinking on taxation and the place of government, into the twenty-first century. Henry Thomas Buckle, a Victorian philosopher, thought that it was probably the most important book which had ever been written.[1] These are judgements with which few, if any, neo-classical economists might disagree. Alan Greenspan, the former long-serving head of the American Federal Reserve, described Adam Smith as 'a towering contributor to the development of the modern world', and the most important influence in his life.[2] *The Wealth of Nations* has been used by economists and neoliberal reformers to legitimise their reforms, to create an equivalence between the private sector and the public benefit that is purported to arise from the unhindered pursuit of self-interest, and to condemn the presence of government as malodorous and oppressive. In the hands of high-profile contemporary advocates of the virtues of the market, such as Milton Friedman, Robert Nozick and Friedrich Hayek, the capture of the moral high ground in public sector discourse has been extremely successful in most Western nations. It has been sufficiently persuasive to convince governments that greater market freedoms are the natural state of affairs, and that government intervention is artificial in general and, in economic affairs, indefensible. In a highly controversial thesis, Naomi Klein argues that Friedman's influence was also crucial in providing the necessary free market justifications and motivations for the American government to undermine several democratically elected governments in South America and put in their place authoritarian regimes more sympathetic to American business interests. In Chile, which is among the most notorious of these interventions, Friedman self-righteously claimed that the 'really important thing ... is that free markets did work their way in bringing about a free society'.[3]

The ongoing reform of the public sectors and especially public services of many advanced Western democracies, to transform them in the image of the private sector, has clearly confirmed the belief of these governments that the way in which the business world conducts its affairs and the values by which it is driven are best. Brereton and Temple conclude that 'any notion of the private sector having something to learn from the values and practices of the public sector has come to be seen as risible'.[4] Discourses created around the market by neoliberalism have fostered the illusion that exchange transactions provide the only reliable measure of the worth of social interactions. Not only are market exchanges projected as providing the most efficient method possible for satisfying wants and enhancing utility, they also operate without the need for coercion or intervention by any outside body.

Particularly effective in establishing the legitimacy and appeal of neoliberal discourse is the way in which 'the market' provides a metaphor which is able convincingly to conflate both the abstract and concrete, to provide a 'totalising structure' for society based upon market values. The infusion of market-based values beyond economic exchanges into society in general amounts to a process of 'universal commodification' in which neoliberals have relied upon the:

> powerful and persuasive images of market rhetoric in which the term 'market' becomes a polysemic symbol. Thus … through a process of slippage between referents, the image performs ideological functions by standing for various forms of abstract relationship … The market model mediates between experience and reality by offering itself as a new interpretive schema, which in due course becomes a routinised form of understanding ourselves and others.[5]

Despite the overwhelming dissemination of market values throughout government and civil society, it is in times of social, political and economic crisis that the public's rising demands for answers, and sometimes salvation, from government reveal that they still believe that ultimate and unavoidable responsibility for the well-being of society and of individuals must ultimately reside with the government, and that this cannot be transferred and abdicated to the private sector. No amount of blame shifting and attempts at avoidance will deflect public anger should government be seen to be negligent in its stewardship of the well-being of its citizens. The public look past the unelected in the market place and the government bureaucracy to those whom they entrusted with great powers and for which they expect them to answer. Thus, the hegemony of neoliberalism has been challenged by recent prominent market failures, while the 'war on terror' waged by the American government after September 2001 has confirmed the benefits to society of selfless duty and self-sacrifice – the antithesis of the market's self-interest.

The scenario provided in the prelude to this chapter dramatically highlights both the limits of self-interest and the contributions of public interest motives to society's well-being. Self-interest, while always present in some form, is likely to be a motive of varying impact. However, the *exclusive* motive of self-interest proclaimed by public choice advocates and like-minded liberals is far from the exclusive, or even the dominating, motive of the behaviour of all people in all circumstances. Even at the height of the neoliberal purges of the late twentieth century, there still remained a keen, if not always openly expressed, appreciation that not everything has a monetary value.

Belief in the virtue of self-interest

The starting point for most neoliberals' amour with markets is Adam Smith's apparently unconditional recognition that:

> Every man is ... by nature, first and principally recommended to his own care; and as he is fitter to take care of himself, than of any other person, it is fit and right that he should do so. Every man, therefore, is much more deeply interested in whatever immediately concerns himself, than in what concerns any other man.[6]

The individual, therefore, stands at the centre of liberalism, in both its classical and contemporary forms. It seeks to create for human behaviour a discourse of normality predicated on selfishness.

Eighteenth-century liberalism turned on its head the long-standing traditional conception of society, which had been sustained by church doctrine for centuries, according to which individual significance was in direct proportion to each person's contributions to the well-being of society. The centrality accorded by liberalism to the individual and their freedom was embodied in what Berlin refers to as a negative conception of liberty – as freedom from coercion. Herbert Spencer's earlier, and highly influential, conception of negative liberty admitted both economic freedoms, associated with the ability to use one's property as desired without external restraints, and the political freedoms of freedom of speech and voting. John Stuart Mill also saw the 'only freedom which deserves the name is that of pursuing our own good in our own way, so long as we do not attempt to deprive others of theirs'.[7] According to such doctrine, nothing must be put in the way of individuals to do as they feel compelled to do to satisfy their desires. Freedom is the converse of coercion, which Hayek defined as being forced 'to act not according to a coherent plan of his own but to serve the ends of another'.[8] Any situation under the benign providence of the market should be judged 'good' if it allows individuals to obtain what they seek and it is the product of mutual agreement.[9]

Individuals are seen by the liberal as the engine of wealth creation and of national prosperity, thereby providing the only sure means of promoting the common good. Personal liberty, to the extent that it does not impinge on the ability of others to enjoy similar opportunities for liberty, must be pre-eminent if individuals are to be able not only to use their abilities and initiative in their own best interests but also that of society. Each individual, wrote John Stuart Mill, 'is the proper guardian of his own health, whether bodily or mental or spiritual. Mankind are greater gainers by suffering each other to live as seems good to themselves, than compelling each to live as seems good to the rest.'[10] Without the contributions made possible by unfettered individual efforts, society either would not exist or it would condemn everyone to a greatly diminished standard of living.

The benefits to society from an unconscious and voluntary yielding to self-interest were seen by Adam Smith as necessarily greater than might arise from any intentional efforts on the part of a sovereign authority to accomplish the same thing.[11] While the state unintentionally and unavoidably had a propensity to incur costs, markets always unintentionally produce benefits: individuals would always be better judges of what was best for them than 'any statesman or lawgiver'.[12] Similarly, in views that differ little from today's more fervent advocates of the market, Josiah Tucker in 1756 was impressed with the way in which 'the universal mover in human nature, self-love, may receive such a direction ... as to promote the public interest by those efforts it shall make towards pursuing its own'.[13] This coincidence of benefit between self-interest and the public interest also preoccupied Bernard de Mandeville in his well known and influential *The Fable of the Bees*. Through his analogy of the bee hive, Mandeville reinforced the view that the well-being of the social collective depended *entirely* and enduringly on allowing self-interest to work its intent unfettered and undiminished:

> Thus Vice nurs'd Ingenuity,
> Which join'd with Time and Industry,
> Had carry'd Life's Conveniences,
> Its real Pleasures, Comforts, Ease,
> To such a Height, the Very Poor
> Liv'd better than the Rich before.[14]

This 'possessive individualism' has been given two main features by MacPherson. Firstly, individuals need to be considered as the sole owners of their abilities for which they owe nothing to society. They are entitled to use whichever capacities they possess for their own benefit as long as they do not infringe upon the rights of others to do likewise. Freedom is interpreted, therefore, as domination over things and not of individuals. Secondly, society is not seen as a set of relationships held together by duties and responsibilities. Instead, it is composed of free and equal individuals related to each other only through their possessions, where 'the relation of exchange ... is seen as the fundamental relation of society'.[15]

Economic freedom, and hence a free market, encourages independence and individual responsibility – the very antithesis of the dependency and avoidance of personal responsibility that state intervention is said to produce. Government intervention was criticised by Hayek for the way it denied people the opportunity to be self-reliant and to enjoy the self-respect which is the product of individual achievement. A culture of dependency promoted by the 'provision state' or 'nanny state' could suffocate individual initiative under the weight of government regulation and paternalism.[16] Distributive justice, he warned, comes to take the 'place of the justice of individual action'.[17] In her famous 'The lady's not for turning' speech in the House of Commons on 10 October 1980, Margaret Thatcher intoned that the healthy society upon which a vibrant economy depended could not be created by the state. Rather, she argued:

> When the state grows too powerful, people feel that they count for
> less and less. The state drains society, not only of its wealth but of
> initiative, of energy, the will to improve and innovate as well as to
> preserve what is best. Our aim is to let people feel that they count for
> more and more.

In order that they might further press their case for minimal government interference in the lives of private citizens, liberal theorists such as Hayek and Friedman as well as conservative political parties have attempted to create a fundamental, naturalistic association between market freedoms, personal liberty and political participation.[18] By allowing each individual the unfettered freedom to pursue their economic interests, according to Hayek, political power would be dispersed among a great number of agents, which would in turn deny governments the opportunity to concentrate political power and thus to threaten the liberty of all.[19]

According to Butler, the fear of centralised political power, of being at the mercy of the whims of government, was the essence of liberalism for Friedman.[20] It was also a view frequently aired to defend the American citizen's right to bear arms, for instance after the shooting deaths of 32 students at Virginia Tech in April 2007. John Stuart

Mill, in a passage which has informed and inflamed much of the debates about the role of the state, warned that experience:

> proves that the depositories of power who are mere delegates of the people [ie liberal democratic governments] ... are quite as ready ... as any organs of oligarchy, to assume arbitrary power, and encroach unduly on the liberty of private life ... all tendency on the part of public authorities to stretch their interference, and assume power, a power of any sort ... should be regarded with *unremitting* jealousy.[21]

So important was unrestrained individual initiative that Hobhouse, Milton Friedman and his wife Rose all saw economic freedom as the essential requirement for political freedom.[22] Indeed, to criticise the free market and to oppose its unlimited extension throughout society is for Friedman 'a lack of belief in freedom itself'.[23] While ever economic freedom is guaranteed, he argued, 'freedom of speech, of religion, and of thought' are possible.[24] According to him, once economic freedom is constrained by government actions, then all other freedoms will suffer a similar fate and may eventually be fatally threatened: markets were the only sure source of freedom for the individual, the only sure means of holding political oppression at bay.

Belief in the freedom of the market

Herbert Spencer described markets as having God-given qualities, that they showed similar characteristics to 'the self-adjustment of planetary perturbations, and in the healing of a scratched finger ... and in the increased sensitiveness of a blind man's ear'.[25] Public choice advocates also attribute a mystical quality of perfection to markets. For them the main question is:

> whether the rules by which individual actions are co-ordinated are such as to transform actions undertaken by participants in their own private interests into outcomes that are in the interest of others. We know that this curious alchemy is in fact worked by the market.[26]

The supremacy of markets over all other competing forms of resource allocation is said to be derived from their natural ability to assemble and transmit a vast amount of information about the preferences of consumers and the production functions of suppliers which encourages least-cost practices and the efficient distribution of scarce resources amongst competing users. Accordingly, ideal markets are characterised as supreme examples of information efficiency. In a freely operating market economy, there are vast numbers of agents seeking, providing and acting upon information. Each agent, who is acting in his or her best interests, can only do so while every one else is also free to act in a similar manner. In contrast, neoliberals see government as an unnatural means of allocating scarce resources among competing uses and, thus, must be inefficient in its ability both to collect, assimilate and act upon information and to deliver services efficiently and effectively. According to Jackson and Price, government suffers from a:

> lack of clear objectives, ambiguous incentives ... and inadequate cost control systems all coupled with political interference ... In the absence of the profit motive and the disciplinary powers of competitive markets, slack and wasteful practices can arise ... Resources are absorbed by elaborate and often ineffective control mechanisms rather than being devoted to the service itself.[27]

Government is something forced on markets from the outside and, thereby, interferes with and degrades the naturalistic workings of the market. If government intervention restricted some market players in comparison to others, however venal their intentions and actions, then the imperfections in information which would arise would reduce the efficacy of the market. Efficient resource allocations can only occur when free agents are fully apprised of opportunities in the market. The slightest interference, it is suggested, has the potential to set in motion a set of seemingly anarchic reactions, the intentions of which are known only unto themselves and which any further efforts by governments to regulate will only worsen. Accordingly, governments should only play a part when there has been a 'rare' occurrence of market failure: when the market has been incapable of providing the product or service required.

Herman de Mandeville warned that whereas the private 'vice' of self-interest is best left alone and not fettered, to leave public vices unchecked is to place all in peril. In contrast to most enthusiastic supporters of the untrammelled self-interest facilitated by markets, who seem to presume that of itself this stems from virtue and results in even greater virtue, de Mandeville was further convinced that the full benefits of self-interest, and the markets through which it found expression and fulfilment, would only be realised by tolerating the worst aspects of self-interest, short of physical injury to others:

> Fools only strive
> To make a Great an Honest Hive
> T'enjoy the World's Conveniences,
> Be fam'd in War, yet live in Ease,
> Without great Vices, is a vain
> Eutopia seated in the Brain
> Fraud, Luxury and Pride must live,
> While we the Benefits receive ...
> So Vice is beneficial found, ...
> The Whole Part was full of Vice,
> Yet the Whole Mass a Paradise.[28]

Although sympathetic to liberal fundamentals, Keynes pointed out how, in the context of the market, the suggestion that the pursuit of self-interest will always produce the greatest wealth and happiness relies upon a number of unrealistic and even dishonest assumptions. Most especially Keynes refers to the assumptions that there is perfect knowledge to inform decisions and that there is always strong competition between suppliers – when in reality even in the most competitive markets ignorance reigns. In these circumstances, Keynes concludes that 'It is *not* a correct deduction from the principles of economics that enlightened self-interest always operates in the public interest'.[29]

Market limits

Neoliberals believe that market failures occur far less often than those associated with the delivery of services by government. According to neoliberals, *true* market failures are exceedingly rare, certainly much less common than potentially catastrophic government failures. One widely quoted example of this denial is Milton and Rose Friedman's refusal to accept that the Great Depression of the late 1920s and 1930s was anything other than a failure of government.[30] This belief in the near infallibility of the market is possibly not surprising, given that the neoliberal definition of market failure tends to be so tightly hedged with conditions that it ensures that most market crises, which may otherwise be termed as failures, are reinterpreted in a less threatening manner. Among critics of this blind faith in the largesse and perfectibility of markets, Donahue instead has identified six sources of market failure: incomplete or insufficient information in market exchanges; excessive transaction costs; absence of a market; market power, such as monopolies, which distort prices; externalities which are not reflected in prices; and the inherent contributions of some services towards public good.[31]

Hayek did concede that the market might not be able to provide 'collective' or public goods and that these would then become the responsibility of government to finance, although not necessarily to deliver. When this occurs, he urged his readers to remember that 'we are resorting to an *inferior* method of providing these services because the conditions necessary for their being provided by the more efficient method of the market are absent'.[32] Thus, the burden of proof for the need for government intervention should always be with the government. Government failures are to be regarded as the norm, as inherent to the nature of government, whereas the market, in most circumstances, will naturally and reliably provide consumers with the products and services that they demand. In virtually all circumstances, according to Friedman, the greater information efficiency of the market will compel responsive adjustments to any imperfections, even in the most extreme circumstances. Accordingly, he argues that government can never be better than the market.

Clarke and Pitelis question this argument, as does Galbraith, suggesting that a careful consideration of evidence of the workings of the market 'makes this belief less self-evident'.[33] Further, changing the form of ownership of a service from public to private does not mean that efficiency must be and will be enhanced. Instead, and contrary to the neoliberals' undiminished enthusiasm for the market, it is far from clear from the experience of the past three decades of the major liberal democracies which have transformed their public services that the performance of the market is overwhelmingly superior to that of the state.[34] This is confrontingly suggested with the examples of market failure provided in later chapters.

Single-minded advocates of the superiority of the market in organising economic and social relations are reluctant to recognise even that, when the very existence of society and the market might be threatened, it is not the market which history has shown is able to save the situation but the active intervention of the state. Paradoxically, as markets are given more freedom by governments, the more often they are coming to depend on government to save them in a crisis. Pigou uses the example of pollution to demonstrate how the market, by not including all the costs associated with economic activity – that is excluding negative externalities – has consistently failed to protect the environment.[35] Consequently, as fears of global warming seem to be alarmingly vindicated, government has had to intervene and legislate practices which will reduce carbon emissions, actions that business is reluctant to initiate and which the unalloyed workings of the market might even forbid. In 2006, after an extensive review of the evidence for climate change, Britain's Stern Review on the Economics of Climate Change concluded that climate change had resulted from the persistent failure to recognise the full cost of economic growth and, thereby, constituted the greatest market failure ever known.[36]

In China, mounting evidence of the toxic damage to the natural environment and to the lives of its citizens who live in dangerously polluted cities, itself the consequence of little or no government regulation of the industries that have driven that country's phenomenal growth over the past decade, has finally convinced the Chinese government that it needs to intervene decisively to ensure that the private sector is forced to take seriously their public interest responsibilities. In the worst of China's polluted cities, birth defects rose by 40 per cent in the short period between 2001 and 2006, with major physical deformities now afflicting over 6 per cent of new babies.[37] With 16 of the world's 20 most polluted cities now in China, and with more than 750 000 people estimated to die each year from the effects of air pollution, President Hu announced at the 17th Congress of the Chinese Communist Party in October 2007, that his government would adopt a 'scientific outlook on development'. Instead of anarchic economic growth, in future the emphasis would be on sustainability and social harmony to ensure that economic growth was no longer 'realised at an excessively high cost of resources and the environment'.[38] Pan Yue, vice-minister of China's environmental protection agency, warned that China's economic progress would soon end if it was not realised that the environment would not be able to maintain the present pace of pillage.[39]

Child and Finn are particularly scathing of the weaknesses of markets in these circumstances. Child argues that markets, by their nature, are immoral, that they cannot but produce great inequality and generate significant negative externalities such as pollution. Unlike liberals for whom the harnessing of human greed and selfishness can only be for the common good, Child warns that markets do not serve society and its members well.[40] Monbiot has similarly observed that:

> Unless taxpayers' money and public services are available to repair the destruction it causes, libertarianism destroys peoples' savings, wrecks their lives and trashes their environment. It is the belief system of the free-rider, who is perpetually subsidised by responsible citizens.[41]

The Nobel laureate and economist Kenneth Arrow also regards the neoliberals' embellished view of markets as self-serving and a negligent distortion of the reality. Market failures occur frequently when the pursuit of private interests deflects the efficient use of society's resources and the equitable distribution of the goods that result.[42] Contrary to idealistic praise of the benefice of the market, the elevation of the supposed virtues of the market over that of the potentialities of the state conveniently, and possibly dishonestly, represses the fallibility of the market, a condition inherent to any institution arising from human inventiveness and need. Rarely, notes both Arrow and Latham, are consumers as well informed and markets as efficient as they are presupposed by economic theory.[43] Instead, it often suits the purposes of powerful market players to withhold information from consumers or to collude to ensure that the market is prevented from operating freely. This was something which Adam Smith was keen to recognise when he reminded his readers how 'people of the same trade seldom meet together, even for merriment and diversion, but the conversation ends in a conspiracy against the public'.[44] The perennial sagacity of Smith's understanding of both human nature and of business was only too obvious when in 2007, following discovery by its regulators of an agreement to orchestrate prices between four of the largest glass makers in Europe, the European Commission imposed fines of nearly €500 million. The European competition commissioner, Neelie Kroes, said that the fine will make it very clear that the European Union 'would not tolerate companies cheating consumers'.[45] Legal proceedings during the 1990s in America and elsewhere against the tobacco industry disclosed a high level of collusion and a dirty tricks campaign orchestrated for at least the previous 50 years by the major tobacco firms to keep from consumers knowledge of the disastrous effects on their health of prolonged cigarette smoking. This has enabled them to escape government regulation of their products which would have controlled this tragic example of market failure. Many are concerned that similar disclosures may await mobile phone users and that, after all, the electromagnetic radiation emitted by their phones is harmful to their health.[46]

Although effusive in his praise of self-interest and allowing individuals to pursue this through the market unhindered by government, Adam Smith saw this also as the source of abuses. Abuses orchestrated by the private monopolies which characterised mercantilism in the eighteenth century were of especial concern to Smith, as was the tendency for businessmen at every opportunity to contrive markets exclusively for their benefit while arguing disingenuously that the public good was best served in this manner.[47] Smith made it very clear that he was primarily motivated to write *The Wealth of Nations* to expose the evils of a market system where merchants had a tendency to create powerful monopolies which betrayed the avowed virtues of markets. The interests of:

> the dealers ... in any particular branch of trade or manufactures, is always in some respects different from, and even opposite to, that of the public. To widen the market may frequently be agreeable enough to the interest of the public; but to narrow the competition must always be against it, and can serve only to enable the dealers, by raising their profits above what they naturally would be to levy, for their own benefit, an absurd tax upon the rest of their fellow citizens.[48]

Abuses visited upon consumers by the monopolistic practices of unscrupulous businessmen who were under the lucrative protection of government prompted Adam Smith to proclaim the merits of a freely operating market and the need to restrict and restrain government wherever possible to ensure that it was not in a position to favour a few at the cost of the many. The dishonesty of politicians in the eighteenth century when Smith was writing and their close ties with a small number of very powerful, wealthy businessmen was sufficient to convince Smith that such governments should not be trusted with great powers. This did not mean that he was opposed to government intervention under any circumstances, especially if there were sufficient controls to ensure that it was done transparently, honestly and fairly. The way in which Smith criticised mercantilism and his demand that the eighteenth-century state withdraw as regulator and protector of private enterprise is very different from today advocating the withdrawal of the state from economic planning and the broad superintendence of the welfare of citizens. Thus, it is possible to interpret Smith's opposition to government less as opposition to the *institution* of government and instead his disgust for the way in which government at the time he was writing had become the implement of 'the mean rapacity, the monopolising spirit of merchants and manufacturers' to further only their own interests.[49]

Smith's recognition of the possibility of market abuses did not seem to deflect either the Friedmans or Hayek. For them a private monopoly was able to be more responsive to changes than the purportedly more moribund, slothful public monopolies, and was therefore always to be preferred. Private monopolies which are also the most efficient should be tolerated, irrespective of the resulting defects in market freedom. Consequently, any possible reservations about the market and intimations of its limits were not to be allowed to intrude in government plans to privatise those core infrastructure assets and public utilities which were unavoidably natural monopolies. For the Friedmans, the monopolist has no social responsibility to consumers, other than to obey the law as must everyone. To force monopolists to exercise their rights for socially desirable ends and not in their own interests would be to destroy free society.[50]

The concerns expressed by Adam Smith, about the tendency for the powerful in business to ingratiate themselves with government so that they might persuade it to use its powers for their own benefit, were for Thorstein Veblen just as apposite in the twentieth century where the state operated most obviously in the interests of wealthy elites: 'the chief – virtually sole – concern of the constituted authorities in any democratic nation is a concern about the profitable business of the nation's substantial citizens'.[51] Preservation of their wealth through political influence, political intimidation and capture of the politically powerful, warns Harvey, is the enduring and undiminished concern of these financial elites into the twenty-first century.[52] This has required them to be highly adaptive to different and peculiar circumstances, and to use their considerable resources and common interests to shape dominant political, social and economic discourses such that these create a set of understandings which normalise institutions and practices that inexorably privilege their own interests, irrespective of the short-term consequences for others. Nowhere is this strategy more obvious or more successful than the private health insurance industry in the United States which, with the largest number of lobbyists of any industry per member of Congress, continues to be successful in convincing government to deny American citizens a universal health care system.

Harvey is convinced that, since the late twentieth century, consequences such as this have been the express intention and result of neoliberalism: the primary end of neoliberalism has not been to transform international capitalism, as proclaimed.[53] Rather, neoliberalism has never been anything other than a project to restore the power of one class: power which they believe had been gradually dissipated throughout the twentieth century by the public interest priorities of the welfare state. In considering the motives for the marketisation of the Australian state, Cahill and Beder also have characterised the neoliberal onslaught as the means by which powerful capitalist interests could influence state policy to benefit them at the expense of labour.[54] These highly organised and influential interests sought to dismantle the social and political institutions which gave Australia a unique social identity but which diminished the wealth and power of the capitalist class. Privatisation by Australian governments was, in particular, a means to destroy union power. Cahill and Beder conclude that neoliberalism in Australia 'has been a class-based project through and through – driven by business interests and state elites'.

The imperfections and limits of markets could be further explored with reference to a variety of services where the benefits of the state and the shortcomings of the market are particularly obvious and less conjectural. The intention at this point, however, is not to describe every activity from which the market should be excluded or, conversely, should be the responsibility of the state. Instead, the aim of the rest of this chapter is to traverse the *circumstances* which implicate the limits of markets and of self-interest.

The limits of self-interest

Not only, reassures public choice icon James Buchanan, does the market enable each member of society to exercise their freedoms as they individually desire, but the act of mutually beneficial exchange simultaneously enhances the interests, and thus the well-being, of third parties without transgressing on their freedoms. According to Spencer, the act of exchange between two parties 'ends with themselves – it does not affect the conditions [that is freedoms] of the bystanders at all'.[55] The reality, however, can be somewhat different, for it is not unusual for market transactions, in and of themselves, to generate significant harmful effects for others and which may ultimately require the intervention of government.

With market exchanges taking place within and dependent upon society for their efficacy, it is unlikely that they will have no impact on the interests of others who compose society. Nor will the market exchanges between freely contracting individuals in a complex modern economy guarantee that all the effects of these exchanges will be beneficial and that any negative effects are quarantined to these particular individuals. When internal and external costs and benefits diverge significantly, individuals and organisations in the market do not always make optimal decisions either for those directly involved in transactions or for other unrelated parties, with the possibility of socially undesirable outcomes arising. As previously noted with respect to pollution, the drive to maximise their own utility may see individuals and organisations do things in the market which are costly to others. Notoriously, to improve Enron's apparent market performance and, thereby, enhance their prospects of ever-higher levels of remuneration, senior executives invented financial transactions which were meant to deceive investors and other stakeholders while at the same time manipulating market signals. In one, now infamous, example of the venality of Enron's senior management (examined in greater detail in chapter 5), during 2000 they and other energy companies fabricated an artificial crisis in the supply of electricity to California by creating the impression that there was a great shortage of power. To meet this shortage the state government had to pay a premium to Enron and others, and the Californian public was forced to pay higher energy bills than might otherwise have been necessary.

The confronting negative externalities which the unlimited pursuit of self-interest may produce are increasingly manifested as ever-worsening social problems which can soon become the concern of all. Nowhere today is the opportunity for this to occur more obvious than on the internet. In the twenty-first century, computer technology allows individuals and businesses to pursue their self-interest in a manner and to an extent not previously available. It is now possible for anyone to delve into the vast resources and market power of the internet to satisfy almost any desire, whether it be finding a rare book or pursuing a sexual practice which may be illegal in liberal democratic societies. However, the internet as the ultimate manifestation of the importance of the unfettered, uncensored pursuit of self-interest has also brought into stark relief the opportunities that this creates for individuals to do so at great cost to the public interest.

In addition to the increasing concern about the ability of a substantially unregulated, anarchic internet to provide seemingly unlimited opportunities for the sexual abuse of children, its contributions to the spread of terrorism and socially destructive gambling in particular have also generated significant debate about the balance between self-interest, personal freedoms and the public interest. In the wake of September 11, and later attacks in Madrid and London, law enforcement authorities throughout the world have exposed numerous cases of terrorist groups using the privacy of the internet to contact others with whom they were plotting their next attack and to arm themselves with bomb-making techniques. The shooting deaths over several months in 2007 of eighteen young British men, including a boy aged 11 years, provoked a public outcry not only at the murders but at the way in which the social website YouTube was being used by gangs of British youths to publicise their activities and to glorify their ability to gain access to and use a large number of illegal firearms. This has led to calls for greater control over activities carried on the internet. The dangers which an unregulated internet might present to the public and the denial of responsibility for any lethal consequences by businesses which operate the sites were tragically demonstrated in November 2007, when a Finnish schoolboy who murdered eight of his classmates and teachers used YouTube to proclaim his intentions. When it was suggested to YouTube's owner, Google, that it may have been able to prevent the killings if it had a policy to vet each upload of material, Google said that it refused to become a censor of the web and to stifle individual freedom of expression.

Despite mounting evidence of the damage to the public interest that some internet activities have caused, most governments are still not prepared to intervene in a market which powerful internet companies such as Google regard as the ultimate manifestation of political and economic freedom. In 2006, however, Google was accused of hypocrisy when the company colluded with the Chinese government to censor material which offended the regime. In one high-profile case, Google was accused by the prominent Chinese scholar and opposition politician Guo Quan of assisting the Chinese government in suppressing nascent opposition parties by excising his name from Google after he established the New Democratic Party. Guo Quan accused Google of becoming 'a servile Pekingese dog wagging its tail at the heels of the Chinese communists'.[56]

A British parliamentary committee in 2007 referred to the internet as 'a playground of criminals', such was the freedom they enjoyed from effective regulation of their activities.[57] The House of Lords committee accused both business and government of treating the internet as a 'wild west' which resulted in millions of internet users exposed to serious criminal intent. Today, the committee warned, organised criminal groups are 'highly skilful, specialised and focussed on profit'. So sophisticated were these criminals, the chairman of the committee urged that governments should not 'just rely on individuals to take responsibility for their own security. They will always be outfoxed by the bad guys.' To protect individuals from their own ignorance, and society from the mounting social costs of gambling and the fraudulent practices which were endemic to it, the House of Lords committee suggested a more active role for government with the establishment of a new 'e-crime' police unit.[58] Imposing limits on individual freedom on the internet, warned the committee, was both necessary and an obligation of government in the best interests of the social collective. In 2006, the American government demonstrated its uncharacteristic concern for the wider public interest effects of unrestricted on-line gambling by making it illegal for companies with gambling sites overseas to make their services available to Americans.[59] For some British executives of on-line gambling companies, this came as a surprise when they were arrested at American airports later that year. On-line gambling remains illegal in France. There may indeed be the need for the state to remind individuals that the freedoms that they enjoy are still exercised within wider societies.

The individual and society

All the major political philosophers, from Plato and John Locke to Robert Nozick and John Rawls in the late twentieth century, have been concerned about the status of the individual and the relationship between the individual and society. Depending upon their understanding of the precedence of the individual or of society, so the rights and obligations of individuals, and hence the quality and conditions of their liberty, were determined. The individual, as found in the works of the great classical liberal theorists such as Hobbes, Locke, Burke, Bentham and Paine, is prior to society; hence their emphasis on untrammelled self-interest and the benefits that this supposedly has for the social collective.[60] Society exists to serve the individual and to protect their freedom. Society, argue Milton and Rose Friedman, can never be over or above individuals. It can have no goals except those that its composite individuals agree will be its goals.[61]

Unlike classical liberals such as Locke, who believed that individuals and society were not the same thing and that their natures were essentially opposed, David Hume believed that individuals can only truly be themselves, develop their natural capabilities and thus fulfil themselves, if they are within society. 'Man', declared Paine, 'did not enter society to become *worse* than he was before, nor to have fewer rights than he had before, but to have those rights better secured'.[62] The importance of collective society to each individual's well-being, especially when in need, was very clear to Adam Smith:

> All members of human society stand in need of each other's assistance, and are likewise exposed to mutual injuries. Where the necessary assistance is reciprocally afforded from love, from gratitude, from friendship, and esteem, the society flourishes and is happy. All the different members of it are bound together by the agreeable bands of love and affection, and are ... drawn to one common centre of mutual good offices.
>
> [Man has] a natural love of society, and desires that the union of mankind should be preserved for its own sake, and though he himself was to derive no benefit from it ... Its disorder and confusion

... is the object of his aversion ... He is sensible too that his own interests are connected with the prosperity of society, and that the happiness, perhaps the preservation of his existence, depends upon its preservation. Upon every account, therefore, he has an abhorrence at whatever can tend to destroy society.[63]

Contrary to his apparent condemnation of non-individualistic institutions, Buchanan was unable to deny that 'we live together because social organisation provides the efficient means of achieving our individual objectives and because society offers us a means of arriving at some transcendental common bliss'.[64] He also warned that social order 'would collapse overnight if all persons ... should suddenly commence to behave strictly in accordance with the utility maximising models of orthodox choice theory' – that is, *only* with self-interest.[65]

In contrast to present-day neoliberals, for Plato and Aristotle and other early political theorists, society as a 'natural entity' existed before the individual. Individuals were born into society; to be a member of society was the natural condition of each individual. Thomas Aquinas, in his *On Princely Government*, refers to humankind as naturally a social animal which was 'destined to live in a community'.[66] Individuals were bound as a political community by their commonalities – not as the means exclusively to facilitate individual utility as portrayed later by Jeremy Bentham and John Locke. These understandings from early political philosophers were still sufficient even for Fukuyama who, echoing the views of Hobhouse nearly a century earlier, portrayed the human species as driven to 'create moral rules that bind themselves together into communities'.[67] According to this view, then, the liberty and freedoms that each person enjoys depends upon the needs of society.

In a speech on liberty in late 2007, the new British prime minister Gordon Brown – who was born in Adam Smith's birthplace, Kirkcaldy – sought to reaffirm the importance of individual liberty to British society and British history. At the same time, however, he reminded his audience that individual rights were embedded in the social values of benevolence, civic society and a sense of a common purpose, that is a common destiny.[68] According to this view, the well-being of society must always be given pre-eminence, the freedoms of the individual must always serve the wider interest, for it is only when society is stable and its future secure that its members also have the conditions which would allow them to live freely and fully. No individual rights existed independent of or prior to society. For Brown, a form of liberty which was entirely about selfishness was alien to that which had developed in the past three centuries of British history. The British nation was founded upon 'a moral sense underlying shared purpose' which was sustained only so far as individuals recognised that they had responsibilities for others. The market society can only ever make us strangers to each other.

Similarly, for Hobhouse:

> organised society is something more than the individuals that compose it ... In any human association it is true ... that the whole is something more than the sum of the parts ...
>
> In discussing society, we are liable to two fallacies. On the one hand we may be tempted to deny the reality of the social group, refusing to conceive it as a distinct entity, insisting on resolving it into its component individuals as though these individuals were unaffected by the fact of association. On the other side, in reaction from this exaggerated individualism, we are apt to regard society as an entity distinct from the individuals, not merely in the sense that it is an aggregate of individuals viewed in some special relation, but in the sense that it is a whole which in some way stands outside them.[69]

Elevating the primacy of society *over* the individual was, and continues to be, anathema to many resolute neoliberals. Most early modern liberal political theorists, including Locke and Bentham, but not Adam Smith as noted earlier, believed that to live as part of a society was not the natural condition of individuals. Instead, they characterised society as a deliberate creation of individuals which allowed a very different view about the standing, and thus the rights, of individuals relative to it. Most famous is Locke's conception of individuals as having once lived in a state of nature when society did not exist, where each individual had certain natural rights and was responsible for both his or her own sustenance and safety, with no responsibilities to any others beyond their immediate family. At some time, the uncertainty and impermanence of life in a state of nature, but most especially the threats from others to one's property and liberty, induced individuals to agree to surrender some of their freedom to form into larger groupings: thus the beginnings of society.[70] They entered a social contract.

Irrespective of their position on the primacy of the rights of the individual, all liberal theorists recognise that market exchanges and the rights that they promote depend for their efficacy on a sophisticated, effective legal framework provided by society to enforce the contracts upon which the market depends and to protect the property which is the focus of most market exchanges. Markets, after all, are nothing more than social institutions, and their successful operation depends upon ingrained social habits and cultural traditions which give legitimacy to market exchanges and to their overarching political and legal institutions.[71] Property rights and any other rights arising from the enjoyment of property were rights which were conferred on individuals by society, and as such were described as 'artificial' (that is, man-made) rights protected by social rules and conventions which were designed to create the greatest social happiness.

The common good

Opponents of the neoliberal's aggressive individualism and relentless self-interest see a sense of community as not only necessary for stable, efficient markets but as both an essential civilising force and the moral requirement of democracy.[72] Single-minded dedication by individuals to their material welfare is condemned as the antithesis of the moral behaviour essential to the success of any society, and thus markets, where there needed to be a sense of mutual obligation.[73] Whereas liberals accept as fundamental the right to self-determination and the contributions that this can make to social justice and to the welfare of all, those who place community at the centre of society ('communitarians'), see the power of self-determination as circumscribed and made possible by social institutions and structures. The idealistic Kantian conception of the individual who is under no compulsion to assume obligations not of their own choosing, especially those which are the consequence of the commitments expected of them as a result of the social situations in which they find themselves, offends the communitarian's experience of how the world actually operates. Our lives, contends Sandel, are not devoid of moral obligations, however much modern society may make it easy for individuals to transfer these to others. The moral and social obligations which we either assume or which are expected of us give form and meaning to our lives, something which the liberal's 'thin' conception of the individual cannot provide. We are 'situated selves', not autonomous, detached voyeurs indifferent to the fate of everyone around us.[74] According to this view, it achieves little to divide obligations, as does Rawls, into natural obligations, such as the need to refrain from violence, and voluntary obligations, such as those associated with parenthood. What counts is the existence of obligations, however derived or defined, but especially those conferred on elected governments on behalf of individuals.

For the communitarian, the overwhelming obligation of government, as Thomas Aquinas observed, is 'the ordering of the common good'.[75] This is not achieved by the liberal's mathematical summation of individual preferences which flow from the primacy given to selfish individual rights; nor by Bentham's utilitarian conception of government whose object should be to provide the conditions which will deliver the greatest happiness for individuals and not make decisions about what is good or bad for the individual and the social collective.[76] According to communitarians, enhancements to individual happiness do not provide the only test of right and wrong. Through participation in social and political communities, and by engaging in democratic discourse between the governed and the governing, communitarianism promises active citizenship and the identification of common interests which can generate a store of social trust, instead of the alienation and exclusion which are seen by its critics to be the legacy of the selfish individualism of neoliberalism.[77]

Under a communitarian approach, individuals develop a strong sense of responsibility which is derived from their place and participation within the community. Benefit to the community, to the public interest, is used as the benchmark of individual aspirations. Outside their community, and without the responsibilities which membership entails, the individual has little meaning and even less importance. Those in ancient Athens who chose to remove themselves from the state and to live a life of selfish detachment were known as *idiotes* – the term from which the modern word 'idiot' is derived. Freedom for the Athenian was taking their share of the responsibilities of public life, not retreating to privacy.

These sentiments resonate strongly with Hobhouse:

> The happiness and misery of society is the happiness and misery
> of human beings heightened or deepened by its sense of common
> possession ... Its conscience is an expression of what is noble
> or ignoble in them when the balance is struck ... The greatest
> happiness will not be realised by the greatest or any great number
> unless in a form which all can share, in which indeed the sharing is
> for each an essential ingredient.[78]

Anthony Giddens' 'Third Way' approach to government can be seen as an attempt to meld features of liberalism and communitarianism. Giddens emphasised the importance to the well-being of a society, and to each individual of which it was composed, of coincident contributions from governments, markets and civil society; and the need to ensure a dynamic balance between these three elements. An overemphasis on one or two of these could only ever be at the expense of the others. Thus, should the interests and values of the market be allowed to assume too great an importance, then civil society must suffer and ultimately the economy, for a strong economy depended upon a strong society. The Third Way required neoliberalism's emphasis on the rights and economic freedoms of individuals to be matched with a corresponding recognition that with rights come responsibilities. The Third Way would not be a further development of neoliberalism, but rather the means of correcting its more significant deficiencies. Most especially:

the neoliberal idea that markets would almost everywhere stand in place of public goods is ridiculous. Neoliberalism is a deeply flawed approach to politics, because it supposes that no responsibility needs to be taken for the social consequences of market-based decisions. Markets can't even function without a social and ethical framework – which they themselves cannot provide.[79]

Reflecting the unease of public intellectuals such as Giddens, neoliberal antagonism towards anything above a minimal government presence has meant that neoliberalism has come to be seen as an extreme right-wing political ideology, synonymous with the label neoconservatism, which has replaced the paternal communitarianism of the traditional conservative right. In place of a belief in the importance of preserving social and political cohesion in the process of wealth creation, the unchallenged sovereignty of the market in the neoliberal mantra perpetuates a form of claimant politics characterised by 'extreme relations of domination and subordination'.[80] This introduces a perverse paradox in the modern capitalist market society. Usually, cautions John Ralston Saul, 'there is an assumption in any social contract that the constituted elites are protectors ... of that social agreement. The idea that a civilisation could function with its elites as the principal abusers of the contract is impossible. And yet this is precisely what we have.'[81]

It has been noted earlier that, ultimately, self-interest must also serve the public interest, for the blatant exercise of self-interest solely to benefit the individual can destroy the very structures upon which it is dependent. No market can exist without some commitment to the public good, that is, the presence of a degree of moral virtue. Theories such as public choice which depend upon the characterisa-tion of individuals as entirely selfish – prompting O'Toole to refer to their followers as 'arid pessimists'[82] – might therefore be seen as flawed from the very outset. While Adam Smith agreed that the pri-mary interest of each individual is their 'own care', each still must be careful to 'humble the arrogance of his self-love, and bring it down to something other men can go along with ... [for] if he should jostle, or throw down any of them, the indulgence of the spectators is entirely at an end'.[83] For most, Smith continues, the need to consider others is not artificial or forced: 'How selfish soever may be supposed, there are evidently some principles in his nature, which interest him in the fortunes of others, and render their happiness necessary to him, though he derives nothing from it, except the pleasure of seeing it'.[84] To give unquestioned obeisance to the values of the market with its regard for material things, according to Smith, would threaten an individual's moral virtue, which is evidenced in a capacity for sympathy or empathy towards others. Thus, although it may appear difficult to reconcile the ethic of sympathy in *The Theory of Moral Sentiments* with the ethic of selfishness in *The Wealth of Nations*, in each case Smith argued (as did David Hume) that the enduring requirement of a successful life and a strong society is the voluntary, even natural, presence of a concern for the public good.

Both Smith and Hume, as products of the Scottish Enlightenment, were very clear about the importance of mutual obligation, without which society would surely and soon collapse. At no time can Smith be seen to be unconditional in his admiration for the contributions of markets to the well-being of individuals and society. Markets – for indeed Smith never referred to markets as 'the market' – were only one part of society, not its entirety as the more extreme liberals such as Hayek and Buchanan propose. Similarly, Smith saw material well-being as only one aspect, albeit a very important part, of an individual's identity. Throughout *The Wealth of Nations* he prefers to talk about 'commercial society', rather than reifying markets as 'the market', thereby recognising that markets were constituted by individuals living in a system of complex co-ordination, the long-term well-being of which was to be advanced by markets. Accordingly, the fundamental concern of *The Wealth of Nations* was not about 'markets' as social abstractions, nor a debate about the merits of 'the market' verses the state. Morrow has argued that Smith's insistent concern in *The Wealth of Nations* for benevolence and the welfare of individuals make it first and foremost a work of moral philosophy, in which the contribution of moral values, such as concern for others, is not a constraint on the behaviour of individuals, but the essential condition for societies and the co-operative behaviour upon which they depend.[85]

higher allegiance to the public interest, they also contributed towards community cohesion.

In the absence of the values of service and loyalty to the community Brereton and Temple reported that it was not uncommon for many individuals to feel a sense of loss – however much some writers may believe that a public service ethos is a myth.[100] According to the British Public Administration Select Committee in 2002, governments should regard this public sector ethos as the fundamental set of values which must always inform public sector reform.[101] Integrity, duty, impartiality, justice and the public interest were also the values and practices which were to guide the behaviour of any organisation providing public services. Rejecting the claim that public services are not intrinsically different from those found in the private sector, that it did not matter who provided the services as long as they were made available and of good quality, the Public Administration Select Committee instead concluded:

> It does matter what a public service is … Whatever the shortcomings of the public sector as it is, there is something necessary, special and distinctive about those services which are provided as public services. They carry with them intrinsic assumptions about equity, access and accountability … The public realm, of collectively provided services and functions, needs to be recognised for what it is – an essential component of a good society.[102]

Duty, described by Godwin as the 'application of the capacity of the individual to the general advantage', is the essence of the trust that citizens have in the public sector.[103] Fukuyama calls duty a shared 'language of good and evil', while Rousseau saw duty as the natural accompaniment to the creation of civil society, obligating each to help the other.[104] A sense of duty is an intrinsic moral force that cannot be created at a whim or something which will readily respond to extrinsic inducements. Rather, it will be the product of a long process of culturation whereby individuals come to accept that there are higher allegiances and obligations than solely to oneself or to one's supervisors. Duty requires an individual to act in a particular way because it is the morally correct thing to do and not because it is consistent with any doctrine of self-serving, utility-maximising behaviour. Out of a sense of duty, as powerfully illustrated in the scenario preceding this chapter, individuals will sacrifice their lives to preserve the lives of their fellow, anonymous citizens. Indeed, as Gary Younge suggests, to fight and die for one's country is 'the ultimate form of public service' and duty.[105] O'Toole notes that the idea of public service and the moral virtues of duty and sacrifice upon which it depends is 'as old as philosophy itself', featuring in both Plato's *Republic* and Aristotle's *Politics*.[106] Aristotle put aside the selfish, ephemeral accumulation of wealth as the aim of a good life in preference for duty and honour. A respect for duty in an Aristotelian world is inescapable if one is to live an honourable and worthwhile life.

Recent public sector reforms, however, have operated on the premise that the public sector is no longer the place for the values of the selfless public servant, but rather those of the business man and business woman. In 1998, at the height of the Australian public sector reforms, the federal Minister for Education argued that the public service's responsibility to ensure a better society was best achieved by moving the public service 'from service provider and prescriptive regulator to the role of managing change, providing frameworks and *overseeing* the protection of the public interest'.[107]

The relentless hegemonic spread of a corporatist culture in the public sector has severely tested belief in a public service of high professional integrity which was regulated by normative standards of moral conduct, as opposed to the mandated policies and institutions that promoted blatantly self-interested behaviour justified by measures of performance borrowed from business. At no time is this more evident than when failures of the market in previously public services have had especially brutal and tragic consequences. Thus, rail crashes in Britain, resulting from the negligence, apathy or poor organisation of private contractors working on rail lines, have provoked calls for a return to a pre-privatisation public service culture for the railways and for their renewed commitment to the public interest and sense of personal responsibility.

After nearly three decades of penetrating public sector reforms, from departmental permanent secretaries down, public servants in both Britain and Australia are now expected to operate on the premise that giving priority to economic considerations is the only responsible way to husband scarce public resources in the presence of ever-rising demands for government services.[108] Inefficient management is proclaimed as not only wasteful but also that it leads to an inequitable distribution of increasingly scarce resources. Thus, as long as public servants adhere to the new priorities, reformist governments see little difficulty in melding 'performance accountabilities' – which are overwhelmingly financially based – with traditional public service values. However, while ever the self-interest of the public servant is promoted as the means of furthering the public interest, selfless service will come to be seen as less relevant and possibly, following public choice warnings, even a dangerous deception. Modern public sector reforms explicitly accept that self-interest drives public servants, and that it is incumbent upon government to expose and harness this fundamental characteristic in the public interest. According to this view, premising government on the mirage of public interest not only denies the public the benefit of explicitly harnessing the energies emanating from self-interest but allows public servants to divert benefits to themselves which would otherwise go to the public.

According to O'Faircheallaigh, the result of 'contract relations' replacing 'trust relations' for both government and society has been a decline in trust.[109] Relationships created through contracts displace long-standing, and less formal, relationships and erode the trust which these relationships made possible. New associations arising from contractual agreements cannot expect to enjoy the same level of confidence and understanding contained within the relationships which they replace.[110] In the process, public confidence in the ability of the public service to provide independent advice to their political masters – upon whom they depend for the renewal of their contracts and the conferring of rewards – is corrupted. Notably, the contributions provided by the continuity of the public service as the nation's collective memory of government and the political independence that this afforded public servants have also suffered by the employment of government appointees on short contracts. Politicisation of senior management positions in government by the appointment on limited contracts of sympathetic experts or party stalwarts has accentuated public sector short-termism and degraded the institutionalised independence which has been expected of the public service as advocates of the public interest and which has provided a counter to the ebullient political plotting by governments.

Further, with the blurring of the differences between public servants and the employed officials working on behalf of political parties, there has also been accumulating evidence that senior public officials appointed by government during their tenure in government are more concerned about the interests and partisan policies of political parties than the broader public interest. According to some studies there have been increasing opportunities for, and instances of, systemic corruption, while the appearance of 'spin doctors', or political appointees who seek to justify every fault of their employers, is well known and mocked.[111] Should governments be intent on adopting an entrepreneurial style of management, concern has been consistently expressed that 'it must be recognised that while "economic efficiency" might be improved in the short term, the longer term costs associated with this apparent improvement may well include antipathy to reducing corruption, fairness, probity and reliability'.[112]

——

Contrary to the enthusiastic pledges by reformist governments that they remain committed to traditional public service values of honesty, integrity, equitable service to the public and the provision of frank and comprehensive advice to ministers, qualitative dimensions of public sector performance have instead been shown to have suffered from competition with more efficiency-orientated, measurable accountabilities. Not everyone is easily convinced of a natural symbiosis between a culture of service and one of quantifiable performance. Indeed, so great can be the differences in objectives between concern for democratic values, such as justice and equity, and efficient management that Cook and Levi describe them as possibly 'irresolvable'.[113] The result, observes Saul, is that 'social morality is subordinated to the efficient functioning of the system [and] the social contract is subordinated to the financial contract'.[114] This concern is at the heart of the British Conservative Party's new policies released throughout 2008. Instead of the Labour government's obsession with measurable performance targets, and the resulting quagmire of bureaucratic rules and forms, public servants such as police and teachers would be allowed to use their professional judgement.

The traditional public service may have had its defects when measured against benchmarks of efficient performance, decision-making transparency and openness, but it did at least provide some guarantees of a common set of values and stable expectations for the citizen in their interactions with the executive.[115] While ever traditional public service values dominated, there still remained an implicit faith in the ideal that the public service would treat all whom it served in an equitable, honest and fair manner. Individuals entrusted to act on behalf of a community of citizens undertake a commitment to fulfil the duties and obligations of their office, irrespective of personal preferences and the desires of influential interest groups. With the explicit elevation of the motive of self-interest in the public services and a new regime of accountability measures which requires precise performance metrics, no longer can the virtues of service and duty be relied upon as much as they may have been in ensuring dedication to the public interest, even allowing for the not infrequent imperfections and failings of these qualities in practice.

When governments promote self-interest as the preferred characteristic of the behaviour and contributions of individuals, and accept that the values and practices of the marketplace are superior to those of public bureaucracies, they are no longer expected to take prime responsibility for the well-being of their constituents. This responsibility is now said to lie chiefly with each individual and not, as in the welfare state which had provoked the neoliberal response, with government. The belief that, in the first instance, individuals should take responsibility for themselves and that markets were the best means to facilitate this has provided governments with the permission and the justification to reduce their interventions on behalf of individual constituents. This politically expedient consequence of neoliberal self-interest, its relentless malleability according to political exigency, and the uncertain extent to which it could be taken, has been the most contentious aspect of neoliberal reforms on the roles which governments are now expected to perform.

'Social values more noble than ... profit'

President Hoover, Mr Chief Justice, my friends:

This is a day of national consecration, and I am certain that my fellow-Americans expect that on my induction into the Presidency I will address them with a candor and a decision which the present situation of our nation impels. This is pre-eminently the time to speak the truth, the whole truth, frankly and boldly. Nor need we shrink from honestly facing conditions in our country today. This great nation will endure as it has endured, will revive and will prosper.

So first of all let me assert my firm belief that the only thing we have to fear ... is fear itself ... nameless, unreasoning, unjustified terror which paralyzes needed efforts to convert retreat into advance. In every dark hour of our national life a leadership of frankness and vigor has met with that understanding and support of the people themselves which is essential to victory ...

Plenty is at our doorstep, but a generous use of it languishes in the very sight of the supply. Primarily, this is because the rulers of the exchange of mankind's goods have failed through their own stubbornness and their own incompetence, have admitted their failures and abdicated. Practices of the unscrupulous money changers stand indicted in the court of public opinion, rejected by the hearts and minds of men. Stripped of the lure of profit by which to induce our people to follow their false leadership, they have resorted to exhortations, pleading tearfully for restored conditions. They know only the rules of a generation of self-seekers. They have no vision, and when there is no vision the people perish.

The money changers have fled their high seats in the temple of our civilization. We may now restore that temple to the ancient truths.

The measure of the restoration lies in the extent to which we apply social values more noble than mere monetary profit. Happiness lies not in the mere possession of money, it lies in the joy of achievement, in the thrill of creative effort. The joy and moral stimulation of work no longer must be forgotten in the mad chase of evanescent profits. These dark days will be worth all they cost us if they teach us that our true destiny is not to be ministered unto but to minister to ourselves and to our fellow-men.

Recognition of the falsity of material wealth as the standard of success goes hand in hand with the abandonment of the false belief that public office and high political position are to be valued only by the standards of pride of place and personal profit, and there must be an end to a conduct in banking and in business which too often has given to a sacred trust the likeness of callous and selfish wrongdoing.

Small wonder that confidence languishes, for it thrives only on honesty, on honor, on the sacredness of obligations, on faithful protection, on unselfish performance. Without them it cannot live. Restoration calls, however, not for changes in ethics alone. This nation asks for action, and action now. Our greatest primary task is to put people to work. This is no unsolvable problem if we face it wisely and courageously.

It can be accompanied in part by direct recruiting by the government itself, treating the task as we would treat the emergency of a war, but at the same time, through this employment, accomplishing greatly needed projects to stimulate and reorganize the use of our national resources ...

It can be helped by the unifying of relief activities which today are often scattered, uneconomical and unequal. It can be helped by national planning for and supervision of all forms of transportation and of communications and other utilities which have a definitely public character. There are many ways in which it can be helped, but it can never be helped merely by talking about it. We must act, and act quickly.

Finally, in our progress toward a resumption of work we require two safeguards against a return of the evils of the old order: there must be a strict supervision of all banking and credits and investments; there must be an end to speculation with other people's money, and there must be provision for an adequate but sound currency ...

If I read the temper of our people correctly, we now realize, as we have never realized before, our interdependence on each other: that we cannot merely take, but we must give as well, that if we are to go forward we must move as a trained and loyal army willing to sacrifice for the good of a common discipline, because, without such discipline, no progress is made, no leadership becomes effective.

We are, I know, ready and willing to submit our lives and property to such discipline because it makes possible a leadership which aims at a larger good. This I propose to offer, pledging that the larger purposes will bind upon us all as a sacred obligation with a unity of duty hitherto evoked only in time of armed strife. With this pledge taken, I assume unhesitatingly the leadership of this great army of our people, dedicated to a disciplined attack upon our common problems.

Action in this image and to this end is feasible under the form of government which we have inherited from our ancestors. Our Constitution is so simple and practical that it is possible always to meet extraordinary needs by changes in emphasis and arrangement without loss of essential form. That is why our constitutional system has proved itself the most superbly enduring political mechanism the modern world has produced. It has met every stress of vast expansion of territory, of foreign wars, of bitter internal strife, of world relations ... I shall ask the Congress for the one remaining instrument to meet the crisis ... broad executive power to wage a war against the emergency as great as the power that would be given to me if we were in fact invaded by a foreign foe ...

In this dedication of a nation we humbly ask the blessing of God. May He protect each and every one of us! May He guide me in the days to come!

(Inauguration speech of Franklin Delano Roosevelt, at the time of the Great Depression, Washington DC, 4 March 1933)

THE 'PROPER' ENDS OF GOVERNMENT

One of the most disputed questions both in political science and in practical statesmanship ... relates to the proper limits of the functions and agency of governments ... There has grown up a spirit of resistance ... to the interference of government, merely as such, and a disposition to restrict its sphere of action within the narrowest bounds.

(John Stuart Mill, *Principles of Political Economy*)

The essential, core roles assumed by governments and the justifications for these have changed little since the creation of the modern state. These fundamental responsibilities, the functions which according to John Stuart Mill are 'universally acknowledged to belong' to government,[1] have been essential in ensuring social stability and security for individuals and their property, whether by providing necessary protections from fellow citizens or outside powers. In many cases, these vital functions can only be carried out by government organisations whose values and aims cannot, indeed must not, be those of the market.

This chapter highlights the peculiar and unique concerns of government, with particular reference to those 'public goods' which cannot be provided easily or enduringly by the private sector. It also acknowledges the inability to decide conclusively what governments should be doing. Mill recognised that the functions of government tended to grow as civilisation advanced, and that it was unrealistic to expect that governments would not do more. Rousseau was only too aware that identifying the precise roles which government must perform to achieve good government, that is specifying the 'proper' ends of government, was probably an impossible task for the simple reason that:

> everyone wants to answer it in his own way. Subjects extol public tranquillity, citizens individual liberty; the one class prefers security of possessions, the other that of person; the one regards as the best government that which is most severe, the other wants the State to be feared by its neighbours, the other prefers that it should be ignored.[2]

It is possible to identify three broad categories of activities to suggest when it is appropriate to have recourse to the state, that is when the limits of the market may have been realised. The first category of activities, which are not the concern of this work, could be regarded as those which are clearly the province of the market; they are activities which define the very nature of markets, and with which markets have always been identified. In these cases, markets are best when transaction costs are low, contract requirements are easy to specify, and where the quality of the service provided can be determined with some precision. The nature of these products and services is such that in a liberal democratic state there is little possibility, in normal circumstances, that governments would need to take responsibility for their provision, although this has occurred. Of these, the provision of an immense array of consumer goods, such as clothing, is most obvious. For the vast majority of goods consumed by individuals to be delivered in an efficient manner and meet market demand, all that is needed is for the market to be allowed to operate freely. Even here, however, it is not unusual for government to take an active role.

Many consumer products require an effective regulatory presence by government, most especially where the products might be a danger to the purchaser or to unsuspecting others. Medicinal drugs, motor vehicles and firearms are just some of the many products that fall within this first category but for which the market is not the sole arbiter of the conditions under which the products will be provided.

The second category of activities are those where the *presumption* is that the market will supply the products and services required but where the presence of government may also be seen as appropriate, even necessary. This category encompasses the most contentious range of activities, for it recognises that the neoliberal reforms have made the boundary between the state and private interests far more permeable. As a result, there is the possibility of great variation and dispute about the activities which should involve the state in either payment or delivery. These activities most notoriously have come to include services which are essential for each member of society and which throughout most of the twentieth century were substantially the domain of government – notably education and public utilities such as gas, water and electricity. The consequence of the liberation of market discipline for those unable to pay for essential services was tragically demonstrated in 2007 when a New Zealand woman, who was dependent upon a mechanical respirator for breathing, died soon after her electricity supply was cut off after she failed to pay her bill to the private electricity provider. In early 2008 the German-owned energy company npower was also heavily criticised by the British energy regulator, Ofgem, for its readiness to cut the supply of gas to British domestic consumers who had not paid their bills. The chief executive of Ofgem cautioned private energy suppliers, at a time when the prices of gas and electricity had undergone unprecedented increases (npower had itself announced a 19 per cent rise), to ensure that 'they are offering the best support to people in debt or danger of falling into debt'.[3]

The third category of activities are those which are most clearly, and thus widely accepted to be, state responsibilities. Activities in this category encompass pure public goods such as defence. A feature of these is that governments are unable to restrict access to the benefits they provide, since they fall to everyone. Even here, however, the state's fiercest critics have been pushing the state to find the critical limits of markets. In this regard the privatisation of prison services and air traffic control systems, the rising private involvement in defence and the contracting out of child protection services have been particularly controversial. With this category it is often difficult to specify outcomes or how to measure and achieve them. It is these activities which especially highlight the limits of markets and the insufficiency of self-interest, either to promote unproblematically individual well-being or the common good.

According to the more extreme neoliberal beliefs, all activities are legitimately the province of the private sector. There are few if any services to which the government has an exclusive right. Government should retreat into the shadows, emerging only to ensure that the rules of economic engagement are honoured by participants and not take a dominant role in the provision of services. The result has been that no longer do governments in Anglo-American liberal democracies necessarily see themselves as the exclusive champion of the public interest with respect to the delivery of some services which they had provided for much of the twentieth century and which most citizens regarded as their right. In the individualised world of the neoliberal, the greater role which individuals are expected to take in protecting their own interests places them in a more intimate relationship with the private sector, but at the same time closes off avenues of protection. The entrepreneurial, dynamic, business-like government of the neoliberal is only possible, it is suggested, if it is allowed to become more like its private partners and less like outmoded, no longer relevant images of government. In the more extreme neoliberals' radical vision for the liberal democratic state, government is only to ensure that the structures are in place which allow individuals the opportunity for self-fulfilment.

The rise of the modern state

Government agencies and their effects permeate every aspect of our society in the pursuit of 'peace, order and good government',[4] so much so that in the modern state it is difficult to identify the precise boundaries of government. Accordingly, it is undeniable that the actions of government in liberal democracies such as Britain and Australia are remarkable for their depth of penetration and breadth of coverage. Even in the United States, the supposed paragon of market virtue and extreme individualism, the government still maintains a significant presence. According to Thomas Paine, whereas society resulted from our 'wants', government was the product of our 'wickedness': 'the former promotes our happiness *positively*, by limiting our affections, the latter *negatively* by restraining our vices'.[5] For most practical purposes the terms 'state' and 'government' are regarded as synonymous, with a more nuanced approach taken by some writers who prefer to regard the liberal democratic state as composed of both the elected government and the institutions it requires to order and discipline individuals who constitute the second component of the state, civil society, the collection of free and autonomous individuals living lives of private endeavour, for the most part in mutual harmony.[6] The partisan nature of particular governments will mean that they may be replaced; whereas the state, as an association of individuals who share a set of cultural and historical characteristics within a sovereign territory, will endure. The essential characteristic of the state for Max Weber, famously, was its monopoly of the forces of physical coercion exercised through legal and social institutions.

Over most of the past millennia, the foundations and expectations of government were remarkably stable in comparison with the present realities. Not until the mid-nineteenth century did it become accepted that governments might assume an active role in the daily lives of their citizens, apart from ensuring that the community, often a city-state, was secure from the intrusions of outside forces. Any governing institutions essentially served the interests of a small, privileged and vastly wealthy minority of the population for whom the remainder existed to serve unquestioningly. In the eighteenth century, Enlightenment thinkers in Europe and America challenged this traditional, and usually divinely ordered, view of government, proposing instead that governments only existed with the permission of the people over whom they ruled and not according to the churches' interpretation of the wishes of God. Instead of the great bulk of the populace having no right to question those who ruled over them, it was now claimed that all had a set of natural rights, only some of which they were prepared to trade for the protection of the state. This conception of government questioned the absolute authority claimed by most monarchical governments and the bases of this authority. Rather than God pronouncing upon the legitimacy of governments, it was the long-suffering people who now had the right to pass judgement on governments and, consequently, to determine their legitimacy. Individuals who now saw themselves with a natural right to liberty, happiness, equality before the law and freedom from oppression were unlikely to be satisfied with governments who denied the sovereignty of the individual over that of the state. Thus began the long struggle between liberty and authority which Mill saw as the most 'conspicuous feature' of modern history and the modern state.[7]

The essential features of democratic government have been enshrined in either written constitutions, as in America, Australia and France, or the uncodified political customs and understandings of Britain. The written constitutions which underpin the government of a number of liberal democracies testify to the enduring concerns of government and the expectations of their citizens. They provide the overarching conception of the role of government and the importance of the state. In 1733 Lord Bolingbroke described a constitution as 'that assemblage of laws, institutions and customs, derived from certain fixed principles of reason, directed to certain fixed objects of public good, that comprise the general system, according to which the community hath agreed to be governed'.[8] Constitutions for many countries provide for clear restrictions on the powers of government, the consequence of which should be to promote the welfare of those who live under the constitution.[9] Hence the American Constitution established that the people of the United States had created their union to 'establish Justice, insure domestic Tranquility, provide for the common defence, the general Welfare, and secure the Blessings of Liberty'.

Modern constitutions enshrined citizens' expectation that in return for surrendering some of their liberty in the interests of the common good that they would receive tangible, positive benefits. The spread and excesses of industrialisation in the early nineteenth century served to destroy these illusions and to alienate large sections of the population who found themselves at the mercy of powerful industrialists and landowners. As the new class of capitalists began to supplant the aristocracy, who usually had a strong sense of obligation for the welfare of their tenants, and to deny the bulk of the population a share in the newly created wealth, governments were forced to redress some of the imbalance. In addition, the worsening living conditions which accompanied unregulated industrialisation and urbanisation eventually made it necessary for government to intervene to ensure that there was a sufficient supply of educated, healthy workers to meet the needs of industry. No longer was it sufficient for the government to remain neutral and limit its role to ensuring that impediments were not unduly placed in the way of individual initiative and wealth creation. Instead, the state was forced to protect those least able to look after themselves from the excesses of self-interested, untrammelled markets and to promote a more equitable distribution of the benefits of wealth. The resulting surge in social legislation in the latter half of the nineteenth century was testament to not only the social consciences of a few influential individuals but also to the self-serving foresight of those whose position, power and wealth were most threatened by glaring social and economic imbalances.[10]

Greater activity by the government in what had been the domain of private individuals did not signal, however, relinquishment of a preference for a minimalist role for government. Adam Smith's analogy of the 'invisible hand',[11] whereby market mechanisms were to see to the most efficient use of resources, retained a firm grip on most governments until well into the early twentieth century when only the savagery of modern war was able to slacken this hold temporarily. In the reconstruction which followed World War II, the same collective mentality and national cohesion which had been essential to the successful prosecution of the war effort was transferred to the social sphere with the rise to maturity of the welfare state in Australia and Britain, although less so in the United States. Until the late twentieth century, liberal democratic governments continued to take on more responsibilities in response to the demands of their citizens and their rising affluence. Citizens came to expect frequent interactions with their government. This was especially so in a nation-building state such as Australia.

With a very small population thinly distributed over vast distances, the assumption by government of responsibility for public utilities and infrastructure services was widely seen as essential to the social and economic development of Australia. Thus, in the 40 years prior to Federation in 1901, public capital formation progressively exceeded private. The public sector financed railways, irrigation schemes as well as urban transport and sewerage systems, water supplies and, in time, gas and electricity.[12] After Federation the state governments at times required Commonwealth financial support in order to promote progress. For example, neither private enterprise nor the states had the financial resources to link the east and west coasts by rail, even though this was thought to be a national strategic priority for economic and defence purposes. Accordingly, in 1912 the Commonwealth undertook construction of the rail link from Port Augusta to Western Australia.[13] The Commonwealth was also instrumental in the construction of roads in remote and sparsely populated areas. Realising the limited means available to the less populous states, the Commonwealth's *Main Roads Development Act* of 1923 provided for grants to the states for the building of new roads and the improvement of existing national roads.[14] The Commonwealth government also moved to establish the Commonwealth Bank in 1911. This was in response to Australians' awareness that their economic and social well-being were vulnerable to the selfish priorities of other countries, particularly after economic catastrophes of the late nineteenth century had been caused predominantly by irresponsible British banks. When the legislation was introduced in Parliament, it was described as a 'bank belonging to the people, and directly managed by the people's own agents'.[15]

It is often suggested that the twentieth century was dominated by the battle between state provision of services, epitomised by socialism and Marxist political philosophy, and the market, epitomised by America's form of capitalism and liberal political philosophy. Indeed, the fall of the communism in Russia and throughout eastern Europe in the last decades of the twentieth century signified for Francis Fukuyama 'the end point of man's ideological evolution and the universalism of Western liberal democracy': we had reached 'the end of history'.[16] It also settled, he suggested, the precedence of the market over the state. Oliver Letwin, speaking for the British Conservative Party in May 2007 while launching a more 'socially focussed' image for the party, also proclaimed that the struggle for political supremacy and legitimacy between socialism and capitalism had been decided in favour of the market, and that the debate which now engaged both the Conservatives and Labour was no longer about how much the state should do for individuals but about the enabling role which was now assumed for the state; how the state could best provide the circumstances which enabled individuals to fulfil themselves.[17] Meanwhile, announced Letwin, 'the free market has won ... and we now need to focus on our society: not just the way we run our economy but the whole way we live'.[18] The free market may have swept most of its competitors before it but it was only able to do so by being embedded in a powerful, resilient political doctrine – liberalism.

The state and the liberal mind

From the eighteenth century, understandings about the role of the state and the importance of the market, but especially allowing it to operate free from political interference, were most heavily influenced by the principles of liberalism. Modern liberalism can trace its essential philosophy to constitutional disagreements which occurred within Britain and France from the seventeenth century. The constitutional crises in England – firstly civil war beginning in 1642 and then revolution in 1688 – prompted the first significant efforts by Thomas Hobbes (1588–1679), Adam Smith (1723–1790) and John Locke (1632–1704) to formalise beliefs which later in the nineteenth century were to become identified with liberalism.

According to Hayek, Adam Smith's *The Wealth of Nations* published in 1776 signalled the birth of liberalism.[19] However, it is in the writings of Locke especially that the main principles around which liberalism was later to coalesce can be discerned. Particularly important was his belief in inalienable natural human rights which did not presuppose, nor should they be altered by, any form of government. These rights were independent of government and absolute in their rendition within any form of government. In his *Two Treatises on Government* he concluded that:

> the natural liberty of man is to be free from any superior power on earth, and not to be under the will or legislative authority of man, but to have only the law of nature for his rule ... The liberty of man in society is to be under no other legislative power but that established by consent in the commonwealth, not under the dominion of any will, or restraint of any law, but what that legislation shall enact according to the trust put in it.[20]

Locke, and indeed Hobbes, was writing at a time when government was often tyrannical, when only a few individuals had any say in it, and all were at the mercy of this privileged elite. Accordingly, the theories of government of the early liberal writers were bound to reflect this immediate influence. Their argument for natural rights which were independent of the largesse and beneficence of governments was their only means of denying the legitimacy of oppression. In the eighteenth century, the ideas of the French social philosophers Montesquieu and Rousseau, as they endeavoured to justify the revolution of 1789 and to explain its later excesses, provided fresh impetus to liberal doctrines. That the experiences and precise political prescriptions of these writers should now unquestionably govern the lives of individuals would of course be unrealistic and disingenuous.

From the writings of early liberals, 'classical' liberalism emerged in the nineteenth century with the works of John Stuart Mill, Jeremy Bentham and, most notoriously, Herbert Spencer's confronting remedies for society's ills. Amongst the fundamental beliefs of classical liberalism were the benefits of 'minimal' government, the sanctity of private property, freedom from arbitrary rule, and the importance of allowing individuals responsibility for their own lives.[21] According to Spencer (1820–1903), the 'liberty which a citizen enjoys is to be measured, not by the nature of the governmental machinery he lies under, whether representative or other, but by the relative paucity of the restraints it imposes on him'.[22] The state should do nothing other than protect the freedoms of individuals – Spencer's 'principle of equal freedom'. Thomas Jefferson, in his inaugural address in 1801, urged that once government had provided citizens with the necessary protections against violence from their neighbours, it should then leave them to 'regulate their own pursuits of industry and improvement'.[23] Always, assured Mill:

> the great majority of things are worse done by the intervention of government, than the individuals most interested in the matters would do them ... if left to themselves ... [P]eople understand their own business and their own interests better, and care for them more, than the government does ... This maxim holds true throughout the greatest part of the business of life, and wherever it is true we ought to condemn every kind of government intervention that conflicts with it.[24]

While Mill and Spencer may have viewed state intervention with similar apprehension, they differed significantly in their attitudes towards those without property or the means of subsistence. Mill believed that those who had the most also benefited the most from the protection of the state and, thus, should pay more for this protection.[25] In marked contrast Spencer thought that whenever the state sought to mitigate the distress of individuals by levying higher taxes on the rich it had exchanged its role as protector for that of the oppressor of those who took responsibility for themselves. The state was never to take from the prosperous in the mistaken view that it must assist the desperate.[26] Robert Nozick – again unlike Adam Smith, who believed that a society would only endure if the least fortunate were not forgotten – also rejects the idea of the state taking responsibility for achieving social justice if this relies upon a conception of distributive justice in which voluntarism and individuality are corrupted.[27] The state, according to Nozick, should limit itself to ensuring that entitlement rights, once confirmed as just, are secure. For the government to levy taxes on members of society, but in particular upon those with property, is to deprive them unjustly of the fruits of their labour and deny them their right to liberty. This, concluded Nozick, contradicted the very reason for the formation and perpetuation of society. Government should force no-one to come to the assistance of others, either directly or indirectly through forced levies on property – that is taxes.

For the modern liberal, the successor to classical liberalism, the hegemony of the market may promote a superior form of society where individuals are left largely to their own devices, but this does not mean that all social legislation is to be condemned nor, most contentiously, that government should not intervene when the economic threat was sufficient. Instead, there will be some acts of government which should be tolerated for purposes of selfish protection if it prevents social disaffection that would otherwise threaten the liberty and economic freedoms of the majority. Thus, in 1933 at the height of the Great Depression, when the very existence of capitalism seemed to be threatened by the collapse of thousands of banks throughout America, the United States government passed the Glass-Steagell Banking Act which provided government guarantees to protect bank deposits. Nor, as a later section demonstrates, has the state been reticent to intervene to protect the financial pillars of the capitalist state by either compensating investors and depositors of failed banks or by bailing out formerly powerful financial institutions whose collapse would threaten the survival of many others.

George Soros warned that the need for such interventions was becoming more frequent with the accelerated propensity of innovative financial instruments to destabilise global markets and threaten global financial disaster. Indeed, financial crises are becoming not only endemic to international capitalism but increasingly and rapidly communicable to other markets.[28] These concerns were clearly present when in August 2007 the central banks of France, Germany, Japan, America and the European Central Bank felt compelled to protect their financial markets with the injection of substantial sums when they were threatened by exposure to the financial collapse of the sub-prime housing market in America. In two days, the main central banks injected more than US$660 billion to calm worried investors. For some, rescues such as this or the American government's resuscitation of the home mortgage companies Fannie Mae and Freddie Mac in 2008 were only further evidence of the blatant hypocrisy of the financial markets and of their political protectors. 'No industry', complained Martin Wolf, 'has a comparable talent for privatising gains and socialising losses. Participants in no other industry get as self-righteously angry when public officials – particularly, central bankers – fail to come at once to their rescue when they get into (well-deserved) trouble.'[29] Meanwhile *The Guardian* decried the way:

> Financiers constantly tell the rest of us to leave them alone. The best regulation, we are told, is the lightest regulation; any more and they will take their ball and will play elsewhere. Apart from when they are in trouble, that is …
>
> If an obscure German institution or a well-established French bank finds itself caught out by … tighter credit conditions … that is surely their business alone – just as it was all their own business when times were good.[30]

As the full effects of the credit crisis of 2007–08 began to be felt in the previously prosperous housing market, and the market value of the major building firms in Britain plummeted, they also called upon the government to 'do something' to save their industry. Matt Ridley, the chairman of the British bank Northern Rock which the Bank of England narrowly saved from total collapse in September 2007 by injecting £16 billion of taxpayer money, had confidently pronounced in 1994, well before his public humiliation, that the 'little-known ninth law of thermodynamics states that the more money a group receives from the taxpayer, the more it demands'.[31]

In liberal eyes, Keynesian macroeconomics showed only too clearly how intervention by government leads to the need and demand for more intervention. When government took responsibility for achieving full employment, rather than ensuring the security of the political and economic institutions which provide the means for this to be achieved, they were inexorably drawn into more forms of intervention, with each requiring yet more intervention and oppression.[32] The problem in preserving a free society then becomes 'how to ensure that coercive powers granted to government in order to preserve freedom are limited to that function'.[33] Friedman warns that danger, not deliverance is, and ever has been, the consequence of more government.

State limits and private partnerships

Bentham referred to the proper province of government as the 'agenda' of government and other functions as the 'non-agenda'. Mill referred to the 'necessary' and 'optional' functions. Agenda, or necessary activities, relate not to those 'which private individuals are already fulfilling, but to those functions which fall outside the sphere of the individual, to those decisions which are made by no-one if the State does not make them'.[34] For Keynes, government functions were either 'technically social' or 'technically individual'.[35] The functions which constitute Keynes's technically social functions were regarded by Mill as being 'inseparable from the idea of government', for they enable individuals to accomplish things that they would be unable to accomplish by themselves.[36] For the neoliberal conservative, if markets are by default the preferred option, then government should only take on that which the markets cannot or will not do. That is, following classical liberalism, the government fulfils a residual function. The less attractive, yet unavoidable, effect of this for Galbraith is clearly seen in the 'shameful' state of American cities, where it seems that government will only step in at the last moment and only under the most extreme pressure to ensure that residents do not live in a state of constant fear and debased living conditions. The result of this 'private affluence and public squalor', in the case of America, was endemic violence and the degradation of its cities.[37] Tony Blair, contrary to his enthusiasm for the market, reminded the British public that the 'state of our public services defines the nature of our country. Our public realm is what we share together. How it develops tells us a lot about what we hold in common.'[38]

Irrespective of the neoliberals' capture of Adam Smith as the ultimate vindication of their demands for a minimal state, he was very tolerant of a wide and 'elastic' range of activity for government. For example, Smith was prepared to forsake the benefits of the unhindered operation of the principle of economic advantage in international trade if a higher good resulted, such as national security. Accordingly, Smith's vision for government was not absolute and applicable at all times. Instead, it very much reflected contemporary conditions and concerns. Consequently, the role of government today should not be expected to conform to some mythologised, eighteenth-century Smithian marketised ideal, when he clearly saw that the contributions of the market must be subservient to the needs of the greater good. Of and by itself, a particular activity engaged in by government was not necessarily illegitimate according to market principles if it met other, higher, needs.

Mill also believed in the 'universal rule': that government should intervene when it produced a greater benefit, 'when the case of expediency is strong'. He rejected the merciless, unyielding approach of his contemporary Spencer – who stipulated a very precise, limited and unvarying role for government. For Mill there were no prescribed, unambiguously sanctioned roles for government which were invariable over time and according to circumstance. Rather:

> the admitted functions of government embrace a much wider field than can easily be included within ... any restrictive definition, and that it is hardly possible to find any ground of justification common to them all, except the comprehensive one of general expediency ...
>
> In the particular circumstances of a given age or nation, there is scarcely anything, really important to the general interest, which it may not be desirable, or even necessary, that the government should take upon itself, not because private individuals cannot effectually perform it, but because they will not.[39]

Although admitting various possible forms of government intervention, the market still remained for all liberals the natural means by which the general interest was promoted. Profound public sector reforms of the late twentieth century confirmed this abiding sanctity of markets for liberals. It 'seemed obvious' to Mitch Daniels, President George W Bush's budget director, 'that the business of government is not to provide services, but to make sure that they are provided'.[40] Indeed, the role of government has been transformed in many cases from that of the provider of services, with responsibility for both delivering and paying for services, to that of purchaser, where the service is delivered by the private sector on behalf of government and the public but paid for by government. This has been achieved in a number of ways, including contracting out a vast array of services once provided by government agencies.[41] The private sector's provision of sophisticated information technology is one of the most profitable examples. It is also one of the most controversial, as a result of widespread unease about placing in private hands immense amounts of sensitive personal information, especially when there have been numerous instances where even governments have been unable to ensure the integrity of their information systems. Similar fears were expressed in Australia when significant outsourcing of the Commonwealth government's information technology functions was first contemplated in the late 1990s.[42] A report by the New South Wales Auditor General in 2002 warned of the considerable risks associated with outsourcing of information technology, and of the need to ensure that agencies are clear why they should do so.[43] The previously inconceivable opportunities for the security of private information, collected and held by governments, to be compromised, opening the way especially for identity fraud, was dramatically exposed in November 2007 when the British Department of Revenue and Customs was unable to account for two compact discs which had been sent through the mail to the National Audit Office. These discs contained highly detailed personal information concerning the 25 million citizens who received child benefits, information which included their addresses and bank account numbers, along with details of their children.

Also very popular with reformist governments in their marketisation of the state have been joint infrastructure projects with the private sector in which private companies might design, build, finance and sometimes operate a facility which provides a public service. In Britain these are known as either the public private partnerships (PPP) or the private finance initiative (PFI). A PFI involves the government contracting with the private sector to provide services which the government will pay for from taxation revenues, but it does not involve the transfer of ownership of any assets to the government. PPPs, the preferred generic term used in Australia for infrastructure projects with the private sector, provide governments with the opportunity to gain equity in a company or an asset.[44] More than 44 countries have used PPP arrangements to provide economic infrastructure such as roads, ports, airports, water treatment facilities and power generation, and social infrastructure such as hospitals and schools.[45] In Britain PPPs, which involve private companies designing, building, financing and sometimes operating a facility which provides a public service, were introduced on a modest scale by the British Conservative government in 1992. Subsequently, they were greatly expanded by New Labour in order to bring much-needed investment to public services, especially in the areas of hospital and school building programs. There are now over 800 PFI/PPP projects in operation in Britain, accounting for around £54 billion of investment, 12 per cent of government infrastructure projects, and over £200 billion of long-term debt repayments by government. In Australia, the Victorian government has entered into 16 major PPP contracts valued at over A$4.5 billion, or 10 per cent of aggregate public sector investment. This accounts for more than one-third of the total number of PPP projects in Australia.[46]

The purported greatest advantage of PPPs is the *apparent* transfer of the debt and associated risk for the construction of large infrastructure projects to the private sector.[47] This politically enhances the government's financial credentials to the electorate in the short term since, in the case of Britain, PPPs do not appear in the budget against the Public Sector Borrowing Requirement, thereby allowing the government greater freedom to borrow for other purposes. This accounting practice was heavily criticised in a biting report by the British trade union organisation UNISON in 2001, at the height of the Blair government's infatuation with the market.[48] Entering into agreements with the private sector to build and operate large public sector projects on behalf of the government, such as hospitals, is usually justified by their proponents on the basis of improvements in quality, accessibility and cost. Partnerships with the private sector were to enable governments to ensure the provision of services which, it was strenuously and aggressively argued, would not be affordable and, therefore, not provided if they had to be funded by government.

What has often escaped the public's attention, if not that of the national and state treasuries and their political masters, is the potentially greater long-term financial costs of the projects to the taxpayer while ever PPPs and PFIs encourage private firms to design projects which are meant to generate the highest profits possible. Also overlooked is the inability of government to transfer attendant risks to the private contractor. A Victorian parliamentary committee warned that the:

> extent to which there can be complete allocation of risks between the government and private sector parties to PPPs is questionable, given government's ultimate responsibility for public services and its inability to transfer what might be described as its political risks and obligations to the electorate … [R]esponsibilities … will ultimately be linked back to government if problems with projects or services are encountered.[49]

The very significant financial dilemmas now confronting Coventry hospital, which was built as part of a British PFI project, are but representative of many similar examples in Britain and Australia which have quickly emerged in the wake of a program of rapid expansion in contracting with the private sector for the delivery of public services since the early 1990s. It also demonstrates, argues George Monbiot, how the neoliberal demands for a minimal state and maximum freedom for business are in practice but fraudulent deceptions, for these policies continue to be dependent upon very significant government support; it has rarely been a matter of *either* government *or* the private sector during the term of a PPP or PFI agreement. In the mid-1990s, the Coventry local health authority was faced with the need to spend £30 million to refurbish its main hospital. With funding in short supply and the private sector uninterested in the limited opportunity for profit from the project, the authority found that it could generate more private sector interest by having the existing buildings demolished and replaced by a new building – estimated to cost £174 million. Ultimately the building cost £410 million, initially resulting in annual payments to the private contractor by the local health authority of £56 million. These costs are required to rise with the retail price index over the 30-year life of the contract. The financial strain of trying to meet the ever-rising annual costs has seen the local health authority, in actions reminiscent of other cities, close hospital wards, dismiss staff and remove beds from other wards, all in an attempt to reduce the much greater financial deficits that it now faces.[50]

Similar problems with PPPs were encountered in Australia with the Metropolitan Women's Correctional Centre and the Latrobe Regional Hospital in Victoria, and the Port Macquarie Base Hospital in New South Wales, all of which were later returned to government control. Built in 1994 under a PPP between Mayne Nickless and the New South Wales government as a 'Build, Own, Operate' (BOO) project, the Port Macquarie Base Hospital was a prominent example of the Greiner Liberal government's belief in the inherent superiority of the private sector in providing services to the public, whether these services be primarily commercial in nature or a core public service such as hospital care. After just over a decade of troubled operations and mounting local opposition, the state government was eventually forced to assume responsibility for the operation of the hospital. The government was praised on all sides for reversing what the Nurses' Association called a 'failed experiment', one which had cost far more than if the government had built and operated the hospital. The failure was a potent reminder for many that while ever the motives of the private sector are the pursuit of profit, citizens such as the residents of Port Macquarie would always be treated as 'second class citizens for private partners will only want to concentrate on aspects that are most lucrative'.[51] With financial gain, rather than providing quality health care, the priority, the least profitable, high-cost services were most often provided at publicly owned hospitals and the more profitable treatments carried out at the Port Macquarie Base Hospital.[52]

Not only did the PFI project in Coventry and the private hospital at Port Macquarie fail to provide a service at a cost comparable to that if the hospitals had remained in the public sector, the involvement of the private sector in fact resulted in a diminished capacity to deliver sufficient services and of the quality required. In the case of the Port Macquarie Base Hospital, operations were cancelled at short notice and long waiting lists soon developed. Meanwhile, problems at Coventry hospital have given the lie to the promises of those in government and in the Treasury who aggressively imposed this PFI program, and many others, on the British taxpayer. Other studies of British National Health Service trusts, notably the Norfold and Norwich hospital, have arrived at similar conclusions.[53] While ever profits must come before the interests of the public, declares Monbiot, it will not be unexpected if PPPs and PFIs deliver poorer services than if these had been the responsibility of the public sector: 'Beds are crammed together in hospitals which look and feel like giant morgues; operating theatres are flooded with sewage; children try to study in permanent building sites ... The experiment keeps failing, but the government keeps repeating it.'[54] Private firms engaged in PFIs have also been shown to benefit outrageously at the taxpayer's expense should there ever be the need to vary the conditions of the original contracts. Thus, Britain's National Audit Office found in its 2008 report *Making Changes in Operational PFI Projects* that private firms were using these opportunities to charge prices which could vary by more than ten times for the same operation. The simple matter of replacing a lock varied at one PFI hospital between £30.81 and £486.54.[55] After two decades of major PPP projects in Victoria, the costly deficiencies and recurring failures meant that the Victorian Public Accounts and Estimates Committee was unable to judge whether PPPs delivered better value for money than traditional government provision.[56]

Irrespective of the problems experienced with PPPs, measures of financial efficiency which inevitably favour private firms still dominate decisions to award substantial infrastructure contracts. However, comparisons of economic efficiency made between the state and the market have systematically and knowingly overlooked the inequity in terms of efficiency. To expect public sector agencies to manage as well as the private sector is to assume that when both are managed at similar levels of efficiency that they are also operating under the same constraints of equity, transparency, consultation and accountability; indeed, that the functions of the public and private sectors are comparable. Yet, public sector performance dimensions are often unavoidably more dense and complex than private sector equivalents, where they exist. For many public services, it may be very difficult, if not impossible, to obtain precise measures of the relationships between inputs and outputs, or even to identify discrete outputs. Identifying and quantifying the usually more amorphous outcomes – for example safer cities as a result of greater spending on more police – is even more fraught with uncertainty and dispute. When government compares unfavourably with the private sector it may be that their greater obligations prejudice performance assessments in purely economic terms, the primary means by which goal achievement is measured in the private sector. Instead, the efficiency of public services delivered by government is a combination of economic and social efficiencies, such as carrying out road construction in a manner which ensures that fragile ecosystems are not endangered, or including extra safety measures in dam construction.

The difference in standards which apply to core service delivery by the public and private sectors, although not given much credence by neoliberals, was realised by Weber, who made a distinction between formal and substantive rationality. While the former is entirely dependent upon rational calculation, substantive rationality refers to a course of action which:

> will be interpreted in terms of a given set of ultimate values ... or ... the content of the particular ends to which it is orientated ... [T]he merely formal calculation in money terms may seem either of quite secondary importance or even as fundamentally evil in itself.[57]

Even though most Western societies may be an association of self-interested individuals, there is an underlying shared belief that the purpose of a social collective should be the preservation and improvement of the welfare of its members.[58]

Irrespective of the efforts of neoliberals to convince citizens that political accountability is no longer the most important requirement of those in the service of government, with preference given instead to accountabilities derived from an entrepreneurial paradigm, this has not been able to dislodge the public's belief that accountability:

is not to be equated with efficiency or with satisfactory experience
of public services by parent, patient, passenger, traveller or whatever.
It has a deeper meaning in expressing the fundamental relationship
between individual, community or collectivity and government.[59]

The House of Commons Home Affairs Committee, in its investigation
of the extent and use of electronic surveillance in British society,
warned governments that ultimately the merits or otherwise in
terms of national security would depend upon maintaining public
trust.[60] The stewardship entrusted to government brings with it a set
of duties, derived from the expectations of the community, which
transcend and encompass far more than simple financial rectitude.
Johnston has reminded us that the 'customer-focused efficiency and
economy model ... is a very different creature than the traditional,
legitimate, political, citizen-oriented model based on the public
interest and public law'.[61] Citizens are far more than 'consumers' of
either public or private sector goods and services. Instead, citizenship
carries with it a broad range of privileges and responsibilities, of
which the consumption of goods and services is only one small part.
Consumption is not the defining characteristic of citizenship, nor
of the agenda of government. Government is expected to represent
the interests of all citizens, only some of whom may be a consumer
of a given product or service. For George Monbiot 'we need a state
that rewards us for co-operating and punishes us for cheating and
stealing ... and [is itself] punished when it acts against the common
good'.[62]

The agenda of the market state: an exploration

Some irreducible government presence will always be necessary to
forestall the consequences of anarchy which might be permitted by
the market. Whenever individuals 'are allowed to pursue their genetic
interests without constraint, they will hurt other people. They will
grab other peoples' resources, they will dump their waste in other
peoples' habitats, they will cheat, lie, steal and kill.'[63] Even the
minimal nightwatchman state envisaged by the severest opponents

of interventionist government still requires someone to take responsibility for pure public goods, such as defence, and to ensure that the necessary legal institutions are in place to enforce market agreements. Hayek reassured his readers that in 'no state that could be rationally defended would the state just do nothing'.[64]

Public goods for Smith and Mill encompassed those public works which were not sufficiently profitable for individuals to provide, but which had the potential to benefit all and for all to suffer in their absence; those which were necessary to facilitate the 'commerce of society' and of 'commerce in general'. These included: highways, bridges, canals, coinage, the post office, street lighting, enforcement of contracts, and protection against deception which involves threats to property. Smith also supported protection of the young and mentally incapable, standards for weights and measures, public sanitation and public education.[65] Of these, state responsibility for public sanitation provides a particularly potent example of a public good which benefits alike those who contribute and those, known as free-riders, who have access to a service without payment; and with neither being disadvantaged by the benefit which the other receives because all live free from the threat of life-threatening epidemics. Indeed, those who contribute to the public good of community health must be prepared to accept that externalities, or spill-over effects, such as contributing to the health of others, may be a precondition for them to get the full benefit of their contributions. Any attempts to exclude the free-rider from participating in the benefits of a healthy city – for instance by condemning them to live in unsewered, filthy ghettos – threatens all members of the community should there be an outbreak of a highly contagious disease in such areas: disease such as cholera is no respecter of persons, however rich and powerful. The easy transmission of pathogens means that in effect the very bloodstream of each individual is a public good and properly the object of coercion and intervention by government which is in everyone's best interest.[66] Thus, most states have legislated to force the quarantine of anyone with a life-threatening, contagious disease. Despite what would seem the obvious benefits of the state actively engaged in ensuring healthy living conditions, Herbert Spencer was still able to disagree, complaining that public sanitation tended to favour the poorest, who pay the least for the service and thus its provision through tax levies should be opposed.[67]

Galbraith, who accepted that there is an irreducible minimum role for government in a civilised society, lists only four reasons for government intervention: protection of the planet; protection of vulnerable workers; protection against dangerous goods; and, most exceptionally, to address the inbuilt destructive tendencies of capitalism, including its propensity to marginalise the less fortunate.[68] 'In the good society', he argued, 'no-one can be left outside without income, be assigned to starvation, homelessness, untreated illness ... Those in need have enough to suffer without being socially stigmatised.'[69] Similarly, Kenneth Arrow, another Nobel laureate economist, has expressed his apprehension about the excesses of a society in which the pursuit of maximum profits drives out any concern for a broader social interest. Even Hayek, who had lived through the Great Depression of the 1930s and World War II, was prepared to admit that the state should play a part in ensuring against extreme privations or hazards of life such as sickness by helping to organise – although not take full responsibility for – a system of social insurance that might also allow the return of a productive member to society.[70]

Nearly two decades after Margaret Thatcher was forced out of Number 10, these concerns were surprisingly recognised by the British Conservative Party which, in 2007, coined the term the 'framework state' to describe their vision for Britain. With particular reference to the British situation, Oliver Letwin described the conservatism of his leader, David Cameron, as:

> a fundamentally different approach to society from ... [the] centralist,
> provider state. Instead of failed efforts to improve society and our
> quality of life by control from the centre, Cameron Conservatism is
> arguing for a framework state ... Instead of being about economics,
> politics in a post-Marxist age is all about the way we live our lives. It is
> about society.[71]

Elsewhere, Cameron referred to the need for government to be less eco-centric and more socio-centric. In particular, he was critical of the alacrity with which profit-seeking enterprises engage in practices, such as pollution, which are costly to society and for which the profiteer is never made accountable. Whenever society and individuals were forced into an unequal relationship with suppliers as a result of the latter's ability to divorce themselves from deleterious indirect consequences of their actions, there needed to be some mechanism to enforce social responsibility and to remind profit maximisers that they had moral obligations to the society which gave them their existence and legitimacy.[72] This post-Thatcher conception of an enabling state confirmed the long-held liberal belief that the state had two essential roles: providing security and stability, and ensuring a framework of support which allows and encourages people to pursue their own self-interest in such a way that would also see them fulfil their responsibilities to the wider community.[73] Some of the functions which might constitute this legitimate province of government are now explored further.

Defending the integrity of the state

It is in the arena of defence, often referred to as a 'pure public good', that the limits of claims on behalf of the market become especially obvious. The most enduring, agreed role of government throughout the recorded history of the state is defending its political and geographical integrity. In its primary motivations and justifications, this is purely a political matter. Accordingly, consideration of economics should not come into the government's provision of some services such as defence; just as politics is not expected to come into the provision of services by the private sector. If market considerations do become major considerations in defence, then they may deny the delivery of the services deemed necessary. If economics and financial considerations were the most important criteria in *all* state action, then there certainly would be no war, of which the extravagance in lives and resources has only worsened as the technology of war has advanced. The market can help in making war sustainable, by ensuring that the necessary resources are used to their best advantage, but it does not decide whether or how war will be waged. The market can have a part to play in the delivery of war-time resources but does not determine whether they will be, or ought to be, provided. Contrary to this political axiom, public choice visionaries especially have been vocal in their advocacy of more pervasive contributions to defence from the private sector.

Representative of public choice views, Tullock's radical support for contracting out significant parts of America's defence capability provides the opportunity to explore the limits of the market in matters of defence. Referring to the extensive presence that the private sector already has in meeting the maintenance needs of the American defence forces, for example the manufacture and supply of ammunition, he sees no reason why similar principles could not apply to the provision of fully operational aircraft carriers such as the USS *Enterprise*. It would be of 'no immense importance whether the holder of the contract for the USS *Enterprise* was the West Point Alumni Association or the US Postal Service'.[74] Even if the arguments used to support such an initiative may have an attractive economic logic, Tullock ignores any consideration or recognition that defence is inherently affected by political, non-financial considerations; that it is not firstly, or even primarily, a matter of getting the best deal. The consequences of the selfish values upon which capitalism depends and which it demands, whereby individuals are expected to employ their talents in the interests of the highest bidder, have confirmed consistently that loyalty cannot be guaranteed by financial incentives. These might provide some assurance of commitment, of which lucrative incentive schemes for senior business managers are telling examples, but this is conditional and uncertain – unlike the unwavering loyalty expected of a nation's military. In times of war more would be expected of private contractors, who would operate the vessels in Tullock's navy to defend the nation, beyond pure economic self-interest. Instead, those who are expected to give their life if necessary in defence of their country refer to the motives of duty, honour, patriotism and service, rarely financial gain.

All that Tullock promised for making America's defence capability more cost-effective may have seemed possible at the time that he was writing, in 2000, after a long and successful period of marketisation of the state and when the influence of public choice supporters was at its zenith. There appeared to be few convincing examples to refute the expansionist claims of public choice advocates, that is until the terrorist attacks of September 2001. Failures by the private contractors responsible for security at American airports, which allowed the terrorists to board several aircraft and carry out their plans, and the subsequent proposals for the reintroduction of federal government agents to guard airports unequivocally confirmed that national security, whether in providing protections from domestic or external threats, was a matter of politics, not economics.

In matters of defence, the possible antagonism between the aggressive pursuit of private profit and allegiance to the state and the public interest has become especially acute for America with the huge presence of private security contractors in Iraq. In late 2007 there were more American private defence and security contractors in Iraq than members of the American army. Private contractors, notably those employed by the security firm Blackwater USA, based in North Carolina, are employed not only to protect private property and business people but also, in preference to the American military's own personnel, for the protection of the most important American officials in Iraq. Mercenaries have been a feature of war since ancient times, but modern states have usually preferred professional national armies. That is until the late twentieth century, when the virtues of the market now rival that of patriotic impulses.

Such a belief is not for all. The size and potency of the private armies in Iraq in 2007 and their influential relationship with the most senior American politicians alarmed Joe Wilson, the last American ambassador to Iraq before the 1991 Gulf War. Echoing Max Weber, he thought it:

> extraordinarily dangerous when a nation begins to outsource its
> monopoly on the use of force [to] a very powerful interest group within
> the American body politic and an interest group that is ... armed.
> And the question will arise at some time: to whom do they owe their
> loyalty.

Congresswoman Jan Schakowsky also expressed the concern that 'the one thing the people think of as being in the purview of the government is the use of military power. Suddenly you've got a for-profit corporation going around the world that is more powerful than states.'[75] For her and many others, the limits of private contributions to America's defence were clearly and alarmingly evident when Blackwater employees killed 17 innocent Iraqi civilians, allegedly without justifiable provocation, and the company and the United States government refused to take any action against those involved, claiming that they were protected by the legal immunity which Iraqi laws then gave to foreign mercenaries.

The custodians of liberty

The highly contentious and sensitive nature of private involvement in front-line defence is similarly evident with the enthusiastic and rapid privatisation of incarceration services as part of the administration of justice. Here again, the essentials of the liberal state can be particularly well appreciated.[76] As noted earlier, liberalism believes that all rights, whether political, economic or social, are solely the province of the individual, never the collective in whatever form it might take, but especially not the state. As an artificial body, a creation emanating from the freely given consent of individuals, the state has no authority or rights other than that transferred from individuals. Thus, the liberal believes that, if the state is but the agglomeration of authority permitted to it by individuals, then they may also give their consent to delegate this power further from the state to private firms. This means that in the case of the privatisation of prisons, detention centres for illegal immigrants and other forms of state-sanctioned incarceration – where this belief finds possibly its most extreme test – the state does not 'own' the exclusive right to punish, but instead administers this right as a trust on behalf of individual citizens. For the private sector to become involved, all that is necessary is that the private contractor is also made to be accountable for the exercise of this same trust. Market supporters see only benefits for those detained, while tax payers can expect their tax burden to be reduced when supposedly more efficient private contractors provide this service.

With equally strong conviction, those who oppose this use of privatisation believe that there is a strong moral imperative that some activities, such as operating prisons and providing blood transfusions, should not be carried out by the market. Private profit should not be involved when it is derived from human suffering. Just as importantly, critics of private prisons see the creation of these facilities as the surrender by the state of its monopoly of coercion which is a manifestation of the source of its legitimacy and its sovereignty. Nothing better expresses the authority and sovereignty of the state than its ability to order the imprisonment and possibly the death of an individual. Private prisons, and other forms of incarceration, are seen by their critics to contradict the long-held maxim that only the state should be able to deprive of their liberty those within its area of control, even though the original decision to imprison is not the province of the private sector.

Critics of private prisons also protest that any arguments for private prisons which rely upon economic justifications fail to recognise, possibly wittingly, the effect the profit motive may have on the nature and quality of the service. With the provision of services such as prison management, which rely heavily upon professional judgement, they argue that it is not possible to specify contractual conditions with absolute precision and prescience given that the self-interest of the contractors will compel them to do only that which has been explicitly stated in the contract and for which they will be paid. Thus, while it may be easy to identify the best way to meet the nutritional needs of prisoners, many other aspects of management may not be able to be specified, thereby making it difficult to ensure accountability and guarantee the provision of a service equivalent to that provided by government, which is expected to be guided in its management of prisons by other than financial motives.[77]

In an endeavour to meet the well-known objections of such opponents of the privatisation of prisons, those who support privatisation argue that there is no conflict between making a profit and respecting the tenets of justice which encompasses the humane imposition of legally sanctioned punishment. With the precise nature and limits of their authority specified in any contract, if this were possible, it would be irrelevant to prisoners who was in charge; prisoners are not concerned with the 'philosophical niceties' of the state transferring its authority to a private contractor, only how they are treated in practice.[78] Concerns that private providers may be tempted to sacrifice the welfare of the prisoners whenever profits might be threatened are further dismissed as illogical: rather than profits providing a motive for poor treatment, the reverse must be the case. Treating prisoners fairly and justly is a good strategy for controlling costs, for it will help to minimise opportunities for friction between inmates and guards which might otherwise result in very costly and dangerous confrontations. This also will avoid the possibility that the government will have to step in to prevent any violent outbreaks in the prison which might subsequently endanger the community outside. These, it is finally suggested, will be strong arguments to convince government of the benefits of renewing their contract with this efficient and reliable provider.

Contrary to this apparent persuasiveness, the stridency and exclusivity of the arguments promoted by supporters of private prisons, in which rarely is the potential for problems recognised, these arguments have been shown by experience to constitute a propagandised appreciation of the benefits of markets. The reality, as presented in chapter 6, is that however poor the management of those detained, it may be very difficult for government to find alternative providers as well as being politically damaging to have to admit error. Nor are governments unable to relinquish their ultimate responsibility for the secure detention of prisoners, something which has been verified on numerous occasions when taxpayer funded police officers have been called upon to apprehend prisoners who have escaped from privately operated prisons.

The sanctity of market confidence

Consistent with their views about the primacy of property protections in ensuring individual liberty, all liberal political theorists have stressed the fundamental role of the state in ensuring that commercial transactions and public confidence in the market are not corrupted and, thereby, threatened by either the fraudulent behaviour of some players or a temporary weakness in some sectors of the market. Most important for the stability of capitalism is the integrity of security markets and the stability and predictability of the financial system which facilitates market exchanges, in which banks amongst other financial institutions have assumed the most prominent and critical role. A major crisis in the security markets or the banking system, which threatens the economic well-being of a large proportion of the population and the prosperity of the nation, is also a political crisis, for those affected will demand action by their elected government to restore order to protect them. If the crisis is sufficiently grave, and the incumbent government is perceived to be negligent in returning prosperity and certainty, it can expect to suffer a high political price – as alluded to by President Roosevelt in his inaugural speech.

Cataclysmic collapses of security markets which have been triggered by an endemic loss of confidence, possibly threatening the very existence of states, have compelled governments to take an active and highly visible role in the regulation of these markets. In the United States, the Great Crash of 1929 and the prolonged economic depression which followed led to the creation of the Securities and Exchange Commission (SEC). The origins of the SEC in a time when confidence deserted the market are recognised in its statutory mission to 'protect investors, maintain fair, orderly, and efficient markets, and facilitate capital formation'. Its accountability to government, in addition to that to the market, is assured by the presidential appointment of five commissioners. Amongst its myriad functions, the SEC is responsible for closely supervising the performance and operations of the security markets, especially the practices of securities firms, brokers and ratings agencies upon whose advice many market participants depend. Regulating the behaviour of the latter has become an especially prominent responsibility of the SEC after a string of severe gyrations in the securities markets in which deceptive or blatantly false information provided by ratings agencies was implicated. Eventually this saw the passage in 2006 of the American Federal Credit Ratings Agency

Reform Act which significantly widened and strengthened the over-sight responsibilities of the SEC over the world's leading credit-rating agencies. The timely need for these reforms was confirmed in 2007 when the aggressive selling tactics of credit ratings agencies were blamed for a credit crisis caused by the implosion of the American sub-prime mortgage lending market. The new Act, emphasised the chairman of the SEC, would promote the reliability of information provided by influential credit-rating agencies by requiring greater transparency in the methods used to arrive at recommendations.[79]

In increasingly complex financial markets, the actions of even one major financial institution have the potential to threaten the existence of many others through the many interlocking financial relationships arising from shared dependencies on arcane and often highly risky financial instruments. When this occurs, governments are expected to take an active role rather than allow the discipline of the market to restore equilibrium and peace in its own time and irrespective of the financial, social and political costs which may result. The prolif-eration of many new, highly complex financial products which have exposed the consumer to unprecedented risks, of which they may not be aware, has required of government ever greater interventions to provide the institutional protections. Beyond the experience of the Great Depression, recent history is replete with examples of govern-ments which were not prepared to allow one part of the financial mar-kets to threaten not just the confidence in these markets but their very existence. Experience has proven that, should public confidence be withdrawn from one sector of the market, by contagion others may be quickly and similarly affected in the absence of any intervention by government.

The central importance of banks to the efficient, predictable operations of markets is recognised with the rigorous regulatory envi-ronment in which they operate and which requires of banks a high standard of financial probity and responsibility to their depositors, to their shareholders and to the society that they serve. Thus, even at the height of the Thatcher government's liberalisation of markets through insistent, aggressive deregulation, the Chancellor of the Exchequer still believed that an:

effective system of banking supervision is as important as the banking system itself. For without it there will not be the confidence on which sound banking depends – from the confidence of the individual depositor that his money is safe, to confidence in Britain as one of the foremost financial centres in the world.[80]

Irrespective of the accelerating marketisation of both society and government over the two decades subsequent to the chancellor's observations, recurring episodes of significant market and economic instability have only served to confirm the perspicacity and appropriateness of this judgement.

At no time in recent years has the action taken by the British government to restore market confidence been more controversial than in September 2007 when the relatively small British bank Northern Rock, a former building society, faced certain collapse after a run by its depositors – the first bank run in Britain in 140 years. Huge losses suffered by American financial institutions which had lent heavily for property purchases by individuals regarded as higher risks (the subprime lending market referred to earlier), made it difficult for banks such as Northern Rock to obtain the funding to sustain their program of rapid growth. Profit warnings by Northern Rock soon followed, precipitating a sudden drop in public confidence. Northern Rock's share price lost 90 per cent of its value in a matter of weeks, and long queues formed outside its offices as worried depositors attempted to withdraw their money.[81] Fearing that its problems would shake confidence in the rest of the British banking system, the Chancellor of the Exchequer sought to reassure investors and depositors that their investments and money were safe – although only up to specific, relatively low, limits.

When the chancellor's initial assurances proved insufficient to allay public fear and restore confidence in the wider banking system, whose share prices had also begun to suffer, in an unprecedented move the government felt compelled to replace the limited statutory protections for some deposits with an assurance to all existing customers that the government would guarantee all deposits with Northern Rock. In response to the rising panic in the financial markets, this guarantee was extended later to all other financial institutions should they find themselves in similar circumstances.[82] Effectively this meant that the bank's commercial paper was to be underwritten by the taxpayer. By January 2008 public support for the bank reached £26 billion with the public, through their government, also assuming responsibility for more than £100 billion of Northern Rock debts. Northern Rock had in effect become a government-owned company. Political commentators and the Conservative opposition, with some prescience, portrayed the guarantee by the new Brown Labour government as the 'nationalisation' of Northern Rock and the return of the socialist sympathies of previous Labour governments.[83] The comprehensive financial reassurances by the government saw a dramatic fall in withdrawals from Northern Rock and confidence begin to return to the market. Without government intervention Northern Rock would certainly have failed in September 2007. Of more concern to the government, in its wake the collapse of Northern Rock may have provoked the fall of other similar financial institutions.

In addition to regulatory intervention, governments have also frequently used taxpayer funds to pay for the failures of significant businesses which were considered to be too important to the well-being of the financial markets to be allowed to fail. Amongst the most high-profile examples is the decision by the United States Congress in the late 1980s to approve US$150 billion to liquidate and reorganise more than a thousand savings and loans associations which, with the deregulation of the financial markets required by the Reagan government from the early 1980s, had been allowed to engage in high-risk activities which made them susceptible to even the smallest fluctuations in funding conditions. The 'savings and loans crisis' was at the time the largest single example of the United States government providing financial assistance to the private sector, although certainly not the first. It followed similar rescues of a bankrupt New York City in 1975 and the Chrysler Corporation in 1979. Although it did not provide any funding, the American government was also intimately involved in the rescue of investors in the hedge fund Long Term Capital Management (LTCM) in 1998. The head of the New York Federal Reserve Bank was able to convince the major creditors of LTCM that it was in everyone's best interests for them to provide US$3.5 billion to avoid an uncontrolled collapse. The government's involvement prompted the House Banking Committee in Congress to summon the head of the bank and his superior Alan Greenspan to explain why 'a private firm designed for millionaires [should] be saved by a plan that was brokered and supported by a federal government regulation'.[84] Both men were only too well aware that should the consequences of inaction threaten the integrity of the financial markets that it was indeed proper for the government to intervene.

The Federal Reserve, at the height of the sub-prime mortgage market meltdown in 2008, again stepped in to protect the integrity of the American banking system by providing over US$150 billion to relieve the worsening liquidity crisis, seen by many to be the most dramatic action taken since the 1930s.[85] Even this would not be finally sufficient to return confidence to the market. When America's two largest home lending companies, Fannie Mae and Freddie Mac lost half their market value in the first week of July 2008, the Treasury was compelled to intervene to prevent the collapse of the American housing industry. The two companies accounted for nearly half of America's home mortgage debt, nearly US$5.3 trillion. Accordingly, assured the Treasury Secretary Henry Paulson, their 'continued strength is important to maintaining confidence and stability in our financial system and our financial markets'.[86] Barclays Capital suggested that Fannie Mae and Freddie Mac were 'so intertwined in the fabric of global capital markets that a failure would cause not just a US recession, but a global depression'.[87] To save the companies, the Treasury proposed to inject more than US$15 billion of capital which would be convertible to shares to be owned by the government. Effectively the American government was buying the debt of these companies in what one Republican senator on the Senate banking committee referred to as 'this unprecedented intervention in our free markets'.[88]

Matters of life and death

Knowing the limits of the market can also keenly involve matters of life and death, although this has not been a prominent concern of the champions of the market. Thus, confidence in the wisdom of the market has seen Milton Friedman and, much earlier, Herbert Spencer support markets as a better means than government regulation to protect the public from potentially dangerous products such as unproven medicinal drugs that pharmaceutical companies may attempt to sell. Spencer wanted everyone to be free to buy whatever they believed to be best for their health; it was not a matter for government to determine what constituted satisfactory health or how this could be achieved.[89]

Arguments such as this, however, have not been sufficiently persuasive to overcome the statist's belief, or even that of Hayek who supported government certification of certain goods and services,[90] that people should not be left to harm themselves if state regulation could prevent this from happening. This expectation was made very clear to the Thatcher government in 1990 when after several deaths from a serious outbreak of bovine spongiform encephalopathy, or 'mad cow disease', the British public demanded that the government protect them from the farming practices which had placed all consumers in danger. In response, the government introduced legislation, the enforcement of which became the responsibility of the new Food Safety Directorate. Earlier in the twentieth century another concern related to bovine hygiene had similarly required the intervention of government. Despite the proven threats to public health from unpasteurised milk, with at least 40 000 people dying from milk contaminated with bovine tuberculosis, it was not until 1949 that a socialist British government enacted the necessary legislation to provide the compulsory protections that self-interested landowners had obdurately and pugnaciously refused to provide.

Most commentators, irrespective of their attachment to markets, believe that the naive citizen who does not have the expertise in pharmacology to ensure their safety when choosing medication, is unavoidably dependent upon access to the knowledge which the greater resources and enforcement powers of government permit.[91] Serious, and not infrequently fatal, problems encountered with medicinal drugs approved by regulatory authorities are legion, with many having to be subsequently withdrawn from the market by government decree

– although rarely, if ever, by the unprompted initiative of manufacturers. This occurred in July 2007 when independent research in the United States and Britain disclosed that the popular drug Avandia, which was used by a large number of diabetics, greatly increased the chances of a heart attack, even for patients who had no previous history of heart problems. Only after this independent evidence was published was the drug withdrawn from sale by the manufacturer Glaxo-SmithKline, which would be expected to have accumulated similar evidence from its own legally required testing.[92] In the same year both the American drug regulator, the Food and Drug Administration, and the Canadian regulator, Health Canada, commenced major investigations into the safety of the drugs Prilosec and Nexium, used to treat stomach ulcers, after it was revealed by independent studies that the drug could be linked to heightened risk of life-threatening heart problems. News of the possible removal of the products from sale resulted in the market value of its manufacturer, AstraZeneca, falling by £1.3 billion.[93]

Irrespective of government intervention or that of other disinterested parties, according to Friedman the ability to choose, upon which competition depends, would ultimately and effortlessly see the consumer of pharmaceutical products protect their own interests by moving away from less safe or less efficacious products, eventually causing the poorer product to be withdrawn from the market *by the market*. For Friedman, the market, unlike democratic political institutions for which decisions to ensure accountability have to be consciously made, has the advantage of having a naturalistic, built-in mechanism of accountability which ensures that its activation is not dependent upon the conscious and, therefore, delayed decision of someone in government. Accordingly, if a producer is unable to meet the demands of market participants in an efficient manner then they will be unable to retain the confidence of the market and will be forced to exit. Similarly, consumers unable to participate in the market on its terms – that is pay the market price – will also have to withdraw and suffer the consequences for their health. In contrast, Hayek was far less enthusiastic in these situations, preferring that government intervene to regulate and if necessary to prohibit the use of substances which were proven to be life threatening.[94] He was not prepared to tolerate the cost in damaged health while the market found its long-term equilibrium.

Although Friedman's argument for individual responsibility seems a logical application of market principles, it overlooks two significant considerations, even if the superior information efficiency of the market is accepted. Firstly, it is unlikely that all consumers will have the same incomes and information and, thus, a similar ability to move between products. The product which has fallen out of favour, because of concerns about possible deleterious effects, will suffer a fall in price while the price will rise as demand increases for safer products. Any obvious fatal consequences aside, most poor consumers will have little choice but to continue to purchase the less desirable, but now less expensive, product thereby possibly prolonging its life, if not their own. Friedman would argue that ultimately this could not continue, for all firms will want the largest and most profitable share of the market that they can obtain by providing products that are in highest demand.

In the case of some drugs, such as antibiotics and the supply of blood products, the consequences of inadequate regulation by government may potentially extend well beyond particular individuals to jeopardise much of society. Thus, if access to antibiotics is not adequately controlled, their abuse allows bacteria to mutate and overcome the drugs' prophylactic effect. Experience in many countries has shown that, left to their own judgement to self-medicate with antibiotics, individuals will tend to over-use them by inappropriately and mistakenly attempting to treat symptoms which arise from viruses. This then places all society in danger, for this inappropriate use of antibiotics by some may remove the effectiveness of these drugs for others who become infected by the now resistant bacterium. In other cases where some drugs are criminogenic – inducing changes in mental states and behaviour which make people more violent and unmanageable – the safety of the community is threatened. To regulate the use of drugs under these circumstances is very much consistent with the views of Smith and Locke, for whom government intrusion was legitimate if it was to protect individuals from the physical threats of others.

The potentially fatal consequences of inadequate government controls over the sale of pharmaceutical products was exposed in China in 2007, during the trial for corruption of the head of China's food and drug agency, the body responsible for licensing all pharmaceutical products and also food sold in China and for export. After the deaths of ten patients in 2006 from the effects of defective yet approved antibiotics and the serious illnesses suffered by another 34 000 people which resulted from consuming approved yet unfit food products, it was discovered that the head of the agency, Zheng Xiaoyu, had taken over 6.5 million yuan in bribes from Chinese pharmaceutical companies to expedite the approval of their drugs for sale in China and for export. The impact of the failure of effective regulation was also felt internationally, when dogs and cats in America died after eating pet food containing fatal additives supplied by Chinese firms. In a display of the government's determination to reassure foreign and domestic consumers of the safety of Chinese products, Zheng was sentenced to death and soon after executed in July 2007. The court in its judgement said that Zheng had not used the 'power given to him by the state and the people seriously and honestly, but instead he has ignored their vital interests by taking bribes. This has threatened the safety of peoples' life and health.'[95]

In addition to deficiencies in the market's ability to regulate itself, its reluctance to introduce innovations which would protect consumers from serious harm when this may impede the competitive advantage or reduce the profits of a seller has occurred time and again in the automobile industry. Ralph Nader's passionate and effective campaigns from the 1960s, which exposed the callous indifference of the large car makers in the United States to the safety of their customers, eventually forced the government to legislate to compel the manufacturers to take responsibility for producing safer products. Nader, firstly in his 1965 book *Unsafe at Any Speed*, exposed the way in which the three largest American automobile manufacturers were prepared to design and manufacture cars as fashion accessories, irrespective of the known dangers which their designs created for passengers and for the general public. Even though poorly designed internal fittings were implicated in many thousands of serious injuries and fatalities, the market dominance of Ford, General Motors and Chrysler meant they were reluctant to change, at least before the entry of Japanese car makers in the 1970s. Not until Nader exposed the extent of the mortality and injury, and campaigned for the government to take action to protect the consumer, was change enforced.

In other cases in the automobile industry, many life-saving devices have found their way from the most expensive cars to the more affordable, where competition is greatest, only after governments have legislated for their mandatory inclusion. This occurred with seat belts and airbags, and it was reported in 2007 that the same thing was about to happen in Europe with anti-skid brakes. The *Times* reported a claim by a road safety group, the FIA Foundation, that forcing motor manufacturers to fit, at little cost, Electronic Stability Control devices to every make of car would save at least 4000 lives a year and prevent over 100 000 serious injuries throughout Europe.[96] The foundation referred to the need to impose this safety device by government directive as 'a classic example of market failure'.

Protection of the most vulnerable

As important as government intervention has been with consumer products, it is with the protection of the most vulnerable in society – the mentally ill, children and the aged – that the unique contributions of government are universally seen as justified. Indeed, care of these individuals by government was explicitly approved by Mill, Smith and Hayek.[97]

In order to determine the suitability of market principles, practices and values for the provision of social services to the most vulnerable, government policy-makers might refer to either the economic efficiency of the market or to the ability of private providers to better implement comprehensive policy goals, of which financial considerations are only one aspect and certainly not the most important. Financial considerations are only meant to serve the overriding objective of providing high-quality services: saving money should be but the means of providing more services and/or higher quality services at the right time and in the right place. In some cases which involve the provision of social services to the most vulnerable individuals in society, not only will reliance upon the market be inappropriate it may also be counterproductive where outcomes are difficult to quantify, a notorious feature of social services. Social services are very different from other goods and services in both the nature of the service provided and the difficulty in measuring the efficacy of provision.

The highly complex, multi-faceted nature of many social services is especially obvious in the care of children made the responsibility of the state. One recent British study led by Kirkpatrick examined the ability of private firms to provide high-quality residential homes for vulnerable children at a cost which compared favourably with state provision of the same services.[98] In the course of their study, the researchers identified a number of highly significant problems with the private delivery of child care which, although they were well known at the time that the contractor was engaged, had had little impact on government preference for private provision of these services. A particularly worrying problem was the difficulty governments faced in obtaining reliable information about the quality of the services provided by private contractors. Contrary to the image of markets as the ultimate mechanisms for ensuring efficient information processing, at this point in the contracting process health authorities found it very difficult to obtain reliable information about prospective providers who promised much but often failed to deliver the services stipulated. More especially, given the complex nature of the task confronting the contractor, local health authorities were unable to specify with any degree of certainty or precision the exact nature of the services that the provider was expected to deliver.

Information deficiencies were not, however, a problem for potential contractors, most of whom employed several members of staff solely for the purpose of negotiating contracts on the most favourable terms. Grimshaw and others also refer to this power imbalance and, consequently, the way in which the private sector is better than public bodies at contract specification and management in their own interests.[99] The local health authorities, in contrast, were always short of qualified personnel to manage the tendering process and to monitor its implementation. The natural consequence of this imbalance saw contracts which disproportionately favoured the contractor. In one case a local government officer observed how 'we pay [the provider] £400 a week ... but we don't know what we're getting for our money ... we don't have a contracting framework that makes us feel like we're in control of the costs, or the standards'.[100] Such contract monitoring was ad hoc, with only one authority in Grimshaw's study able to rely upon a dedicated contract unit. Thus, authorities in Kirkpatrick's study were 'getting stung, left, right and centre'.[101] Even more worrying for those who were responsible for the care of the children, the local authorities' policy goals were not being met. In some cases, instead of the local authority establishing the care plan for each child, they were being dictated to by the contractor.

Similar, urgent concerns about the vulnerability of the public purse in most PFI negotiations associated with the provision of care as a result of information asymmetries were also expressed by the House of Commons Public Accounts Committee in November 2007. The committee noted that there continued to be a shortage of appropriate negotiating skills in the public sector for PFI teams, and called upon the Treasury to 'work with departments to consider whether ... further cost data are needed to enable project teams to negotiate robustly'.[102] Subsequently, in response to a later report by the National Audit Office on the management of PFI contracts, the chairman of the committee lamented how the 'public sector has allowed itself to be taken for a ride ... Public sector contract managers for PFI deals have insufficient commercial experience to negotiate with and develop effective relationships with their private sector counterparts.'[103]

Kirkpatrick's study concluded that reliance upon markets for providing residential care for vulnerable children had been proven to be inefficient, more costly and unsuitable to a service that involved a high degree of professional judgement and frequent personal intervention by social workers. The researchers found that, for these 'high risk' services with 'vulnerable users' to work effectively, social workers were required to establish close relationships with children and their families, the costs of which would be far greater should the service be contracted to the private sector. Instead of market contracts, 'relational contracting' was more appropriate where the service involved considerable professional judgement and where the outcomes were not amenable to financial or other measurement. Relational contracting is appropriate where there is a common value system between the contractor and the contractee, mutual dependence and a high degree of trust, a presumption that the specification of contracts will be incomplete and where there is open communication between the purchaser and provider of services. These features amount to an understanding that there is a shared commitment to the service provided which may involve activities over and above that which is specified in the contract.[104] Successful intervention, measured through changed lives, was not amenable to a financial calculus of success.

———

The essential, and historically immutable, ends of government in a liberal democratic state are rarely disputed, irrespective of political beliefs, and have changed little since Adam Smith. Government is constituted to ensure that individuals are able to live their lives and to enjoy their achievements secure in the knowledge that threatening intrusions by others will not be tolerated, whether these threats come from outside the borders of the state or from within. Ensuring the security of lives and property has long been recognised both by political theorists and in the events of history as the reason why individuals are prepared to surrender some of their autonomy to live amongst others and to allow others the authority to regulate some aspects of their lives. This has required governments firstly to raise armies and, secondly, to maintain public institutions to administer the means by which these protections can be enforced at law, and to extract payment for these from those who most benefit. The third, and final, duty of government for Smith required the provision of public works which had extensive benefits to society, benefits which were not easily identified with specific individuals.[105] Beyond these fundamental contributions of government, rarely has there been agreement. Accordingly, no attempt has been made here to engage in a futile attempt to provide a conclusive set of roles or ends that governments *might* serve in a liberal democratic state. Rather, the intention has been to establish that in the modern state, the precepts of liberal beliefs have been especially important in shaping understandings of the extent to which governments *should* intrude in the lives of individuals, either to take responsibility from them for some of the vicissitudes of life or to command their obedience. This influence, while waxing and waning over the past two centuries, has ultimately triumphed with the transformation of the modern state according to market principles and values.

Without resiling from the core responsibilities which legitimise government, governments in liberal democratic states which have taken furthest the process of reform and transformation in the image of the market have ensured that these market values have penetrated as much of society as possible, leaving the individual to take ever greater responsibility for their lives. Yet herein lies the paradox of the market state, for when things go badly wrong, the more will citizens seek salvation and protection from their government. The worse that things become, and as the private sector attempts to retreat from responsibility or seeks to take advantage of any difficulties to generate profits, the greater are the expectations of citizens of their governments for, by definition, the immediate interests of the private sector must be their own self-interest with the public interest only secondary.

Attractive as the purported benefits of the market may be to those influential enough to put in place their vision of an efficient, slim public sector, the relentless colonisation of the public sector by market doctrines has required, paradoxically, more government regulation in those states where marketisation has been most pronounced. The explosion in the number of government regulators which has accompanied the privatisation of some services, with Britain a particularly extreme example, and the inability of governments entirely to relinquish responsibility for these services bears potent testimony to concerns about threats to the public interest which arise when key public services, often natural monopolies, are placed in private hands.[106] This intimate, undiminished character of the expectations of citizens of their governments after the relentless reform of the public sectors throughout Anglo-American democracies is the subject of part II. Especially prominent examples have been chosen which affirm the importance of the state to the well-being of society and to the individuals of which it is composed; that it is, indeed, in government that we continue to trust.

STRUCTURAL FAILURE: BRITISH TRANSPORT INFRASTRUCTURE

The privatisation of the railways ... represented one of the great
political and economic crimes of the twentieth century, and ... its
victims were not only the railways but ourselves, the taxpayers and
passengers who support them. Ideology was a crucial factor in the
havoc that ensued. Quite apart from the privatisation itself, the way
in which the industry was fragmented was incredibly damaging. The
notion that a relatively efficient industry like British Rail could be
broken into 100 parts, all of which had to be profitable, could only
have been dreamt up by rabid ideologues, more concerned with theory
than practice ... The privatisation was a deliberate decision to break
up the railways with little regard to the consequences.

(C Wolmar, *On the Wrong Line*, p 329)

The problems caused by privatisations in Britain's transport
infrastructure have assumed an unenviable status as the epitome of the
consequences of the ardent marketisation of core public services. Four

fatal rail crashes had their origins in the fundamentally misguided fragmentation and privatisation of the integrated rail industry. The public reaction to these and other failures of rail privatisation confirmed that the state could not abdicate responsibility for such infrastructure, and led to a significant increase in government control over the railways. The failures also demonstrate how far privatisation, as an ideology, has permeated the state in Britain, especially when a Labour government not only refused to countenance re-nationalisation of the railways but in fact extended privatisation as part of its Third Way to include the London Underground. Further problems with privatising essential capital-intensive industries which provide a key part of the transport infrastructure are also illustrated by the example of air traffic control, which this chapter also covers. Within three months of its partial privatisation in 2001, Britain's air traffic control service was in serious financial difficulty and required government support to remain solvent.

The condition of a country's economic infrastructure has been a long-standing concern of governments. As far back as the 1830s, for example, the Duke of Wellington publicly expressed his concern over the dangers of monopoly and mismanagement in the railway companies emerging in Britain and suggested state ownership of rail. It was not until the twentieth century, however, that many private industries were nationalised in Western countries such as Britain and France. Other important infrastructural industries, including telecommunications, rail, gas and electricity were also brought within the public sector. Public ownership was justified at the time on several grounds. In the face of market failures caused by inadequate investment by private transport companies, public control was held to be the only way of developing an efficient industry which would add to the productivity of the economy. Transport, in particular, is a capital-intensive industry which requires long-term investment programs. It may be possible to operate some parts of the transport infrastructure on a commercial basis, but not all can generate sufficient revenue to cover their full costs. Creating public corporations also enabled governments to ensure that those on low incomes received essential services such as water and electricity, thus enhancing the ability of governments to pursue Keynesian demand management techniques in order to stabilise the economy.

In Britain, the Attlee governments of 1945–1951 brought major industries into public ownership, establishing a post-war political consensus over the extent and the importance of the public sector which survived largely intact until the 1980s, when Conservative governments in Britain followed a neoliberal philosophy predicated on expanding the role of the free market and decreasing the importance of the state. The private sector was to be encouraged while the public sector, regarded as inefficient and wasteful, was to be diminished. Thus, the Conservatives began both to deregulate the economy and to develop an incremental but nevertheless substantial privatisation program. In rapid succession, assets of several public utilities such as telecommunications (1984), gas (1986), water (1989), and electricity (1990) were sold into private ownership through share floats.

Contrary to appearances and the confident demeanour of Conservative governments, the privatisation program did not have an explicit or coherent set of objectives from the start. Instead, a political and economic rationale gradually emerged as each privatisation was completed. Early justifications for privatisation were based on economic arguments about the greater efficiency of the private sector and the importance of market disciplines. It was argued that competitive market forces would allocate resources more efficiently than bureaucratic structures. Using economic theories of public choice and property rights to justify the case, the government claimed that privatisation would provide greater incentives for cost minimisation, encourage more effective management and stimulate greater employee effort. While public choice theorists, such as Niskanen and Mitchell, argue that public services become inefficient because they tend to be run in the interests not of the public but of employees and other special interest groups, property rights theory, which complements this public choice model, sees the inefficiency in the public sector as stemming from the absence of property rights. Advocates of property rights theory argue that managerial efficiency is encouraged by the ability of shareholders to trade their shares if disappointed by a company's performance. Shaoul's study of the water industry, however, 'refuted the claim that private ownership would increase the efficiency of the industry and that ownership is the most important factor in determining performance'.[1] Indeed, much of the literature on privatisation now accepts that changing the ownership of assets is neither necessary nor sufficient to improve efficiency. What is important are competitive pressures and, in some cases, the nature of the regulatory regime. Later justifications for privatisation placed greater emphasis on reducing the scope of government and on transferring operating risk to the private sector. Key financial aims became those of reducing the public sector borrowing requirement, and helping to finance tax reductions. Other benefits for the Conservatives included, controversially, weakening the power of public sector trade unions and extending share ownership, both of which were clearly evident in the privatisation of Britain's railways.

The plan to privatise British Rail

The railways were not an early priority for privatisation, indeed they were the last and most complex privatisation carried out by the Conservatives. A decade of privatising activity, which had become a distinctive characteristic of the Thatcher governments, had passed before the sale of British Rail was attempted. Although this delay had various possible explanations, amongst the most important was the unprofitability and subsidy-dependence of the existing rail network and the presumed unpopularity of any major reduction of services. The delay was a reflection of rail's unique features compared to other industries deemed suitable for privatisation. In particular, British Rail was already in a competitive transport market, as a result of losing a substantial proportion of its markets for passengers and freight to road and air transport during the twentieth century, leaving it with a market share of only 6 per cent by the early 1990s. Specifically within the railway sector, however, British Rail was still regarded as a natural monopoly because of the substantial fixed costs of track, signals and stations, and the strong case for unified operation and vertical integration. Over half the costs of operating a railway are associated with infrastructure. In addition, unlike utilities such as gas, electricity and water, which provide essential services and can spread fixed costs across a large number of customers, the service provided by railways is not universal – only a minority of total transport users choose rail.[2] As a consequence, to recover their full costs of operating, rail services throughout Europe have required government support. In Britain, this came partly in the form of subsidies for loss-making passenger services. In addition, capital grants and loans were available to support investment in the rail network, although funds were limited by successive governments. In practice, governments compelled British Rail to finance much of its capital investment with interest-bearing public debt.

British Rail was initially subject to rigorous financial discipline by successive Conservative governments after 1979, thereby allowing significant improvements in both operational and financial performance. An analysis of British Rail's performance in the years immediately before privatisation would have revealed that it was perhaps the most financially successful railway in Europe, with a subsidy of only 0.16 per cent of GDP, compared to the European average of 0.52 per cent.[3] In order to inject business criteria into decision-making, from the late 1970s British Rail had introduced a form of decentralised sector management which by 1992 had resulted in the replacement of British Rail's regional structure with 'business sectors' and 'profit centres'.[4] This culminated in the organisational reform which became known as 'Organising for Quality'. The improved organisational and business structure was accompanied by above-inflation fare increases and by a substantial reduction in the number of employees, which declined by around one third in the 1980s and another 12 per cent in the early 1990s.[5] Such a marked cut in staffing levels should have suggested a need for caution about the remaining scope for achieving economies by simply reducing the size of the workforce. This point, however, had not been appreciated by those who associated privatisation with the automatic achievement of enhanced 'efficiency'.

An attempt in the 1980s to raise the issue of rail privatisation with Margaret Thatcher had, uncharacteristically, been brusquely rebuffed. Although Thatcher appeared to have been converted to the principle of rail privatisation shortly before her removal as leader in 1990, the policy was implemented by her successor. John Major, whose administration lagged seriously and consistently in the opinion polls from the end of 1992, felt under political pressure to prove his government's determination to continue with the free market economic policies of his predecessor and to complete the privatisation program. Further, economic recession and the poor state of public finances at the time increased the short-term value of further privatisation revenue. The foreword to the 1992 White Paper which proposed the privatisation of British Rail asserted that:

> Privatisation is one of the great success stories of this Government ... common to all privatisations has been the harnessing of the management skills, flair and entrepreneurial spirit of the private sector ... The time has come to extend these benefits to the railways ... Our objective is to improve the quality of railway services by creating many new opportunities for private sector involvement. This will mean more competition, greater efficiency and a wider choice of services.[6]

Rail privatisation was expected to benefit the industry through the 'greater efficiency' which private management and ownership would ensure by providing 'greater opportunities to cut out waste and otherwise reduce costs'.[7] There would also be benefits for customers through improvements in 'quality' and, in the long run, benefits for taxpayers through a reduction in public subsidy and, later, payments *to* the government from franchisees running 'profitable services'.[8]

The White Paper did not, however, provide any empirical evidence to support the claim that 'greater efficiency' would result from privatisation. Rather, it simply asserted, in a manner reminiscent of all privatisation justifications, that the introduction of competition and of private sector management would bring benefits. It also claimed, again without evidence, that there would be 'a higher quality of service and better value for money'.[9] This lack of empirical evidence was particularly striking given that the paper did concede that British Rail had made 'significant improvements in recent years', that its efficiency 'compares well with that of other European railways', and that the productivity of its workforce 'is among the highest of any European railway'.[10]

The lack of evidence to justify rail privatisation meant that political motivation assumed greater importance. Rail, along with water, was an unpopular privatisation. It had been viewed, prophetically, as 'a privatisation too far', and the proposed fragmented structure for railways was ominously condemned by a former Conservative Transport Minister as 'such a silly scheme'.[11] One highly acerbic, critical analysis condemned rail privatisation as 'politically motivated, hasty, ham-fisted and ill thought through ... there are few if any other railway systems in the world that are wholly privatised'.[12] Concerned for the viability of the rail network, most senior railway managers displayed strong opposition to the proposed privatisation model. Portraying this opposition as motivated by selfish concerns, and thus unreliable, ministers and civil servants went outside the public service for more conducive advice. During preparations for privatisation in the 1990s, the Major government alone spent £450 million on consultants, many of whom had no prior knowledge of the industry.

Although the Labour Party reflected public opinion in its strong opposition in principle to the 1993 Railways Bill, through which rail privatisation would be enacted, the Bill was successfully brought through parliament, after a 'stormy passage', by the Major government.[13] At the 1993 Labour Party conference, the leadership promised that any privatisation of the rail system which occurred would be reversed by a future Labour government, but this was a commitment that did not survive for long after Tony Blair was elected leader of the Labour Party in 1994. Blair was keen to 'modernise' the party, commencing with rewriting clause IV of its constitution which since 1918 had expressed the party's long-term aim of the 'common ownership' of the means of production, distribution and exchange. Following Blair's success in persuading the party, a new 'Third Way' perspective which was to characterise Labour reforms began to influence transport policy. At the party conference in the autumn of 1996, the commitment to reverse privatisation was conspicuous by its absence. Labour's 1997 election manifesto simply said that the rail system must be run in the public interest with higher levels of investment and stronger enforcement of the train companies' service commitments.

The privatisation model: divide and squander

The scheme devised for the railways, as a key adviser to the Transport Secretary argued, amounted to 'a more comprehensive structural reform than in any previous privatisation'.[14] This was to follow the major organisational and cultural changes developed by British Rail over the previous 15 years which were now viewed, not as a basis for further efficiency gains within an integrated railway, but as an opportunity for an organisational break and major splintering of the rail industry. The key element in the 1993 Railways Act was the separation of infrastructure and train operations, which broke up the vertically integrated structure common to railways throughout the world. This separation – which had been under discussion since at least the early 1980s – had encountered severe criticism, even in circles sympathetic to privatisation. At a Centre for Policy Studies conference in 1988, for example, it was pointed out prophetically that the track authority would occupy a monopoly position, and so would have no incentive to be efficient, would be likely to let assets deteriorate, and would be at the centre of an overly-complex system'.[15]

This, nevertheless, was the model for which the Major government had opted, despite the risks implicit in creating a monopolist infrastructure supplier. Influential in the decision was dissatisfaction with the privatisation precedents of British Gas and British Telecommunications, which had been transferred to the private sector as monolithic organisations. In contrast, the government regarded electricity privatisation as more successful: the state monopoly had been split up and a higher level of competition introduced at an early stage, with less need for state regulation.[16] The disaggregated form favoured for rail privatisation also created a more attractive environment for potential train operating companies to operate in by removing a massive sunk cost element which would have resulted from the inclusion of infrastructure as a part of their operating responsibilities.

The most zealous supporters of rail privatisation hoped to see both open access to the network for train operators and the sale of specific train paths. However, franchising was adopted as a second-best solution after it came to be appreciated that on-rail competition would destroy private sector interest in bidding for train routes. Support for franchising drew upon the franchising theory which originated with Sir Edwin Chadwick's proposed solution to the problems of natural monopoly. A notable nineteenth-century British social reformer, who had endeavoured to improve both the Poor Laws and public health, Chadwick was also interested in economic problems such as the need to protect consumers against exploitation by private monopolies. As an alternative to regulation or public ownership, Chadwick argued that where 'competition *within* the field' was impossible, an auction for the right to operate a monopoly franchise would allow for 'competition *for* the field'.[17] The franchise would be auctioned off to the bidder offering the most attractive terms, such as the lowest price to consumers. Although elegant in theory, the franchising solution entailed many practical problems. Of most concern, the adoption of franchising meant that train operating companies would operate local monopolies, thus undermining the principal reason for adopting the infrastructure model at the centre of the privatised rail system.[18] Further, it required a complex and expensive regulatory system to manage existing franchises and to evaluate bids for new franchises.

Implementation of the 1993 Railways Act meant that an integrated British Rail was broken up to create a very complex, fragmented industry. By 1997 it comprised: Railtrack, the monopolist infrastructure supplier, responsible for 11 000 miles (17 600 kilometres) of track, 2500 stations and 40 000 bridges, viaducts and tunnels; 25 passenger train operating companies; six freight companies (quickly reduced to two); 13 infrastructure maintenance and renewal companies; three rolling stock leasing companies; and various engineering and design companies. The degree of fragmentation introduced by British Rail's privatisation was unprecedented for any railway. Further fragmentation developed after privatisation, when the construction firms that had purchased most of the infrastructure companies began making extensive use of subcontracting. Despite the initial claims made for privatisation in terms of more focused and empowered management, the links between commercial planning and infrastructure planning were weaker than under British Rail's sectorised business system of the 1980s which had eliminated regions, divided staff into business sectors, and given sector managers responsibility for the infrastructure used by their trains. The most significant issue of all was the overall consequences of the mixture of vertical and horizontal separation and of monopoly and competition. In practice, organisational fragmentation, together with the associated increased costs and leakages, was to lead to results far worse than those of British Rail's sectorised relationships.

Regulation of the privatised railway industry

Industries previously privatised by the Conservatives, such as gas and telecommunications, often constituted natural monopolies and retained significant elements of monopoly power after privatisation. This gave these privatised industries the capacity to exploit consumers by charging high prices or providing poor services, so the government had to establish regulatory bodies to protect consumers – commencing with the Office of Telecommunications in 1984. Privatisation therefore entailed, in many cases, the 'replacement of public ownership by regulation, with the state's role changing from being a producer of goods and services to that of the regulator of the producers'.[19] As well as protecting consumer interests with respect to prices and service quality, regulators were also expected to ensure that privatised industries were adequately financed and that competition was promoted within the industries.

Several features of the rail industry meant that such regulation was far more complex both in theory and practice than in previous privatisations.[20] Firstly, rail was unique among privatisations for being a loss-making industry reliant upon subsidy. Thus, the train operating companies were guaranteed an initial subsidy of £2 billion in 1996–97, a figure more than double British Rail's average annual subsidy in the 1980s. This subsidy was planned to fall gradually as the train operating companies made efficiency savings. The Conservatives' grossly over-optimistic plan was that, by 2005–06, the subsidy would be eliminated and the most profitable companies would be paying the government for the right to run franchises. These new receipts would then increase substantially over the decade. The second factor complicating regulation was that, unlike other privatised industries such as gas and water which dealt directly with one set of consumers, two sets of customers were involved in the rail industry: the customers of the infrastructure authority, Railtrack, were the train operating companies; while the rail passengers were the customers of the train companies. An additional complicating factor was a lack of clarity about the requisite capital expenditure and the nature of the services Railtrack should provide.

These unique features meant that the complex structure of the privatised industry was mirrored, to an extent, in its regulatory structure. Two new regulatory bodies were given responsibility for the broad oversight of economic and quality issues respectively. The key economic regulator was the Office of the Rail Regulator, led by an official known as the Regulator, which supervised Railtrack, the monopolist supplier of the infrastructure. The key quality regulator was the Office of Passenger Rail Franchise (OPRAF), headed by the Franchising Director, which was given the job of allocating passenger franchises and of monitoring the performance of the train operating companies. The Franchising Director also assumed responsibility for making subsidy payments to the train operating companies and, in the long run, receiving payments from profitable franchises. A qualitative distinction between the two was that the Regulator was independent of government, the office being regulated by licence, whereas the Franchising Director was regulated by contract and subject to government instruction. The third element of the regulatory system, safety issues, was to be overseen by the Her Majesty's Railway Inspectorate, part of the Health and Safety Executive.

Economic regulation of privatised industries has been generally considered necessary in order to promote efficiency and to protect customers from exploitation. There are several possible regulatory models, but the two most common are setting either the rate of return or a price cap. Both of these models were used to regulate different components of the privatised railway industry. As noted, one of the regulatory system's roles was to protect rail passengers. Thus, the price of several kinds of ticket, representing around 40 per cent of total tickets, was controlled throughout the rail network by OPRAF. This was based on a price-capping formula, linked to the retail price index (RPI) and familiar to other privatised industries such as British Telecommunications. In the case of the train operating companies, the price cap matched the RPI for three years and then fell to RPI minus one (that is a cut in real terms) for the next four. Price capping was intended both to protect passengers and to encourage the train operating companies to improve efficiency. In practice, the price capping encouraged a growth in passengers but added problems to the railway system which had been privatised assuming a decline in demand, based on the recession of the early 1990s. Further, the price capping encouraged the train operating companies to cut costs rather than improve services.

The Rail Regulator's main regulatory task, on the other hand, was to limit Railtrack's rate of return, by establishing a 'regulatory asset base' and setting a permitted rate of return on capital. In the United States, where rate of return regulation has long encountered problems, it is considered to lead to overcapitalisation and a loss of productive efficiency, and to involve the regulator in detailed scrutiny of the industry's costs. In Britain, the regulator was periodically to set track access charges which the train operating companies would pay to Railtrack. Initially, the access charges were established to cover operating costs plus a rate of return on capital – as the means of promoting 'competition and innovation', encouraging the 'efficient use of infrastructure', and providing the 'means for financing investment in Railtrack's infrastructure'.[21] In practice, these objectives proved impossible to reconcile under the privatisation scheme which was adopted, compelling the Regulator to increase Railtrack's funding by granting both increased access charges and direct subsidy from the government, even though there was a lack of both innovation and efficient use of the infrastructure.

The level of access charges was crucial both for Railtrack's profitability and for the viability of the train operating companies which paid them. Most of the train operating companies were unprofitable from the very beginning and, therefore, heavily dependent on their own public subsidies. These effectively represented a substantial but indirect subsidy to Railtrack, which was intended initially to operate without direct subsidy. In 1999–2000, for example, the subsidy of £1.4 billion to the train operating companies represented 27 per cent of their total revenue of £5.1 billion, and constituted 64 per cent of the £2.2 billion in access charges paid to Railtrack.

Costs and infrastructure investment

The Major government claimed that rail privatisation would produce benefits through greater efficiency providing more 'opportunities to cut out waste and otherwise reduce costs'.[22] The 1992 White Paper gave no details as to how these costs might be reduced, and even one of the key advisers on privatisation accepted, after the White Paper had become the 1993 Railways Act, that the net effect 'of the new rail charges is to increase costs overall'.[23] Indeed, the new organisational structure of the privatised system had major implications for costs. These may be summarised as interface costs and cash leakages.[24]

Interface costs arise when many companies are involved in a supply chain, with upward pressure on prices as each company aims to squeeze a profit out of its contribution to the system. Thus, whereas the public-owned British Rail had obtained additional trains by simply ordering them from its own workshops, under the privatised system the supply chain would involve a train manufacturer, a ROSCO, a train operating company and Railtrack, with each link in the chain adding an element of profit. The dramatic impact of interface costs on rail can be demonstrated by comparing British Rail's costs before privatisation with the total costs of the railway companies in the privatised and fragmented network. British Rail's costs in 1993–94, the year before its reconstitution as an infrastructure provider, were £3.6 billion. A decade later in the industry's costs had more than doubled.[25] Although part of the increase could be accounted for by passenger growth, substantial interface costs were involved.

The second key change in railway finances was the tendency for cash to 'leak' from the system in the form of the interest payments and dividends required to finance debt and equity respectively. Railtrack alone, for example, distributed dividends totalling £709 million between 1995–96 and 2000–01, equivalent to 41 per cent of the total operating profits of £1.7 billion generated over the six years. As a private company it was not surprising that Railtrack's initial focus was on producing highly attractive returns for its shareholders; that profit rather than the public interest motivated management. Thus, maintenance and renewal of the network was habitually neglected. Deliberately under-priced by the Major government in order to ensure a successful flotation, Railtrack's share price immediately rose from the offer level of £3.90 in 1996 to a peak of £17.68 by the end of 1998. Railtrack's management highlighted this triumph by insisting that the closing share price be posted daily in all signal boxes.

The interface costs and leakages built into the privatised system were not only important in themselves, but were to prove crucial to investment performance with regard to the key railway asset – the infrastructure. Hopes for infrastructure investment centred on Railtrack, which was responsible for track, stations, bridges and viaducts, and freight terminals. The 1992 White Paper had stressed that the government 'wants to ensure that Railtrack continues to invest to maintain and improve the network. Investment will largely be financed from charges to operators.'[26] The company was meant to be encouraged to invest through the rate of return it could achieve for shareholders and through bonuses for senior managers. Doubts soon surfaced, however, about Railtrack's capacity to produce higher investment to maintain and improve the network, since 91 per cent of the access charges paid by train companies were fixed and so gave little incentive to Railtrack to increase network capacity. Further, Railtrack's initial operating licence was so weak that, amazingly, the company was not in fact contractually required to maintain and renew the infrastructure.

Despite the complexity of its operations, and the diversity and quantity of crucial infrastructure assets, there was no comprehensive asset register showing the rail infrastructure's condition. Such a register was regarded as essential both for Railtrack's management of assets and for the Regulator's monitoring of the company's stewardship. Rather than the traditional policy followed by British Rail and other European railways of replacing assets at set time intervals, on the advice of financial consultants from McKinsey, Railtrack implemented 'Project Destiny' which instead focused on the assessed condition of its assets.[27] For example, heavily used points were meant to be replaced more often than those on less busy routes. But this required a co-ordinated program of inspections and maintenance. The results of the new approach, which was to have a major unintended impact upon the destiny of Railtrack, were soon only too apparent. After a prescient investigation into maintenance and renewal expenditure, the National Audit Office warned of the consequences of the low rate of track renewals. For example the number of broken rails increased by almost 25 per cent to 937 in 1998–99, compared with 755 in 1997–98. Railtrack had forecast only 600.[28]

When Tom Winsor became Rail Regulator in July 1999, he attacked Railtrack for giving excessive priority to the interests of its shareholders. He thought that his predecessors had not used their powers sufficiently, and was determined to adopt a more forceful approach to regulation.[29] One of Winsor's most publicised decisions was the enforcement order and fine imposed when Railtrack refused to accept the target of 12.7 per cent for a cumulative reduction in the number of trains arriving late. A record £40-million fine was threatened, but on a graduated basis to encourage the company's management to improve performance. Railtrack achieved a 10 per cent reduction in lateness and so the fine actually paid was only £10.8 million.

The limits of this aggressive diplomacy were, however, revealed when Winsor declared himself in favour of incentive regulation aimed at reconciling Railtrack's commercial aspirations with the public interest. Railtrack shares rose slightly after Winsor's remarks, on the basis that the Regulator had no objection to the company making strong profits. What Winsor said echoed previous comments by Gerald Corbett, Railtrack's chief executive, that there were two very different approaches to the regulation of Railtrack – legal enforcement or incentive-based regulation – and that reliance on the former would increase the cost of capital to Railtrack and limit its capacity to raise finance. The stronger the desire of the Regulator and the government for network development, the greater the probability of leniency and flexibility and the greater the opportunity for safe operations to be jeopardised.[30]

The safety implications of privatisation

Privatisation had very serious implications for safety on the rail network, the second aspect of quality of service of vital importance. British Rail had been staffed by an integrated workforce, 'bonded by a culture of co-operation in working for one railway'.[31] Inspectors were employed by British Rail to cover all aspects of its work, and major improvements in safety resulted from swiftly and uniformly applying the lessons learned from accidents and through investment in new safety measures. The rail network and the management of safety within it was 'the product of 175 years of steady evolution'. There were fewer deaths in railway accidents in each successive post-war decade: from 344 deaths in the 1940s, to 337 in the 1950s, with a dramatic reduction to 75 in the 1980s, and just eight up to the year of the privatisation of the industry in 1996.[32] Thus, by the 1990s British Rail's safety record was 'generally, exemplary' with the last fatalities attributable to a broken rail occurring in 1967.[33] Tragically, this remarkable safety record of British Rail in the 1990s was to be fatally undermined by rail privatisation.

The 1992 White Paper appeared to take safety seriously:

> Safety – of both the travelling public and the workforce – is of
> paramount importance. There will be no change in the commitment
> to ensure the continued safe operation of the railway. The Government
> intends to establish a framework of safety regulation which will
> guarantee that necessary safety performance is maintained and
> observed across the railway.[34]

Close inspection of the document reveals that, in common with the rest of the White Paper, the two-page section on safety was thick with optimistic projections but very thin on detail. In order to provide the missing detail for the new safety framework to accompany rail privatisation, the Major government asked the Health and Safety Commission, which oversees the Health and Safety Executive, to make 'a thorough study of the safety implications of the proposals set out in this White Paper, and to make detailed recommendations'.[35] The commission's report entitled *Ensuring Safety on Britain's Railways*, published in January 1993, was accepted by the Major government and laid the foundations for a new regulatory regime for railway safety. It was based on the concept of the 'safety case', where all companies in the rail industry had to assess potential risks and put forward strategies for minimising them. The safety cases of both the train operating companies and the infrastructure companies would be assessed by Railtrack, which would have its own safety case scrutinised by the Health and Safety Executive. This arrangement was universally unpopular within the industry and ultimately proved to be fundamentally flawed. Railtrack felt that it was being burdened with 'a role to which it was not suited', while the other rail companies feared that Railtrack 'could exercise control over them by masking commercial considerations under the guise of safety considerations'.[36]

The proposed new safety regime did not alleviate concern about the potential conflict between safety considerations and the profit motive in the privatised rail industry. Serious issues were raised about the impact rail privatisation would have on safety even before the 1993 Railways Act had been passed by Parliament. In early 1993, an academic paper drew attention to the likelihood of conflict between the objectives of reducing costs and maintaining safety standards. Harman argued that in a 'situation where efficiency in resource use is an important goal, achievement of very high safety standards may conflict with meeting other aims'.[37] Further warnings came in April 1993 when the House of Commons Transport Select Committee reported on the privatisation plans, emphasising that the railways 'provide extremely high standards of safety for passengers', but that there were important provisos to consider if these standards were to be maintained. These provisos, along with issues raised in other critical analyses, proved to be prescient. The Select Committee warned that great care would be necessary from all parties in the fragmented industry to ensure that safety remained a primary objective of maintenance, operational practices, and employee culture and morale.[38] Two months after the Select Committee reported, a critical analysis of safety in the privatised industry compiled by former British Rail senior managers was published. They warned that the proposed fragmentation of the industry would lead to safety problems as there would no longer be clear direct lines of command, experienced staff were being made redundant in preparation for privatisation, and there would be pressure on Railtrack to contain its safety monitoring costs.[39]

The warnings given about the possible effects of rail privatisation on safety, in the diverse range of reports discussed above, proved all too accurate. British Rail's safety culture was fragmented and weakened by privatisation. Further, each company in the industry had an incentive to reduce costs, dramatically illustrated by the treatment of the infrastructure companies' workforces. The construction companies which purchased these companies quickly made substantial savings on employees, with the number of permanently employed maintenance workers falling from 31 000 in 1994 to a maximum of 19 000 in 2000. At the same time, the perverse incentives and penalties of the complex rail contracts meant that Railtrack and the train operating companies between them employed over 300 staff whose responsibility it was to apportion blame when the inevitable delays occurred from poor and delayed maintenance on the system. The loss of permanent maintenance staff was partly compensated for by recruiting untrained or poorly trained casual workers through extensive subcontracting. As a result, the total number of firms employed in railway maintenance and renewals work increased to between 2000 and 3000, the majority of which were subcontractors whose accountability was uncertain and dispersed.[40]

The problems with the fragmentation of the industry and the management of contractors were highlighted in a major report published by the Health and Safety Executive in March 1996. *Maintaining a Safe Railway Structure* raised serious concerns about the way Railtrack was managing the process of selecting, monitoring and controlling its contractors. It found that Railtrack had a sound framework for the selection and control of infrastructure contractors in its safety case, but that much greater effort was needed to secure the effective operation of safety systems in practice. This report was highlighted by the Transport Select Committee in a study of railway safety published in July 1996. The committee forcefully argued that:

> The Health and Safety Executive report is a matter for serious concern. Close attention must be given by the Health and Safety Executive to ensuring that the new client/contractor relationship ... does not lead to a reduction in the standards of maintenance or pose a threat to passenger and staff safety. We are concerned that the continuing use of contractors by Railtrack should not lead to a repeat of incidents highlighted by the Health and Safety Executive. Continuing random checks on contractors by the Health and Safety Executive are needed for the maintenance of public confidence in the safety of the rail network.[41]

Four fatal accidents

The sagacity of the critical reports on rail safety in 1996 was tragically confirmed by four major fatal rail accidents between 1997 and 2002. All had their origins in the fragmentation of the privatised industry and the neglect of safety considerations arising from loss of accountability between organisational boundaries. The first two were investigated by public inquiries but, despite campaigns by survivors, no such inquiries have been held into the third and fourth crashes. Further, as the following analysis of the crashes makes clear, while rail companies have been fined, not one individual has been held responsible and successfully prosecuted. This applies both to the management of the privatised rail companies and to those ministers, civil servants and advisers responsible for introducing the damaging scheme. The closest thing to a 'trial' of those ultimately responsible for rail privatisation occurs in David Hare's superbly researched, moving and successful play *The Permanent Way* which was based on these crashes.

The first major crash under privatisation was the Southall accident in September 1997. This involved a Great Western passenger train from Swansea to Paddington smashing into a goods train crossing its path in West London. The crash resulted in seven deaths and over 100 injuries. The immediate cause was the failure of the driver of the passenger train to notice the yellow signals which preceded the red signal warning of the goods train crossing at a junction. By the time the driver saw the red signal it was too late to prevent a collision. But the underlying causes of the accident were more complex. The driver should have been alerted to the yellow signals by the train's automatic warning system, but that system was not functioning. Although the problem had been reported to the maintenance depot, the system was only given an inadequate, cursory examination which did not detect the fault, and the train was allowed to continue to operate with the defective equipment.

A public inquiry into the accident, chaired by Professor John Uff, was very critical of the failings at the maintenance depot, but especially the way in which it had been badly managed and under-staffed following a reorganisation in 1996. Uff argued that 'maintenance procedures at Old Oak Common were far from robust ... there was, in September 1997, a lack of attention to details, some of which were safety-critical'. The inquiry concluded that the responsibility for the non-functioning warning system lay with Great Western, 'first in having inadequate maintenance procedures to eliminate known faults, and secondly through inadequate procedures for communicating and taking action'. This was compounded by the lack of co-ordination between Railtrack and Great Western Trains over the reporting of faults in the train.[42] In July 1999, Great Western Trains was fined a then record £1.5 million for breaches of the 1974 Health and Safety at Work Act. The driver, who survived, was originally charged with manslaughter, but the charge was later dropped. The judge rejected an attempt by the prosecution to charge the train company with cor-porate manslaughter as there was nobody in management who could be clearly identified as having a 'controlling mind' responsible for the accident.

Before the Uff inquiry had concluded, Southall was followed by the far more serious accident at Ladbrooke Grove, in 1999, when 31 people died and 425 were injured. An inexperienced Thames Trains driver ignored a red signal light and crashed head-on into another passenger train two miles out of Paddington station. While the primary cause of the accident was the driver passing through a red light, there were significant contributory factors resulting from privatisation.

One key issue was the repeated, serious incidences of drivers passing signals in the Paddington area. The signal which the driver went through had been subject to eight similar incidents in the previous six years, mainly because it was partially obscured by a bridge. Inquiries had been held earlier by Railtrack into the two most serious incidents on the same line, which occurred in 1995 and 1998, but the company did not implement key recommendations — such as the need to improve the visibility of signals for drivers in this difficult area. According to Railtrack's own safety procedures, signal sighting committees should have been convened because of the high number of incidents in the Paddington area.

The inquiry after the accident, chaired by Lord Cullen, concluded that the failure to convene signal sighting committees was 'persistent and serious' and 'due to a combination of incompetent management and inadequate process'. Cullen was also critical of the very weak training program of Thames Trains which had 'no specific criteria ... to determine whether the driver had competently handled a situation; there was a lack of definition as to how frequently the driver should have to perform in similar situations before being assessed as competent'.[43] The driver's training course lasted only 33 weeks, compared to a minimum of 43 weeks under British Rail, and did not include instruction about the risks of passing signals at problem spots such as SN109, the signal culpable for the crash at Ladbroke Grove.[44] Furthermore, the accident occurred after the driver had been working solo for only two weeks. The fines eventually levied suggested Railtrack was twice as responsible as the train operating company: Thames Trains was fined £2 million for health and safety breaches in 2004; and Railtrack's successor, Network Rail, fined £4 million in 2007.

The safety problems of the fragmented industry were illustrated most graphically with the accident in October 2000 near Hatfield, when the 12:10 pm train from London King's Cross to Leeds was derailed by a broken rail, resulting in four people being killed and 70 injured. According to Wolmar, at Hatfield:

the part played by the fragmentation and sale of the railways is very clear. The whole ghastly tale of mismanagement, greed, and incompetence that caused the Hatfield disaster was a result of the crazy structure for the railways created by John Major and his ministers ... Hatfield was the epitome of the failings created by rail privatisation.[45]

That the crash took place on a stretch of line where a fault had been discovered 21 months earlier, and which had been earmarked for renewal for nearly two years, highlighted both Railtrack's lack of knowledge of the state of the infrastructure and its very poor management of contractors. Tragically, although the defects were discovered by the maintenance contractor, Balfour Beatty, and reported to Railtrack, renewal work was fatally delayed with the result that at Hatfield 90 metres of rail fractured into 300 pieces.

Renewal work on the line, which was the responsibility of the large construction firm Jarvis, was paid on a job-by-job basis, while simpler maintenance contracts had a fixed price. Railtrack thus had a financial interest in both minimising the work allocated to Jarvis and in keeping the line closed for as short a time as possible in order to keep penalty payments to a minimum. The farcical and ultimately fatal result of the perverse incentives of privatisation was that, at the time of the crash, a new length of rail had been lying beside the defective track for six months ready for installation.[46] The rail would have stood a much greater chance of replacement under British Rail's preventative maintenance regime, which had ensured that no accidents had been caused by broken rails since 1967.

After the accident, Railtrack, grossly handicapped by the lack of anything resembling a full asset register, was unable to establish whether there were more broken rails in the system. Its alternative, which plunged the company into what proved to be a terminal crisis, was to introduce over 1000 speed restrictions in an attempt to accommodate the deficit in accumulated maintenance and renewals. The widespread paralysis led to a crisis of confidence in the railway system and the departure of Railtrack's chief executive Corbett. The severity of the problems experienced prompted psychotherapy terms to be applied to the railway system, with one senior figure arguing that it was experiencing 'a nervous breakdown'.[47] The proportion of trains arriving on time fell from 89.7 per cent in 1997–98 to 78 per cent in 2001–02, while the proportion of trains run by long-distance operators arriving on time fell from 81.7 to 70.2 per cent over the same period. Under the much-maligned British Rail, by contrast, performance had improved steadily in the 1980s and early 1990s, with the proportion of all trains arriving on time averaging 90 per cent by 1993–94.

At their trial in 2005 for the Hatfield accident, both Railtrack and Balfour Beatty were found guilty of serious breaches of health and safety legislation. Record fines for a rail accident were levied, with Balfour Beatty ordered to pay £10 million (later reduced on appeal to £7.5 million) and Network Rail, which by then had replaced Railtrack, to pay £3.5 million. Both companies were also required to pay £300 000 in costs. Justice Mackay said that he regarded 'Balfour Beatty as one of the worst examples of industrial negligence in a high risk industry I have seen'. Despite this scathing indictment, five senior managers from the companies were cleared of corporate manslaughter on the judge's direction.

Although a huge effort was made to deal with the maintenance backlog after Hatfield, problems of track maintenance were again highlighted in May 2002 by the fatalities at the Potters Bar derailment. A train from London to King's Lynn derailed at a set of points just south of Potters Bar, killing seven people and injuring 76. Investigators soon established that the points, numbered 2182A, were the cause of the crash. The maintenance supplier, Jarvis, which at the time was the largest single contractor for rail maintenance and renewals work, suggested that sabotage could be responsible. This claim deeply upset survivors and those who had lost relatives, including Nina Bawden whose homage to her husband preceded this chapter, and it was clearly refuted by the Health and Safety executive's report into the accident.

The report made it very clear that there was no evidence of sabotage, and that the points had failed because they were 'not fit for purpose'.[48] In October 2003, after receiving much adverse publicity for Potters Bar and subsequent, serious track incidents, and with its share

price plummeting, Jarvis withdrew completely from its rail maintenance contracts. In April 2004, two years after Potters Bar, the chief
executive of Jarvis finally accepted liability, apologised for the company's promotion of the sabotage theory and offered compensation to
victims. Nina Bawden received £1 million. The survivors were very
distressed, however, that no prosecutions of responsible individuals
have followed the crash.

From this analysis of the related issues of costs, infrastructure
investment and safety in the privatised rail system, it is clear how
profit considerations, combined with a complex and fragmented
system, undermined the railway network and led to a serious decline
in safety. The parliamentary reports which predicted safety problems
even before the 1993 Railways Bill was passed proved all too accurate.
In the case of the Ladbroke Grove and Southall accidents, the interactions between privatisation and the underlying causes of the accidents
are demonstrable but complex. With the Hatfield accident, however,
the responsibility played by the fragmentation and privatisation of the
rail industry was starkly transparent. The accident not only exposed
the serious flaws of privatisation, but also contributed significantly to
the collapse of Railtrack.

The collapse of Railtrack

The ultimate failure of rail privatisation and the reality of the
deception within the justifications for rail privatisation may be
analysed by examining the collapse of Railtrack. The replacement
of Corbett as chief executive by the company's finance director did
nothing to remedy the underlying problems it faced. These had
been masked before the Hatfield crash by the company's ability
to survive scathing denunciations by regulators and the offer of
more generous treatment by both the Labour government and by
Regulator Winsor. Indeed, Corbett's establishment of a regulation
department of 25 people at Railtrack, to campaign for a favourable
regulatory settlement, proved so successful in the short run that
Winsor, in his published 'final' conclusions on the company's future
revenue requirements in October 2000, recommended that the total

of grants and access charges be raised to £13.5 billion, including £4 billion in direct grants. This implied a rise in annual income from £1.8 billion to £2.7 billion for the period 2001 to 2006. The importance of the £4 billion in direct grants awarded to Railtrack is shown by the fact that access charges would have risen by 62 per cent over the new five-year period in the absence of grants. Railtrack was even to be compensated for overspending on renewals and for cost overruns on the huge West Coast main line renewal project. With grants and the indirect subsidy to the train operating companies, Railtrack expected to have up to £10 billion of government support from 2001 to 2006, thus mocking the original stated aim of the privatisers that they would create a subsidy-free railway.

Despite the substantial increase in income granted to Railtrack, its position was far from secure. With tragic irony, Winsor's 'final' conclusions had been published in the very month of the Hatfield crash. Railtrack's spiralling costs meant that by April 2001 it had been forced to agree to a revised financial settlement with the rail Regulator and the government which granted it £1.5 billion in subsidy. Despite declaring a loss of £559 million in March 2001, Railtrack's management displayed crass insensitivity by recycling £138 million of the subsidy to shareholders as dividends. This action only added to major doubts about Railtrack's survival as a private sector company. Its share price had suffered a progressive decline from a peak of over £17 in 1998, followed by a collapse in the first half of 2001 when it fell below £3. Railtrack suffered the embarrassing fate of ejection from the FTSE 100 after its market value fell to around £1.5 billion. Railtrack's borrowing had risen from £3.3 billion at 31 March 2000 to almost £4 billion one year later as it attempted to remedy the maintenance and renewals backlog. In addition to Railtrack's inadequate maintenance and renewal work, its poor project management skills were exemplified by the fiasco of its flagship investment project, the upgrading of the West Coast main line route. The project's initial budget was £2.1 billion but it was poorly scoped and managed with costs escalating towards £10 billion. On 7 October 2001, faced with these blowouts and increasing demands for subsidy, Transport Secretary Byers refused to give further financial support and obtained a court order placing an insolvent Railtrack in administration.

Railtrack's collapse revealed fatal flaws in the privatisation model, flaws which had been concealed in the short run by the company's generous treatment while it focused on profit maximisation rather than infrastructure maintenance and renewal. Its collapse destroyed the belief of the privatisers that a profit-maximising company could invest to maintain and improve the network while operating without subsidy, and guaranteed that Railtrack's successor would require far more public support.

The Third Way for rail privatisation

The British Labour Party was elected in 1997 on a pragmatic election manifesto which promised to apply the principle of 'what works' in policy-making. In transport and many other policy areas it adopted the political philosophy of the 'Third Way'. The most notable champion of the Third Way, and strong supporter of 'New' Labour, Anthony Giddens has promoted this approach in several books. As a guide to economic policy, Giddens argued that the Third Way encompasses a 'new mixed economy ... utilising the dynamism of markets but with the public interest in mind. It involves a balance between regulation and deregulation ... and a balance between economic and the non-economic in the life of society.'[49] This approach meant that the Labour government ruled out re-nationalisation of the railways. Instead, it aimed to combine private finance and public subsidy with stronger regulation. Accordingly, in November 1997 it issued new objectives for OPRAF, which regulated the train operating companies. These included securing a progressive improvement in the quality of rail passenger and station services, and managing rail franchises in order to promote the interests of passengers. Then, in July 1999, OPRAF was subsumed into a new body, the Strategic Rail Authority (SRA), which was given the important additional duties of planning the strategic development of the rail network and promoting integration between different types of transport. Prime Minister Blair argued explicitly at a rail summit in 1999 that the

SRA's creation represented a 'third way' beyond the sterile debate between wholesale privatisation and old-style state control.

Railtrack's collapse into insolvency provided the Blair government with the perfect opportunity to re-nationalise the rail infrastructure, and then to re-integrate the train services as franchises expired. Instead of re-nationalisation – which would have reduced costs, including the cost of borrowing, and allowed public control of investment in the railways – the government opted for the time-consuming alternative of placing Railtrack in administration in the hope of creating a company limited by guarantee without shareholders. In the short run, this led to confusion and uncertainty in the rail industry, morale was lowered, and enhancement projects were delayed. Placing Railtrack in administration for one year also proved to be very costly. In 2002, the Blair government paid out over £1.3 billion, which included compensation to Railtrack shareholders, and payments to the administrators Ernst and Young, which exceeded £755 000 per week. In addition, being risk-averse, the caution of the administrators in operational matters had added at least £1 billion to the annual costs of running the rail infrastructure, thus contributing to a very substantial increase in rail expenditure by the government. The increased network expenditure led the Rail Regulator to authorise a 50 per cent increase in funding for Railtrack's successor, Network Rail, from 2004.

Network Rail is a debt-financed not-for-profit private company with members rather than shareholders. Despite its nominally private status, its key sources of funding are government grants and government-backed borrowing. Government subsidy for British Rail in the decade before privatisation averaged £740 million per year, whereas the total subsidy to the train operating companies and Network Rail is now expected to average between £3 and £4 billion per year in the period 2000 to 2009. Moreover, by 2007, Network Rail's borrowing had reached £18 billion, compared to British Rail's borrowing in its final year of only £2.5 billion. Its annual interest payments were just over £1 billion, while during the current financing period of 2004 to 2009 Network Rail's interest payments are expected to total £4.7 billion, representing 48 per cent of total government grants for Network Rail over this period. Thus, interest payments on private borrowing, guaranteed by the government, are an increasing burden on the company, and almost half of its grants are leaking out of the rail industry to the providers of capital. The company is, in effect, a very expensive mechanism for channelling large sums of public money to financial institutions and private infrastructure contractors.

The failure of the Third Way in rail became more apparent when the Labour government published its Railway Industry White Paper in 2004, which represented its third attempt to reform the rail system in just eight years. The White Paper's foreword contained a damning indictment of rail privatisation which, it argued, had resulted in 'an inefficient and dysfunctional' organisation and 'a failure to control costs'.[50] Despite this formidable criticism, the White Paper reflected extreme government ambivalence as it ruled out both re-nationalisation and any vertical integration of the industry. The astonishing key change, which was implemented by the 2005 Railways Act, was to abolish the recently created SRA – Blair's exemplar of the Third Way approach – and to transfer most of its functions to the Department for Transport. This change meant that, paradoxically, while all rail companies remained in the private sector, the government now had far wider powers of intervention, if it chose to exercise them, than when rail was a nationalised industry.

The Third Way for air traffic control

New Labour's renunciation of any possible re-nationalisation of the railways, focusing instead on a Third Way approach, provided a substantially increased role for the private sector, especially for private finance, with the development of the Private Finance Initiative (PFI) and its associate the Public Private Partnership (PPP). Two of the most infamous PPP schemes introduced in transport were those for the National Air Traffic Services (NATS) and for London Underground. NATS is the third-largest air traffic controller in the European Union. It has been state-owned, operating as a subsidiary of the publicly owned Civil Aviation Authority. It provides vital services at 14 airports in Britain, including take-off and landing, and traffic control for aircraft flying over British airspace. Like much of the transport infrastructure, NATS requires substantial investment if it is to operate a safe and efficient service for a rapidly rising number of airlines operating in one of the world's most congested airspaces. In 1994, the Conservative government issued a consultation paper which argued that NATS should be fully privatised by means of a share flotation in order to raise funds for its investment program, but it did not implement the proposal.

The Labour Party's 1997 election manifesto made no reference to the privatisation of NATS, but in 1998 the Labour government published its own consultation document seeking views on its preferred option of a PPP for NATS involving a partial privatisation. There was widespread opposition to the plan, led by a group of Labour backbenchers who campaigned using the slogan 'Our air is not for sale'. NATS was alleged to be inefficient but, just like British Rail, had made recent substantial productivity improvements by reducing staff numbers at a time when it also coped with a large increase in air traffic. It was because NATS was already an efficient organisation that the proposed PPP raised significant concerns over safety. It was argued that the requirement of private investors to maximise profits could lead to cost reductions, and the only area in which savings could be made would be through further staff reductions. In evidence to the House of Commons Select Committee on Environment, Transport and Regional Affairs, the British association of airline pilots, argued that:

> the UK system is safe and efficient because, as things stand, the safety and operational efficiency of air traffic flows is everyone's manifest priority. With the new goals and priorities which might follow privatisation we could not guarantee that this would continue ... efficiencies will impinge on the numbers of air traffic controllers and the workload that the air traffic controllers have.[51]

The Select Committee found the critics of the proposed PPP to be far more convincing than the government:

The Government has failed, in its evidence to us, and more generally, to make a positive case for the public-private partnership for NATS. It has also failed to give adequate reasons for rejecting the options of establishing the company as an independent publicly-owned corporation, or as a trust or non-share-capital corporation, similar to NavCanada ... The current proposal for a public-private partnership for NATS is, in our view, the worst of all possible options for the future structure of the company. It would lead to operational control of NATS, other than in extreme situations, being ceded to a private investor which is very likely to seek either to cut costs, jeopardising safety, or to increase revenues, by raising charges to its customers, putting airlines and airports in the UK at a competitive disadvantage.[52]

The government was peeved at the committee's critical report, declaring that it was 'deeply disappointed' and reiterating its arguments for the PPP:

transferring a controlling interest in NATS to the private sector will give NATS the commitment, capacity and skills to manage the large and complex investment projects to time and to budget. It will also take air traffic services outside public sector borrowing controls and transfer the responsibility and risks for funding these projects to the private sector. The Government believes that the form of PPP proposed for NATS is coherent, robust and will meet both NATS' needs and the Government's wider policy objectives.[53]

The government's response to the Select Committee's proposed model of a not-for-profit body similar to that of NavCanada, the Canadian air traffic control service, was perplexing, particularly when analysed in the light of Railtrack's later collapse. The government argued that the service needed partial privatisation in order to bring 'shareholder scrutiny to bear on NATS' operational efficiency' and to provide 'strong incentives to improve its performance'. Further, it argued that NavCanada's board consisted of representatives of the Canadian government, airlines, unions and independents, and so was not 'accountable to anyone'.[54]

These responses suggest that the influence of the privatisation ideology in the market state is so strong that it can produce delusional, even schizophrenic, attitudes within government. Further, claims by the government that privatisation encouraged 'shareholder scrutiny' and gave 'strong incentives' to improve performance were made less than six months before the Hatfield train crash in October 2000, which dramatically confirmed earlier criticisms made by both the Rail Regulator and the National Audit Office of Railtrack's very poor performance. The main 'shareholder scrutiny' which Railtrack had received was the approval given to its regular increases in dividends. Moreover, the NavCanada model which was dismissed for lacking accountability was precisely the model adopted two years later when Railtrack was replaced by Network Rail, a not-for-profit company owned by members drawn from the government, rail industry and the public. The main difference was that Network Rail's membership did not include union representatives – the concept of worker participation being a little too radical for New Labour.

Having dismissed the viable alternatives proposed for NATS by its critics, the Blair Government implemented the PPP scheme in 2001. The government retained 49 per cent of the shares in the new company, with 51 per cent being transferred to the private sector: 46 per cent to a strategic partner and 5 per cent to employees. The strategic partner for NATS was a consortium of seven airlines which had paid £87 million less than originally offered, reducing the price to £758 million. In an operation similar to private equity takeovers of companies on the stock market, the airlines only put £55 million of their own money into NATS. They then raised the remainder of the purchase price as loans which would appear as liabilities in the balance sheet of NATS, which assumed the interest and repayment obligations. Borrowing thus soared to nearly £1.5 billion, more than double the asset value, in order to purchase the shares, re-finance a Civil Aviation Authority loan and finance investment.[55]

Far from being a 'robust' scheme as the government had claimed, the NATS PPP was predicated on very optimistic projections about air traffic growth. Within only three months of the partial privatisation, NATS was in financial difficulty because of a fall in trans-Atlantic traffic, particularly after the September 11 attacks. The government was forced to provide short-term loan facilities of £30 million, and then inject an equity stake of £65 million. Just as the government could not allow the rail infrastructure provider to collapse without providing a successor, it could not allow NATS to become insolvent: the safety of millions of air passengers depended upon a continuous, stable and high-quality service. In the full and partial privatisations of Railtrack and NATS respectively, there was no real risk transfer from the public sector to the private sector, as no government could allow such essential transport infrastructures to be subject to the unfettered discipline, or indiscipline, of the free market.

The Third Way and the London Underground

The Third Way approach to London Underground also illustrates how little had been learned from rail privatisation in general, and from the collapse of Railtrack in particular. The Underground was originally built by private railway companies, with the first line opening in 1863. Although an engineering success, the investment needed to maintain and develop the Underground meant that it was not a financial success for the companies involved. Thus, after governments had accepted the need to invest substantial sums in the Underground in the interwar years of the twentieth century, it was included in the Attlee government's 1948 legislation that nationalised much of the transport infrastructure, including the railways.

By the 1990s, the Underground was under attack for inefficiency and seen as a candidate for privatisation. This was despite the fact that, like British Rail and NATS, the Underground's management had responded positively to new rigorous financial controls. Productivity had been raised by reducing the workforce by 20 per cent, with the number of employees falling from 21 500 in 1985 to 16 000 in 1999. However, fares had been increasing by substantially more than the rate of inflation, and by 2000 were double the fares in the Paris and Tokyo undergrounds. The level of subsidy from government was much lower in London, which meant that fares funded a much higher proportion of revenue than in comparable systems in cities such as

New York and Paris. London Underground's subsidy was reduced from £600 million in 1992–93 to £73 million in 1998–99. What London Underground really needed, like British Rail, was sustained subsidy to finance investment. What it received, however, was a very disruptive and expensive re-organisation based on the fragmented railway model.

Labour's Third Way approach to the London Underground was not full privatisation, but partial privatisation through a PPP. This scheme was strongly criticised by the mayor of London, Ken Livingstone, who was elected in 2000 on a platform which included opposition to the PPP project. True to his election pledges, he brought a legal challenge to the PPP in 2001, but lost the case. Livingstone's alternative, based on the successful upgrading of New York's subway system, was for the government to allow London Underground to issue bonds to finance the refurbishment of the tube system. The bond finance scheme would have operated with an annual subsidy of £600 million, while the complex PPP scheme which was imposed on the Underground required an annual subsidy of £1 billion.

Four reports from a variety of sources, including another House of Commons Select Committee and accountants Deloitte and Touche, were very critical about the PPP scheme on both value-for-money and safety grounds. The Select Committee on Transport, Local Government and the Regions, in its February 2002 report, criticised many aspects of the proposed scheme. It highlighted the use of the safety case concept, which had proved to be fatally flawed in the privatised rail system, and cited serious concerns expressed by witnesses appearing before the committee. For example Transport for London, the public sector parent body of the Underground, argued that 'management arrangements for the PPP are so complex that they will jeopardise safety', and the committee noted that 'concerns remain that the pressure to deliver improvements under the PPP performance regime will be even higher and potentially in conflict with safe working practices'.[56] Amongst the committee's very critical conclusions, it warned that:

> The Government must provide the funds to meet the target of a 15 per cent increase in capacity by year 20 of the 30-year programme. The

potentially vast cost to London and the nation's economy of failing to meet that target justifies a considerable increase in Government subsidy.

Our considerations show that the shortage of funds has already constrained capacity improvements and it is likely, therefore, that risk transfer has also been limited. If little risk can be transferred to the private sector then the rationale for the PPP is seriously undermined.

A number of key factors in the assessment of value for money are subjective and difficult or impossible to quantify. There are clear differences in opinion between experts in the engineering, management and finance fields involved in the process about these factors. There is also considerable risk that the cost of the project will be inflated after the first review period where prices are not fixed … We note that the Secretary of State accepted that it will not be possible to provide a definitive answer regarding the value for money of the bids. We therefore recommend that the Government does not approve the PPP deal.

We recommend that the Government should develop alternatives to the PPP in conjunction with the Mayor and Transport for London …

A principal cause of the atrocious state of the London Underground has been the failure of the Treasury to provide adequate long-term funding over a number of decades.[57]

In response to this and another Select Committee report, the Labour government presented its own report in May 2002. On the key issue of risk transfer, it argued that:

Some exceptional risks cannot be transferred to the private sector in a manner consistent with securing the best value for money … risks such as discriminatory changes to the law, acts of terrorism, or a rise in the water table. The infrastructure companies will manage the key risks of ensuring that improvements to the infrastructure are delivered on time, on budget, and to high standards of quality and compatibility … All the finance provided by the bidders' shareholders will be at risk if they fail to perform. There will be no limit on the size of penalties for poor performance.[58]

The government accepted that 'a number of key factors in the assessment of value for money are subjective'. Nevertheless, it still cited the expert advisers who supported the PPP scheme, arguing that 'The Government believes that it would be illogical to dismiss their evaluation just because other experts, who were less closely involved, reached different conclusions'. The result was that the response reiterated support for the PPP, arguing that 'it would be likely to save around £2 billion over the next fifteen years, compared to traditional public funding'.[59]

Having dismissed all objections, the Labour government introduced the Underground PPP scheme in 2003. The complex 30-year PPP contracts, which cost £455 million to put together, fragmented the Underground into four parts. Transport for London remains in the public sector, manages the PPP contracts and provides staff to operate trains and run stations. Three privately owned infrastructure companies are responsible for the maintenance and renewal of the trains, tracks, tunnels, signals and stations. After competitive tendering, two of these companies were established by the Metronet consortium which became responsible for a £17-billion project covering nine out of 12 tube lines. The remaining infrastructure work became the responsibility of another company, Tube Lines. The Metronet consortium was a curious combination of five companies, which were rather more notable for their intimate connections with previous privatisations than for their experience of the complex and diverse work which would be required on the Underground. Metronet included: Bombardier, a train manufacturer; WS Atkins, an engineering firm; Seeboard, a privatised electricity company subsequently taken over by French energy group EDF; Thames Water, a privatised water company; and Balfour Beatty, a building company with rail infrastructure contracts.

Metronet, rather than contracting out work for tender, applied a tied supply chain approach and distributed the work to its own members. Hence, Bombardier gained the contract to replace rolling stock and signals, Balfour Beatty won the job of replacing most of the track, and a joint venture company comprising four of the five shareholders won the contracts for civil engineering and for the refurbishment and modernisation of stations. Consortium members therefore benefited twice from the subsidised payments to Metronet: individually from the contracts awarded, and collectively through sharing the profits made. Despite the complex and expensive performance-based contracts used, it soon became apparent that there were problems with Metronet's work which were strongly reminiscent of those arising from rail privatisation. In April 2004, just one year after Metronet commenced work, it was fined £11 million for poor performance. Much more seriously, in August 2004 a report into the White City tube train derailment damned the company for failing to comply with safety measures put in place in 2003 after a similar accident. In July 2005, it was revealed that Metronet and Tube Lines had together been fined nearly £36 million for poor performance.

Supporters of the PPP scheme argued that the fines and criticism received by Metronet were teething problems as the complex contracts bedded down. In reality, however, they were warnings of the disaster to come. In June 2007, Metronet asked for an extraordinary review by the PPP Arbiter – an additional role allocated to the Rail Regulator – after it predicted a short-term cost overrun of £551 million, increasing to £2 billion by 2010. Metronet argued that the cost overrun resulted from additional unbudgeted demands made by Transport for London. On July 16, however, the PPP Arbiter ruled that Metronet had acted neither 'efficiently nor economically', had higher costs than Tube Lines, and so was only entitled to £121 million in additional payments from January 2008. Faced with this rebuttal, Metronet's board sought administration, a wish granted on July 18. In a further mirroring of Railtrack's collapse, the same administrators, Ernst and Young, were appointed to deal with Metronet's administration.

It quickly became apparent that, despite the optimism conveyed by the government, the PPP had not resulted in a substantial transfer of financial risk to the private sector. It was certainly true, as the government had claimed, that 'all of the finance' of Metronet's share-holders was at risk, but the consortium was financed by only £350 million of equity capital. The bulk of Metronet's capital came from £2.6 billion of debt finance. Further, the PPP scheme guaranteed that 95 per cent of this debt finance would be covered by the public body Transport for London, and the projected cost overrun of £2 billion threatened to eliminate entirely the claimed savings of the scheme over public funding.

The Labour government, now led by former Chancellor Gordon Brown, expected that the Metronet infrastructure contracts would be sold to another bidder. If this were to be achieved, then it was likely to involve offering private firms even more generous terms in the future. The short-term reality was that Transport for London had to make emergency funding of almost £900 million available to the shell of Metronet in order to cover the escalating infrastructure costs, and the administration process, which together were estimated to require an additional £20 million per week.

By the end of the summer in 2007, there was unsettling uncertainty hanging over Metronet's future. Transport for London submitted a bid to take Metronet into the public sector for at least two years, but the government awaited a report from Rothschilds on whether Metronet's contracts had any value remaining above the secured debt. In early September, over 2000 Metronet workers, who were members of the largest rail union, went on strike in order to gain written assurances about job prospects and pension entitlements while the infrastructure companies were in administration. After paralysing most of the Underground for two days, they received satisfactory assurances.

Reconsiderations of the Third Way

The collapse of Metronet into administration and a coincident, major investigation by the House of Commons Transport Select Committee into the London Underground PPP provides an opportunity to reassess the Third Way approach of New Labour. In January 2008 the Select Committee delivered a scathing indictment both of

Metronet's stewardship and of the promised benefits of PPPs.[60] Given the dramatic nature of the committee's unreserved condemnation of the consequences of the Third Way approach of the Blair and Brown Labour governments, in much of the remainder of this section the committee will be allowed to speak for itself.

Setting the tone for its report, the committee argued that:

> Contracts that were supposed to deliver 35 station upgrades over the first three years in fact delivered 14 – 40% of the requirement; stations that were supposed to cost Metronet SSL £2 million in fact cost £7.5 million – 375% of the anticipated price; by November 2006, only 65% of scheduled track renewal had been achieved. They have ended in collapse and chaos. It was a spectacular failure. (paragraph 93)

The committee highlighted a number of fundamental problems with the PPP which contributed to the failure, and which amounted to a comprehensive rebuttal of the main grounds upon which PPPs had been, and still are, proposed and supported by government: Metronet's tied supply chain; the myth of risk transfer; safety; and costs and value-for-money.

The bulk of Metronet's obligations under the PPP were meant to be delivered through contracts with its five shareholder companies. The committee found that this structure has now been 'widely recognised as having contributed to the inefficiencies of Metronet, a conclusion which the PPP Arbiter reached in 2006' (paragraph 13). Even Metronet's former chairman, Graham Pimlott, conceded to the committee that:

> I think that there is little doubt that in the case of stations the contractual arrangements with the shareholders was a very negative factor from Metronet's point of view ... It had to pay money when bills were presented and it did not have the ability to withhold it, for example for performance failure. (paragraph 13)

Shortly before its collapse, Metronet responded to concerns about its tied supply chain by starting to award contracts for station upgrades using competitive tendering. The Select Committee was less than impressed by Metronet's late conversion, arguing that 'we are not persuaded that Metronet's shareholders had any inclination to address the problem of the tied supply chain nor, as the intended beneficiaries of the system, did they have very much incentive to do so' (paragraph 16). The committee's overall judgement on the tied supply chain approach was very critical, arguing that its consequences should have been foreseen and that such an approach ought never be allowed again:

> When the bids for the PPP contracts were being assessed, it should
> have been possible for the Government and London Underground,
> then under national control through London Regional Transport,
> to foresee that Metronet's proposed tied supply chain model,
> which guaranteed the lion's share of work to its parent companies,
> did not include the necessary safeguards. The fact that such a
> management structure was judged to be capable of efficient and
> economic delivery seems extraordinary now that Metronet has
> collapsed but the ultimate recipients of the money which was
> paid to the company have walked away with limited losses. The
> Government must not allow this blurring between the roles of
> shareholder and supplier in future bids to carry out work by the
> private sector. Bids where competitive tendering for sub-contracts
> is proposed are likely to ensure that the best price is obtained.
> (paragraph 18)

The key government argument used in favour of the London Underground PPP was that there would be a significant transfer of risk to the private sector. As a result, the annual returns to shareholders on the three PPP contracts, which were boosted by the supposed risks, were expected to be between 18 and 20 per cent. In reality, as the committee pointed out, 95 per cent of Metronet's borrowing was guaranteed by the public sector, with the result that:

> The return anticipated by Metronet's shareholders appears to have
> been out of all proportion to the level of risk associated with the
> contract. The parent companies were effectively able to limit their

liability to the £70 million they each invested in Metronet ... In the face of this very limited liability it is difficult to lend any credence to the assertion that the Metronet PPP contracts were effective in transferring risk from the public to the private sector. In fact, the reverse is the case: Metronet's shareholders, had the company been operated effectively, stood to make quite extravagant returns. Now that it has failed, it is the taxpayer and the Tube passengers who must meet the cost. (paragraph 25)

It was not only Metronet which gained from the public sector debt guarantee, but also its lenders. Although their ultimate risk was only 5 per cent of the debt, the lenders charged about £450 million more than they would have charged on the same level of government borrowing (paragraph 27). The result, argued the committee, was the worst one possible:

> In terms of borrowing, the Metronet contract did nothing more than secure loans, 95% of which were in any case underwritten by the public purse, at an inflated cost – the worst of both possible worlds. As with the shareholders, what minimal risk was borne by Metronet's lenders was disproportionately well rewarded, at the expense of tax- and fare-payers. Public sector negotiating bodies must be hard-headed in their determination to achieve the best possible terms for financing private sector delivery organisations ... If finance cannot be secured at reasonable terms without guaranteeing the vast majority of the debt, loans direct to the Government, which would enjoy the highest credit rating and significantly lower costs, would seem to be the more effective option. (paragraph 29)

The committee took evidence from a number of witnesses, particularly the trade unions, who argued that the fragmented nature of the PPP contracts was having a detrimental effect on safety for Underground passengers and employees engaged in upgrading work. The train drivers' union argued that the PPP had led to poor communication between the infrastructure companies and their employees, and between London Underground employees and the infrastructure companies (paragraph 84). Gerry Doherty, general secretary of the Transport Salaried Staffs' Association, expressed grave concern that the PPP structure had increased safety risks on the Underground. He drew ominous parallels with the fatal above-ground rail accidents, and warned not to:

> wait until you get the same specific instances that you had on the mainline railway through fragmentation and through privatisation before we do something about bringing the railway infrastructure back into where it should be and get proper control over it. What we are saying is that what happened on the Underground is a mirror of what happened on the railway before we had all of those accidents and before we took action by bringing infrastructure and maintenance back in-house. (paragraph 90)

The fears expressed by trade unions were supported by the Office of the Rail Regulator, which was critical of the PPP's impact on track maintenance and renewals. It argued that:

> The PPP infrastructure companies took time to develop their priorities for maintaining and renewing track and this meant that some of the most pressing renewals work was not done as quickly as it should have been. In April 2006 we took enforcement action to require Metronet SSL to maintain the District Line to an appropriate standard. (paragraph 89)

The committee, clearly impressed by the evidence of safety problems presented to it, concluded that:

> To maintain the highest standards of safety for employees in the longer-term, the Government must work with Transport for London and the unions to identify existing communication deficiencies and ensure that the future structure of the contracts does not contain inherent safety weaknesses … the utmost effort must be made to ensure the clarity of procedures for reporting safety concerns. (paragraph 87)

During the transition of Metronet's ownership from its shareholders
to Transport for London ... passenger safety must be the primary
concern of everyone who is involved. A key role for the Government
in its discussions with the Mayor and Transport for London will
be to ensure that future contracts incentivise the actions that are
necessary to guarantee the highest standards of safety on the network.
(paragraph 92)

The Select Committee was also concerned that none of its witnesses
were able to provide an estimate of the total public cost of Metronet's
failure. The additional costs to the public purse comprise the cost
of administration for Metronet and the cost of inefficient work by
Metronet. In addition to these costs, the inefficiency of Metronet has
meant that the schedules for at least 50 station refurbishments have
had to be pushed into the future, 'which represents a separate cost in
lost utility to passengers' (paragraph 75). Shortly after the publication
of the committee's report, the government provided a good indication
of the cost of Metronet's failure when it agreed to pay £1.7 billion
to settle 95 per cent of Metronet's debts, and a further £300 million
to cover its administration costs. This £2 billion in additional costs
may be compared instructively with Metronet's original bid, which
appeared to cost £500 to £1000 million less than the public sector
comparator for the first 7.5 years of the PPP (paragraph 41).

The committee's report further provided some trenchant conclusions both about the Metronet PPP's failure to provide value for
money, and about the wider implications of the failure. The committee forcefully argued that:

Metronet's inability to operate efficiently or economically proves
that the private sector can fail on a spectacular scale ... The evidence
is clear: it cannot be taken as given that private sector involvement
in public projects will necessarily deliver innovation and efficiency,
least of all if the contracts lack appropriate commercial incentives.
Future assessments of the comparative value for money of private
sector-managed models for infrastructure projects should not assume
a substantial efficiency-savings factor; a detailed assessment should

be made of the suitability of the proposed structure of delivery organisations, of bidders' specific expertise and of the strength of the incentives to efficiency. It is worrying that the Government's confidence in such savings appears to stem from a belief that inefficiency is more endemic and irreversible in the public than the private sector. (paragraph 32)

The committee's report concluded with important warnings for the government about the dangers of relying on private sector delivery in future projects. It concluded, without reservation, that:

If the Government is again tempted by a seemingly good deal from the private sector, it should recall Metronet's pathetic under-delivery and the deficiencies in the contracts that allowed it to happen. (paragraph 97)

Whether or not the Metronet failure was primarily the fault of the particular companies involved, we are inclined to the view that the model itself was flawed and probably inferior to traditional public-sector management. We can be more confident in this conclusion now that the potential for inefficiency and failure in the private sector has been so clearly demonstrated. In comparison, whatever the potential inefficiencies of the public sector, proper public scrutiny and the opportunity of meaningful control is likely to provide superior value for money. Crucially, it also offers protection from catastrophic failure. It is worth remembering that when private companies fail to deliver on large public projects they can walk away – the taxpayer is inevitably forced to pick up the pieces. (paragraph 98)

———

The failure of Railtrack and Metronet recognises that the principle of privatisation is inappropriate for highly capital-intensive infrastructure industries which are dependent upon subsidy and which do not provide a universal and unavoidable service. Infrastructure industries will never be able to cover their full costs from fares, while the competing claims of the holders of capital and the investment needs of the industry mean that there will be constant pressure to save on maintenance and renewals expenditure in order to pay dividends and interest. The key underlying implication for public policy is the extent to which privatisation, and a belief in the superiority of the private over the public sector, should be allowed to permeate the British state when rail privatisation failed to meet the objectives claimed for it by the Major government.

However, a Labour government will not even countenance re-nationalisation, despite strong arguments derived from salutary experience that demonstrate that rail privatisation is inefficient, has damaged passenger interests, and will require a permanent subsidy far higher than was ever provided for its nationalised pred-ecessor. The Labour government has not merely renounced nation-alisation, it has extended its Third Way approach by introducing PPP schemes to other essential transport areas, including NATS and the London Underground. Complex schemes have been designed to subsidise private companies in the provision of public services when extensive experience has now proven that it would be far cheaper and more efficient to keep key capital-intensive services in the public sector.

The ultimate paradox of the market state is that, despite the extensive use of privatisation as a first resort, there has not been a substantial transfer of risk to the private sector in key infrastructure areas, since companies cannot be left to the ultimate market disci-pline of bankruptcy. There had to be a replacement for Railtrack; and NATS could not be allowed to collapse; and responsibility for 95 per cent of Metronet's debt capital still rests with the public sector. Further, the market state requires very complex, expensive contracts and regulatory mechanisms to replace the allegedly inefficient public sector institutions, such as the railways, which had functioned far more efficiently than their successors.

The Select Committee's scathing indictment of Metronet and of PPPs as a substitute for public delivery of services has not, however, dampened New Labour's desire to extend PPP schemes into yet more public services. Just three days after the report was published, the newly appointed Secretary of State for Work and Pensions, James Purnell, announced that voluntary organisations and companies would take on a far greater role in helping the long-term unemployed back to work.[61]

Getting fleeced by the invisible hand

I appreciate the opportunity to appear before this committee. I thank you for devoting your time to this issue, which, I believe, is fundamental to the future of the electric power industry as far as consumer protection is concerned ...

My testimony reflects my personal views only. It is based on forty years of experience with the electric power industry as a regulator, an official in Federal and State government, and as the manager of large public utilities. In my view the real story about Enron is not whether or not they broke the law, but about the influence they had on the lack of law enforcement by the Federal Energy Regulatory Commission, on the rules for deregulation in California and Washington DC and, most importantly, their invidious role in the rip off of California consumers. Enron was by far the leading advocate for the most extreme deregulation of the electric power industry in California and they were the most active participant in the volatile market that resulted ... It is all the more frightening because their profit-making role was largely secret.

We must recognize that the so-called invisible hand of Adam Smith was Enron and their fellow gougers picking the pockets of Californians to the tune of billions of dollars now we are beginning to connect the dots. Prices were sky rocketing in California in late 2000 and early 2001 as a direct result of Enron's influence and participation. At the same time Enron was granted special attention to advise a new Administration in Washington to oppose the price controls sorely needed to protect consumers from the enormous profits they and others were making ...

Some may say that I am singling out Enron and 'piling on' just because they are in trouble for other reasons. That is not true. It is important that Congress understand that a rich and famous company can succeed in achieving terrible results for consumers. This Congress and the several states have before them serious questions inherent in the deregulation of electricity. Is the removal of controls on the price of electric power at wholesale a good idea? Does it make sense to remove the legal obligation of a utility to build or buy enough power to provide reliable electricity?

The words 'competition' and 'deregulation' are seductive. They sound great but the reality we found in California was quite different. A public utility industry whose books are open to public inspection, who are legally responsible for providing reasonably priced electricity, and who did just that for decades, was replaced by companies that operated in secrecy, are accountable to no one (apparently not even their shareholders or employees), could sell or withhold power as they pleased and had no obligations to build new plants ...

Proponents continue to talk of the potential benefits of deregulation. In California we learned who got the benefits – it was the power marketers. As for the consumers, in 1996 when deregulation was launched, the consumers were promised a 20% rate reduction by April 2002. Instead the consumers are paying rates that are 40% higher! ...

It is important to take note that at every step of the rulemaking for deregulation in California from 1996 until today, Enron more than anyone else, used their enormous resources to urge the most extreme positions that resulted in maximum secrecy and lack of accountability. And Enron was a major participant taking advantage of the volatility in prices during the 'Perfect Electrical Storm of 2001' while simultaneously waging an intensive, successful campaign that in six crucial months stopped a new Administration in Washington from doing its job of controlling prices ...

There are some fundamental lessons to be learned from this experience.

Electricity really is different and the system of public utilities with a duty to keep the lights on at just and reasonable rates set by regulators served this country well during most of the twentieth century.

Competition thrives in a surplus. But the private generators thrive in a shortage.

It would be a mistake to assume that Enron was unique and its demise means deregulation is 'cleansed' and there are no remaining concerns.

The Congress should recognize that consumers of all sizes cannot be well served by blind faith in the market. Any market for electric power generation must be combined with sufficient governmental participation to assure that the lifeblood of our society doesn't operate in ups and downs. Such volatility and shortages may be acceptable with oranges or stocks but society simply cannot tolerate it for electricity.

(David Freeman, testimony to the Subcommittee on Consumer Affairs, Foreign Commerce and Tourism of the US Senate Committee on Commerce, Science and Transportation, 11 April 2002, pp 1–9)

THE PRIVATISATION OF
PUBLIC PROFITS: UTILITIES

[R]egulated monopolies, sustained by the State, in the interests of the inhabitants generally, should be controlled by the representatives of the people, and should not be left in the hands of private speculators.

(Joseph Chamberlain, in JL Garvin, *The Life of Joseph Chamberlain*, 1932, p 192)

The privatisation and deregulation of water and electricity public utilities, another prominent and very controversial feature of the marketisation of the state, has brought into particularly sharp relief the pitfalls of this process and the inability of government to transfer to the private sector its ultimate responsibilities for protecting and promoting the public interest. Water is literally essential for life, and electricity has become a vital source of both light and energy for business and domestic consumers in the modern world. The great importance of both utilities to the well-being of individuals and society meant that in many countries both of these utilities were brought into public ownership during the nineteenth and twentieth centuries. In Britain, this began at the municipal level, in towns such as Birmingham, as the quotation preceding this chapter indicates. In the market state of today, the strength of the neoliberal ideology, the high profile of both utilities and their capacity to produce great profits has meant that both water and electricity have been targets of the policies of privatisation and deregulation. This chapter examines problems which have arisen in several countries when these policies have been applied.

Among the damaging consequences of fragmenting and privatising the electricity industries in Britain and New Zealand, the consumers have been subject to substantial price rises as vast profits have been transferred to the private sector. Examination also of the partial deregulation of the industry in California reveals how immense profits were made at the expense of the consumer through extensive, amoral and very often illegal market manipulation by companies, the worst of which was Enron. The opening scenario to this chapter highlights the chaos brought to California by this behaviour, which took advantage of the flawed deregulation experiment. In Britain, another consequence of electricity privatisation was the near total destruction of the local coal industry, while the full privatisation of the water industry in Britain, and the partial privatisation in Australia, has resulted in huge profit transfers to the private sector coupled with serious quality issues.

The establishment of the National Grid in Britain

The origins of the electricity industry in Britain can be traced to Joseph Swan, a prosperous self-educated Newcastle inventor. In December 1878 he revealed to the Newcastle-on-Tyne Chemical Society that a carbon filament in an evacuated glass globe would glow when an electric current was passed through it. Together with another pioneer and American inventor, Thomas Edison, he formed the Edison and Swan United Electric Light Company to manufacture lamps and install lighting systems.[1] There was much speculative activity by companies wanting to offer electric lighting systems, with many private Bills presented to parliament seeking the authority to excavate streets in order to lay underground cables. This prompted a parliamentary committee report in 1879 on the need for legislation to regulate such activity. The first Electric Lighting Act was enacted in 1882, and thus the electricity industry was regulated from its beginnings.

In addition to allowing local authorities or private companies to break up streets, following the concerns raised about consumer exploitation by Joseph Chamberlain, then president of the Board of Trade within the Liberal government, the Act also introduced protection for the public against the abuse of private monopoly power. Maximum prices for electricity were fixed, while local authorities were empowered to purchase electricity companies at written down values after 21 years, although this was later amended to 42 years. The more adventurous local authorities, which saw the opportunity to benefit both consumers and ratepayers, took up the option of providing a supply of electricity in their area. In 1889, Bradford pioneered municipal electrical enterprise, an example followed by St Pancras in 1891, and Portsmouth, Hampstead and Ealing in 1894.[2]

By the early twentieth century it became clear that the fragmented nature of the industry was not conducive to the development of large power stations which were needed in order to exploit the potential for economies of scale. Thus, a new body of Electricity Commissioners was established by the 1919 Electricity (Supply) Act. The commissioners were intended to encourage reorganisation in the electricity industry and to promote, regulate and supervise Britain's electricity supply on a national basis. A major escalation in state intervention in the industry occurred with the creation of the Central Electricity Board by the Electricity Supply Act of 1926. The board, an early public corporation established to operate at arm's length from government, later became the model for the corporations established by the post-World War II Labour government to run nationalised industries. The board was to integrate the country's electricity industry by building and operating a national system of interconnected power stations and transmission lines – which became known as the National Grid.

The 1926 Act was introduced by a Conservative government led by Stanley Baldwin, supported by the Labour opposition led by Clement Attlee, in the face of opposition both from the electricity industry and from free market ideologues, including some Conservative backbenchers. The National Grid's successful completion in 1936 showed that the electricity industry could be developed by a public corporation. In 1948, the Attlee government nationalised the electricity industry, establishing at the same time a British Electricity Authority to operate generating plants and transmission infrastructure and to exercise control over 14 Area Boards. This unified what had become a very fragmented industry, bringing together almost 560 municipal electricity authorities and nearly 300 private companies. While it might be arguable that a post-war Conservative government would also have nationalised the electricity industry, by the time of the Thatcher government in the 1980s any nationalised energy providers had become anathema.

The privatisation of electricity and its consequences

The privatisation of electricity, Prime Minister Thatcher conceded, was the 'most technically and politically difficult' to date, and was also 'the one which went furthest in combining transfer of a public utility to the private sector with radical restructuring'.[3] The first nationalised energy industry to be privatised by the Conservative governments of the 1980s was gas, which was sold to shareholders in 1986. At the same time, recognising the private monopoly position of the company, British Gas, a regulator was appointed to control prices and to gradually introduce competition, but it was not until the 1990s that other companies were allowed to compete with British Gas in offering retail gas sales to consumers. When it came time for the Conservative government to privatise electricity, dissatisfaction within the government with the gas privatisation model ensured that competition was brought into the industry from the start.

The original aim of the Conservative government was to sell off the entire electricity industry, including all of the nuclear power stations. However, it soon became clear that the published operating costs of nuclear plants, as a senior minister admitted, were too low. There had been a substantial understatement of 'the likely true cost of decommissioning a nuclear power station at the end of its life (and to a lesser extent the final cost of the reprocessing or safe disposal of the nuclear waste)'. Thus, despite Thatcher's desire to privatise the entire industry, all the nuclear plants were kept in the public sector as Nuclear Electric to avoid creating uncertainties that would 'frighten off investors' and give the project 'a negative net worth'.[4]

The non-nuclear part of the industry was fragmented into many units as part of the privatisation process in 1990. The former Central Electricity Generation Board (CEGB), which had been responsible for electricity generation and distribution, divided into four companies. The transmission system was vested in the National Grid Company, which was originally owned by the Regional Electricity Companies but later sold in 1996. Two generating companies were established, PowerGen and National Power, and the 12 public Area Boards were replaced by 12 Regional Electricity Companies, which were licensed to supply electricity within their own areas. As in the case of most privatisations in Britain, assets were underpriced in order to encourage a successful sale, which meant that electricity shares were, on average, ten times oversubscribed.

The CEGB, despite the allegations of inefficiency made by the privatisation ideologues, had been profitable before privatisation, earning profits of over £1 billion annually in the late 1980s. From its creation in 1957 until 1989, employment fell in the CEGB by over 55 000 and productivity increased by more than four times. Despite already significant reductions in employees, as soon as the CEGB had been fragmented and privatised the power generators began to make further 'efficiency' savings by making more employees redundant and by reducing the use of coal as a power source. The profits of the CEGB's successor companies increased from £2 billion in 1991–92 to £3.5 billion in 1995–96, as the number of employees fell over this period by 53 per cent, from 40 497 to 21 057 by 1995–96.[5]

At privatisation, 92 per cent of fossil fuel used for power generation was coal, 7 per cent oil, and only 1 per cent gas.[6] This meant that
coal still provided around 80 per cent of Britain's electricity supply.
The National Coal Board had long-term contracts with the CEGB,
which both guaranteed a market for the nationalised coal industry
and ensured a secure source of power for the electricity industry.
Upon privatisation, however, coal was criticised for being uneconomic relative to other sources of power, with the result that the privatised power companies began closing coal-fired generators with a
zeal which bordered on the fanatical. Environmental factors were one
consideration in the move from coal to gas, with gas producing fewer
emissions compared to coal, particularly carbon dioxide. In the first
five years after privatisation, the coal purchases by power stations fell
from 74 million tonnes to 30 million tonnes, while the compensatory
purchases of gas steadily rose.

Such was the drive for profits that although the Coal Board was
achieving huge productivity gains in the 1990s, which saw coal prices
fall by 20 per cent, coal-fired power stations were being closed before
replacement gas power stations were available. This resulted in a foreseeable and significant supply problem, which was met by importing
electricity from the French state-owned supplier EDF. The result was
the bizarre irony that around one quarter of the 'efficiency gains' from
privatising the CEGB 'were transferred out of the country in the form
of additional profits to EDF'. By 1996, gas accounted for 23 per cent
of power generation. Despite the fall in the unit costs of electricity
which resulted from the conversion to gas this was 'not translated
directly into corresponding falls in [retail] prices, but into increased
profits'. Not surprisingly, in the period 1990 to 1995 electricity share
prices rose by over 250 per cent, outperforming the stock market by
more than 100 per cent.[7]

These profits made by the CEGB's successor companies in the
1990s were themselves dwarfed by those of the Regional Electricity
Companies. Their predecessor bodies, which had been attacked for
being inefficient and over-staffed, had made a profit averaging £330
million per year from 1985–86 to 1989–90, representing a 15 per
cent return on turnover. They had also made modest but consist-

ent improvements in labour productivity of around 2 per cent per year between 1970 and 1987. During the post-privatisation period 1990–91 to 1997–98, the 12 Regional Electricity Companies made combined profits of £10.5 billion, representing a 32 per cent return on a much higher turnover as demand for electricity rose. Dividends totalling £6.1 billion were paid to shareholders over this period while at the same time the workforce was reduced by 42 per cent.[8]

A major academic study found that, compared to the counterfactual case of the industry remaining in public ownership, shareholders benefited overwhelmingly from privatisation while consumers only started to benefit moderately from price reductions from 1999–2000.[9] Further, consumers became largely dependent on electricity generated by companies with overseas owners after the Conservative government allowed takeovers in the industry in 1996. By March 1996, only three months after an earlier takeover ban was removed, four companies had been taken over; by 2000 eight of the 12 companies were owned by American power companies. Such was the public concern over the profits and returns to shareholders of the electricity companies and other privatised utilities, even the strongly pro-business Labour Party felt confident of public support when it included a commitment to levy a windfall profits tax on utilities in its 1997 election manifesto. After winning the election, the tax was levied by the Labour government in order to finance its New Deal program to reduce unemployment, with the electricity companies contributing £2.1 billion out of the total levy of £5.2 billion.

The 'dash for gas' was not simply related to falling gas prices, environmental considerations and improved gas turbine technology. Rather, the Conservative governments of the 1980s and 1990s were publicly in favour of a diverse range of energy sources, especially if this provided them with the means to destroy a powerful antagonist, the National Union of Mineworkers (NUM). Two energy economists spelt out the underlying policy objective for coal as the need 'to break the power of the NUM and the perceived stranglehold of coal on the electricity supply industry'.[10] Nigel Lawson, a senior minister in the 1980s, confirmed this, admitting that diversity of supply was 'code for freedom from blackmail' by the NUM.[11]

The psyche of the Conservative Party had been scarred by the events of the winter of 1973–74 when the NUM organised a prolonged and effective strike in furtherance of a pay claim. To manage dwindling coal supplies the Conservative government at the time, led by Edward Heath, declared a state of emergency and imposed a three-day week on industry. With the miners enjoying considerable public support, despite the significant inconveniencies to the public, in February 1974 the Heath government called a general election on the question of 'Who governs Britain?' The response of the electorate was in the negative as far as the Conservatives were concerned, the Heath government losing its majority to be replaced by Labour under Harold Wilson.

Just over ten years later the Thatcher government faced another strike by the NUM, now led by Arthur Scargill, over plans by the National Coal Board to close 'uneconomic' pits. Scargill's claim that the plan would eventually involve the loss of 100 pits and 100 000 jobs was widely denounced as revolutionary 'rhetoric'. However, events were to prove that the rhetoric was only wrong in being a serious underestimate. Unfortunately for the miners, the strike provided the final, convincing justification for the Thatcher government to move against the miners and the coal industry. To Thatcher:

> As an industrial dispute the coal strike had been wholly unnecessary. The NUM's position throughout the strike – that uneconomic pits could not be closed – was totally unreasonable. Never while I was Prime Minister did any other group make a similar demand, let alone strike for it. Only in a totalitarian state with a siege economy – with nationalisation, the direction of labour and import barriers – could the coal industry have functioned, even for a time, irrespective of financial realities and the forces of competition. But for people like Mr Scargill these were desirable things. The impossibility of the NUM's policy on pit closures is a further clue – as if public statements were not enough – to the real nature of the strike itself.[12]

Contrary to the government's denunciation of the aims of the miners and their union, there had been a great deal of co-operation between the government and mineworkers over pit closures ever since the coal industry was nationalised in 1946. At that time there were 980 pits employing 700 000 miners. By 1960, the number of pits had fallen to 698, and to 289 by 1972.[13] The number of pits fell again in the 1970s and early 1980s, reaching 170 pits employing just under 250 000 miners by the time of the strike. Despite this history of co-operative engagement and the existence of a long-established colliery review procedure involving the NUM, the Coal Board's first move was announced without any consultation in March 1984 that the Yorkshire pit at Cortonwood would close. Even Thatcher conceded that this announcement was not 'well handled'.[14] This provocative act was then followed at the national level, six days later, by an announcement of the closure of a further 20 pits and 20 000 more redundancies.

One critic of the Thatcher government's policy saw the importance of the ensuing strike from the point of view of organised labour:

> By any reckoning, the miners' strike of 1984–85 was a watershed in British postwar history. Indeed, it has no real parallel – in size, duration and impact – anywhere in the world. The dispute pitted the most powerful and politicised trade union in the country against a hard-right Tory administration bent on class revenge and prepared to lay waste to our industrial heartlands and energy sector in the process, regardless of cost. It convulsed Britain, turned mining areas into occupied territory, and came far closer than was understood at the time to breaking the Thatcher Government's onslaught on organised labour. The strike was a defensive battle to protect livelihoods and communities that the miners could not have avoided. But it was also a challenge to the destructive profit- and market-led restructuring of economic life then in full flow. And it raised the alternative of a different kind of Britain, rooted in solidarity and collective action, against the individualism and private greed of the Thatcher years – symbolised by the wads of overtime cash her riot squads waved at the miners' picket lines.[15]

The defeat of the miners' strike was followed by an escalation of the pit closure program, even in the Nottinghamshire area where many miners had defied the strike call and remained at work. Many pits were closed down with the number of miners employed falling from around 250 000 at the time of the strike to 65 000 by 1990. Chancellor Nigel Lawson estimated that the government had spent over £2 billion in defeating the strike, a sum he regarded as 'a worthwhile investment for the nation'.[16] In addition, over £1 billion was spent on redundancy payments for miners. Pit closures continued after 1990 under John Major, who was the supposedly more 'moderate' replacement for Margaret Thatcher as prime minister. In 1992, there was another public outcry over the Conservative government's plan to close 31 of the 50 remaining pits, making 30 000 more miners redundant. Arthur Scargill and the NUM suddenly became rehabilitated and it became:

> customary, even in the press, to marvel at how the NUM President's predictions about Conservative intentions towards the miners and their industry – derided as scare-mongering earlier – had been proved right after all. Memories of the months of smear and character assassination ... and the years of hatred and ridicule momentarily melted away.[17]

The government faced a political crisis, with a quarter of a million people demonstrating twice in one week on the streets of London in support of the miners. The NUM voted for strike action in 1993 but the government simply bided its time and postponed the closures for a few months. In a final act, the Major government sold the remaining pits with their workforce of 7000 miners to an entrepreneur, Richard Budge, in 1994. Budge had been heavily criticised for his business practices by accountants Coopers & Lybrand, in a report prepared for the Department of Trade and Industry.[18] The Major government wrote off £1.6 billion of public debt in this very dubious privatisation, which only raised £960 million, thus incurring a loss of over £600 million on the 'sale'.

In a very plausible counterfactual scenario, the money 'invested' to defeat the miners' strike could have been used to develop 'clean coal' technology in order to reduce, or even eliminate, carbon dioxide emissions from coal-fired power stations. Britain could have become a world-leader in the use of clean coal technology. Instead, construction of the world's first carbon dioxide-free coal-fired power station by a Swedish company began in Germany in 2006, with a scheduled target date for the supply of power in 2008.

The pit closures had huge social and economic costs in mining areas, where whole communities were devastated. A major investigation of mining communities published in 2000 found that coalfield communities remained blighted by the impact of pit closures a decade after the event.[19] Ray Hudson, a co-author of the report, commented that:

> Despite being home to around five per cent of the British population, coalfield areas remain marginalised. A decade after their economic, social and cultural life was ruptured by pit closures, they continue to be characterised by high unemployment, long-term sickness and poverty. Government and other initiatives have had, at best, a partial and uneven effect in transforming these areas. Little progress has been made in rebuilding their productive capacity around new industries. Coalfield areas remain in continuing need of strong support from national and European Union programs for social and economic regeneration. But although they are unique places, their experience of dealing with the consequences of industrial decline has wider implications. Not least, they show how important it is for policies and funding arrangements to support the involvement of local people and help release their creativity and talents in renewing their communities.[20]

With the closure of the mines the nation also lost a valuable power source for the electricity industry. Once these 'uneconomic' mines have been abandoned, and crucial maintenance ceased, many become unusable. In the present economic climate, they would once again have been financially viable, given the large rise in both oil and gas prices since the 1990s. Instead, Britain remains heavily dependent upon gas, with 40 per cent of electricity generated in gas-fired power stations. Yet, as its North Sea gas supplies diminish, Britain is increasingly reliant on imports from Europe, where gas prices are linked to the price of oil with both industry and consumers having been affected by higher gas prices. In March 2006 British Gas raised both gas prices and its dividend payment to shareholders by 22 per cent, to be followed by an additional price rise of 12 per cent in September. This has resulted in households in Britain now paying, on average, over £1000 per year for gas and electricity. In addition, oil prices have more than doubled since 2003, increasing from under US$40 per barrel to US$100 per barrel in January 2008.

The privatisation of the British electricity industry had other negative consequences, both nationally and internationally, in addition to the almost total destruction of the local coal industry and the privatisation of public profits with the transfer of billions of pounds from customers to companies and shareholders. Despite all the adverse social and economic effects of the privatisation of British electricity, the electricity privatisation model followed by Britain has influenced both the deregulation experiment in California and the privatisation of electricity in New Zealand, as seen in the later parts of this chapter.

The privatisation of British Energy

The decision by the Thatcher government to retain nuclear power plants was soon revisited in the early 1990s by the Major government as the output and revenue of many of the nuclear power stations increased. By this time, John Major presided over an enfeebled administration and a Conservative Party riven by disputes over both the principle and the extent of Britain's continued membership of the European Union. The government's opinion poll ratings had collapsed to around 30 per cent after it was forced to remove sterling from the EU's exchange rate mechanism in October 1992, an act which destroyed the centrepiece of its economic policy. Newspapers such as *The Sun* demonstrated their fascinating interpretation of impartiality by turning on John Major with a savagery they had previously reserved for Neil Kinnock, leader of the Labour Party. This was followed by a succession of media exposures of the exotic financial and sexual escapades of over

30 Conservative parliamentarians, the cumulative effect of which, when combined with the exchange rate debacle, left the government looking exhausted, sleazy and incompetent.

John Major's response, in an attempt to boost his sagging political virility, was to take the concept of privatisation beyond even the limits established by Margaret Thatcher. Thus, the remnants of the coal industry were privatised in 1994, followed in 1996 by both Railtrack and British Energy. The last two privatisations had much in common. Both were only privatised after a large debt write-off; both organisations required very substantial expenditure on maintenance, which was understated at privatisation; and both ultimately had to be rescued with large amounts of public money which dwarfed the initial privatisation proceeds.

British Energy was established in 1995 by the Conservative government to take responsibility for operating the eight most modern nuclear power plants in Britain. Although ageing, nuclear power plants still produce nearly 20 per cent of the nation's electricity supply. The Magnox nuclear reactors, some of which dated back to the 1950s, were considered too old and too expensive for a private sector company to decommission, and so remained in the public sector as part of British Nuclear Fuels. When in 1996 the Major government privatised British Energy, the flotation was deemed a success, although there were some ominous warning signs of future problems. Not the least of these were the misleadingly optimistic projections about both electricity prices and the company's liabilities contained within the company's prospectus. Instead of operating profitably at the time of privatisation, the financial advisers handling the sale, Barclays de Zoete Wedd, revealed a decade later in March 2006 that losses of between £50 and £550 million per year would have been made over the previous five years had British Energy been operating in the private sector. In the event, the public flotation raised only £1.5 billion, compared to the initial projections of proceeds of between £2.6 and £3.3 billion. Further, the Major government wrote off £800 million of debt in order to save the privatisation. Thus, the proceeds were trivial in terms of the government's budget deficit: they did not even begin to cover the public investment of over £2 billion in just one of British Energy's assets, the new power station Sizewell B.

As with rail, concerns were strenuously raised about the safety implications of privatising nuclear power stations, 'principally that commercial pressures might discourage staff from shutting down plant for safety reasons, or encourage them to restart prematurely'.[21] The urgency of these concerns was vindicated when, barely five months after the privatisation in May 1996, British Energy announced that 'efficiency' savings would be made by cutting 1500 jobs, representing over one fifth of the workforce employed by the company. General safety concerns, and particular concerns about staff reductions, were examined two years after privatisation by the House of Commons Select Committee on Trade and Industry. The committee noted that, as a result of the staff reductions and the increased use of contracting out, there should be 'the fullest co-operation' and 'the greatest possible transparency' between the Nuclear Installations Inspectorate – the body established in 1960 to monitor and licence all nuclear power stations in Britain – and the company. The review concluded that it was vital for public confidence 'that nuclear safety should continue to be, and be seen to be, a dominant priority for those engaged in the civil nuclear industry ... this is an issue which we will be watching closely.'[22]

As in all previous privatisations, a key motive for British Energy's flotation was the desire to obtain short-term receipts. This privatisation was uncommon, however, in that another explicit objective was to create a 'robust company' which would be able to meet 'its liabilities'. The Panglossian nature of these hopes was exposed when the Department of Trade and Industry showed what turned out to be a very prescient concern that British Energy might not be able to meet their long-term nuclear liabilities and that these liabilities would by default have to be met by taxpayers in the future. In 1999, the House of Commons Select Committee on Public Accounts criticised the sale of British Energy for 'the disappointing level of proceeds' from the privatisation and drew attention to the 'uncertainties' relating to the ostensible transfer of nuclear liabilities to the private sector.[23] In particular, this committee raised concerns:

that there remains uncertainty about the size of nuclear liabilities in the future. This uncertainty arises because the technologies for dealing with longer-term decommissioning are untried and because there is currently no costed strategy for the disposal of certain kinds of nuclear waste. We note the Department's recognition that there are no 100 per cent guarantees or room for complacency in the monitoring and managing of these risks in the future and we recommend that they should monitor the progress of the nuclear industry in developing its technologies for undertaking these tasks.[24]

The select committee's emphasis on the 'uncertainties' relating to British Energy's nuclear liabilities also proved to be accurate. The company initially appeared to be profitable, and so its share price increased from the flotation level of £2.40 to a peak of over £7 in early 1999. However, the financial vulnerability of the nuclear power plants soon became apparent. The bulk of a nuclear power plant's operating costs are fixed, in the sense that they will be incurred even if the plant is not operating. This is partly due 'to the need to operate and maintain a nuclear plant's safety systems even if the unit is not generating electricity'.[25] As a result, profits are very sensitive to both electricity price changes and to any operating difficulties. British Energy's share price began to fall in 2000, with the company running into major difficulties in 2002 when it was hit by two problems. Firstly, an increase in overall generating capacity in the late 1990s had reduced the wholesale price of electricity, and it continued to fall in the early 2000s. In addition, the company had to take several nuclear plants off-line to deal with major operating problems, thus losing even more revenue. The result was that the company was making losses, its share price collapsing to around 5 pence and its stock market valuation falling to £31 million – when it had been over £2 billion in 2001. By the autumn of 2002 the company faced the prospect of being placed in administration and so appealed for government support.

There were two major concerns which determined the government's unavoidable response: the significant contribution of the company to the electricity supply; and the safety of the nuclear power plants. The Labour government, as in the case of Railtrack, could have renationalised British Energy. It chose not to, preferring instead to adopt a complex 'Third Way' approach which relied upon large public subsidy to retain the company in the private sector. The government initially provided a short-term loan of £650 million in 2002, but ultimately was obliged to support the company with a £2.8 billion rescue package. The liabilities for dealing with spent nuclear fuel and for the decommissioning of older power stations, which were meant to have been transferred to the private sector by privatisation, were formally transferred to a Nuclear Liabilities Fund in the public sector. In 2008 decommissioning costs for 19 nuclear power plants were estimated to be at least £73 billion, a great deal more than the £17 billion which the British Nuclear Decommissioning Authority estimated in 2003.[26]

A complex capital restructuring was carried out and British Energy was re-listed on the stock market in 2005. The government received 64 per cent of the new shares, with 2.5 per cent going to the previous shareholders, and the remaining shares going to creditors. At the same time, British Energy was required to pay 64 per cent of its available cash flow to the Nuclear Liabilities Fund. By 2007 the substantial increases in the wholesale price of electricity had helped to restore the company to profitability, allowing it to pay the first dividend since the rescue operation. Thus, a nominally 'private' sector company was given the opportunity to return to sufficient profitability to enable it to resume dividend payments through the aid of government subsidy and through the transference of its nuclear clean-up liabilities to the public sector. The extent of the obligations now transferred to the public sector prompted the House of Commons Select Committee on Public Accounts to publish a follow-up to its earlier report in 1999. This July 2007 report was critical of the fact that, as a result of the restructuring of British Energy:

> the taxpayer has been left to underwrite a large and uncertain
> liability, recently valued at £5.3 billion. The Company assumed full
> responsibility for its nuclear power stations, including the associated
> liabilities, on privatisation in 1996. In reality, the Government's

international obligations always meant that responsibility would fall on the taxpayer if the company was unable to meet them.[27]

The select committee was also concerned that without direct responsibility for meeting its liabilities the company:

> may now lack the incentive to reduce the liabilities falling to the Nuclear Liabilities Fund. The Department, working with the Nuclear Decommissioning Authority, should put in place adequate arrangements to confirm that the Company carries out its operations efficiently, reducing the eventual liabilities to be met by the Nuclear Liabilities Fund wherever possible.[28]

The precarious nature of British Energy's newly-established profitability was highlighted in the autumn of 2007 when the company closed down two of its nuclear power plants and delayed the recommissioning of two others because of operating and maintenance issues. Concern was also raised about the loss of skilled employees, on top of the earlier large 'efficiency' savings, with 40 per cent of the workforce due to retire over the next decade. The company's share price fell by 15 per cent, from £5.79 to under £5, as financial analysts downgraded their earnings forecasts. Britain's electricity supply appeared at risk, and there were predictions that British Energy would have to buy its power in the highly costly wholesale energy market in order to meet its supply commitments if the outages persisted. After the destruction of its coal industry, Britain was very vulnerable to continued price rises in imports of both oil and gas and to the operating problems with ageing nuclear reactors. The privatisation of all of Britain's energy industries left the country facing the prospect of a winter in 2007–08 of soaring energy prices and power shortages. Thus, the failure of the privatisation of British Energy exposed the insincerity of the justifications used to silence opponents. The privatisation did not raise significant revenue, nor create a robust, innovative nuclear power industry. Nor were liabilities transferred from the public to the private sector. There had been little of benefit to the public interest.

Energy privatisation in New Zealand

In the 1980s and 1990s, governments in New Zealand pursued a neoliberal philosophy similar to that of the Conservative governments led by Margaret Thatcher and John Major in Britain. This philosophy was predicated on expanding the role of the free market and decreasing the role of the state. The only significant difference was that policies of deregulation and privatisation had been originally promoted in New Zealand by a Labour government in the 1980s – a fact which reveals how far privatisation, and a belief in the superiority of the private sector over the public sector, had permeated states around the world under governments of nominally different political persuasions. The Labour government elected in 1984, led by David Lange, began by introducing extensive deregulation. It removed exchange controls on capital flows, floated the currency and removed agricultural subsidies. Further measures included the abolition of many regulations on business and import quotas, the removal of subsidies and tax exemptions in many areas, reductions in income tax rates, the restructuring of some government departments and government agencies along commercial lines, in some cases in preparation for their sale, and the targeting of inflation as the main objective of economic policy.[29] The privatisation of public assets began in 1987, influenced and aided, as in Britain, by reports from consultants for whom privatisation was a very lucrative policy.

Despite the extensive market liberalisation introduced by the Lange government, in the 1980s the electricity industry in New Zealand was still owned by both central and local government. Electricity was generated by the Electricity Division of the Ministry of Energy, while the retail electricity suppliers were either elected supply authorities or local government departments. New Zealand is in the very fortunate, and climate-friendly, position of being able to produce over 70 per cent of its electricity from renewable sources, mainly hydroelectric. This had meant that, historically, New Zealand had low electricity production costs and therefore low retail prices in relation to other economies such as Japan and the United States. It also had a policy of cross-subsidising domestic users by charging higher rates to commercial users. Early in its privatisation program the Lange government retained the state's control of electricity, but it made an important change to its organisational form in 1987 by creating a state-owned corporation, the Electricity Corporation of New Zealand (ECNZ), from the Energy Ministry's Electricity Division. The new ECNZ was put under the control of some of the most enthusiastic business supporters of the government's structural adjustment program, who urged the government to privatise the corporation and to encourage private power generators. Private generators, however, would have to use thermal power at much higher costs, thereby allowing ECNZ to raise its prices.[30] In order to boost profitability, ECNZ began a program of selling off its oldest and least profitable power stations. A further significant organisational change occurred in 1989 when the Labour government ended the election of members to the electricity supply authorities.

The market liberalisation and privatisation policies of the Labour government were continued by the conservative National government elected in 1990. Among the earliest, the electricity industry was changed fundamentally by a key piece of legislation, the Energy Companies Act of 1992. This required all of the local electricity supply authorities to be corporatised, and so turned into 'energy companies', in preparation for privatisation. In addition, the useful cross-subsidisation of domestic users by commercial users was ended. The results of these innovations for consumers were soon apparent. Whereas, after adjusting for inflation, the price of electricity for domestic users was roughly the same in 1992 as in 1983, the price of electricity for domestic users rose steadily from 1992 until it was 20 per cent higher by 1998. In sharp contrast, commercial prices fell by 15 per cent between 1992 and 1998. There was 'therefore a significant redistribution of the costs of electricity from corporate users to people in their homes'.[31] This change both reflected and also contributed to the extensive redistribution of income from the poor to the rich which occurred within New Zealand. Between 1984 and 1996 the richest 5 per cent of the population increased their share of national income by 25 per cent, and the top 10 per cent increased their share by 15 per cent. The share of national income for the bottom 80 per cent of New Zealanders fell, with the median income of adults falling by over 13 per cent over the decade 1986 to 1996.[32]

Mercury Energy, the largest power company created in 1993 under the provisions of the new Energy Companies Act, was owned by the local community trust, the Auckland Energy Consumer Trust, which had over half of the share capital and appointed four of the nine company directors. In practice, control rested with one of New Zealand's largest law firms, which had the power to appoint the remaining five directors. This law firm:

> had exceptionally close relationships with many of the private
> corporations and individuals benefiting from the structural adjustment
> programme and privatisations. Thus the community trust was unable
> to control the asset it owned, and Mercury Energy began an aggressive
> programme of taking over neighbouring power companies. It took on
> a prominent corporate raider and union basher from Australia, Wayne
> Gilbert, as its chief executive.[33]

Soon after its creation, Mercury Energy made 600 employees redundant and contracted out key functions such as cable maintenance. It raised the price of electricity, increasing profits by NZ$100 million. Unfortunately, the results of Mercury Energy's focus on takeovers and profit maximisation, rather than cable maintenance, became starkly apparent in 1998 when there was a failure of all four of the power cables supplying electricity to the entire central business district of Auckland, New Zealand's main business centre, producing a complete power blackout from 20 February. Even though two of the cables were 40 years old and past their replacement date, the company's grossly over-optimistic prediction was that power would be restored in seven days. Instead, it took four weeks, and much longer in some areas. A full service was only finally restored in mid-April after new lines had been laid and supply cables reconnected. The delay in restoring power was a direct consequence of the zealous labour retrenchment which meant that skilled cable staff had been lost to the electricity industry in New Zealand. Consequently, staff had to be flown in from Australia and even France to retrieve the situation.

At its height the blackout affected over 8500 businesses employing around 74 000 people, and over 6000 apartment dwellers. Restaurants and small businesses had to close, the residents in apartments had to leave, and Auckland University's 30 000 staff and students had to stay at home. City centre businesses estimated that their losses amounted to NZ$60 million per week. Subsequently, Mercury Energy was forced to pay thousands of compensation claims, totalling NZ$128 million. In July 1998, the company announced that it could not afford to pay a dividend when its profit of NZ$82 million in 1997 became a loss of NZ$25 million in 1998. Mercury Energy tried to blame factors such as the weather and excess consumer demand for the blackout, but this denial of responsibility was refuted by the company's earlier warnings to Auckland City Council in 1996 that the cables feeding electricity to Auckland's central business district were unreliable. As a result of the blackout, the National government established an inquiry which reported at the end of June 1998. The inquiry's findings were a damning indictment of Mercury Energy's poor cable maintenance practices:

> While Mercury Energy is a competent distribution company, it did not have the required expertise, operations and management procedures for the 110 kV cables; The cause of repetitive gas leaks and faults was not solved by systematic investigation; A well-developed asset audit and asset management programme for the 110 kV cables did not exist; Maintenance contracts for the 110 kV cables were deficient in terms of their specification, management and monitoring; There was inadequate internal expertise on 10 kV cables and inadequate participation in external forums to remain current with cable operating and maintenance practices; The specification of the 110 kV cables was never checked nor reassessed against the 'as built' conditions; The 110 kV transmission risk in 1997 was materially underestimated and as a consequence actual security of supply was under-planned; The reliance on informal arrangements for the pooling of spares for the 110 kV cables was ineffective as shown by at least one incident prior to 1998.[34]

The inquiry's recommendations focused mainly on the steps Mercury Energy needed to take to improve its asset management. It recommended that the company should 'establish a specific management plan' for its cable system and periodically have the plan 'peer-reviewed by external experts'. It also recommended that:

> Mercury Energy review its practices in respect of its use of external contract services to establish clear and definitive specifications for contract services; Mercury Energy review its strategic plan to ensure that the core business of distribution and security of supply is given appropriate priority and allocation of resources ... Mercury Energy institute periodic technical audits for all major assets associated with the power supply.[35]

Although the inquiry criticised Mercury Energy's corporate governance and accountability arrangements, which had been imposed by the National government, there were very few recommendations in this crucial area. The company was expected to negotiate a 'Statement of Corporate Intent' by 1998, and the government was to consider 'whether, in the public interest, steps are necessary to restore the intended lines of accountability to normal standards in Mercury Energy's corporate structure'. There was no suggestion of reversing the corporatisation of Mercury. Instead, the government was asked to 'consider' a requirement for power companies to publish asset management plans every three years, and to 'encourage' electricity suppliers to develop customer contracts 'that reflect security of supply standards'.[36]

Far from the debacle reversing the trend towards privatisation, the National Party government used the blackout in Auckland to justify increased fragmentation and competition in the electricity industry. Subsequently, the Electricity Industry Reform Act in 1998 forced the separation of the three main sectors of the industry: power generation, supply networks, and electricity retail.

Increased competition and fragmentation were meant to reduce prices and to encourage new companies to enter the industry. In practice, the rush to fragment and privatise had several negative consequences. Most significantly, different elements of the industry became concentrated in the hands of a small number of companies, often under foreign ownership. Electricity retail became largely concentrated in the hands of four companies, the largest of which, TransAlta, had one third of the market. A similar result emerged in the power generation sector, which is now also dominated by a few large companies, the leading one being the American UtiliCorp, with a 30 per cent dominance. This market concentration has led to substantial price rises for both domestic and commercial users. New charges for previously free services have also been introduced. TransAlta, for example, introduced charges in 1999 for reconnection, disconnection and final meter-readings.[37] In addition, there has been extensive retrenchment and heightened job insecurity for the workforce in the electricity industry, the results of which were graphically demonstrated both by the Auckland power cuts and the difficulties in restoring power to the central business district.

Electricity supply in the United States

The United States energy industry is quite unlike those of Britain and New Zealand, whose electricity industries were privatised in the 1990s after being under public sector control for decades. In the United States, most electricity has always been supplied by private companies, but under a variety of regulatory regimes. Private electric utility companies developed rapidly in the United States in the early twentieth century when many small utility companies were taken over and absorbed into large holding companies which exercised monopoly powers to exploit consumers in many states. By 1927, three large holding companies controlled 45 per cent of the electricity industry.

This concentration of market power so alarmed President Franklin Delano Roosevelt that he promised in his 1932 campaign for the presidency to reform the electricity industry so that market abuses would be addressed, and to ensure the supply of power to rural areas which had been neglected by electric utilities. Thus, as part of his New Deal, additional agencies such as the Tennessee Valley Authority were created to provide for the electrification of rural areas, while new regulatory powers were introduced. Amongst the most effective measures, the Public Utility Holding Act of 1935 created a framework of Federal and state law to regulate the holding companies in the electricity industry. In the same year, the Federal Power Act was introduced in order to give the Federal Power Commission the responsibility to oversee and regulate the transmission and sale of electric energy in interstate commerce. At state level, public utility commissions were responsible for the regulation of utilities.

This regulatory system enabled the development of a comprehensive interconnected electricity supply industry in the United States. Smaller generators were replaced by larger power stations which benefited from economies of scale, and electricity prices fell steadily up to the 1960s as supply increased. Electric utility companies were allowed to recover their operating costs, plus a regulated profit margin of around 10 per cent, when calculating prices for consumers. This position changed significantly in the 1970s with the energy crisis following the restriction of oil supplies to Western countries by the Organisation of Petroleum Exporting Countries in 1973. The response in the United States was an uneasy mix of both regulation and deregulation. Increased regulation was seen as necessary because of widespread concerns about both the price and the security of supply of energy. Thus, new Federal agencies were created, including a Department of Energy and the Federal Energy Regulatory Commission, which took over the regulatory powers of the Federal Power Commission in 1977.

During Ronald Reagan's presidency in the 1980s, when many hitherto regulated industries such as telecommunications were deregulated, supporters of deregulation argued that electricity deregulation would both lower prices for consumers and increase the supply of electricity. Accordingly, in 1992 the Energy Policy Act was introduced in order to create open access to the electricity transmission system for all generating companies. Not content with this, independent generating companies argued that they continued to be disadvantaged by the secure position of entrenched, vertically integrated utility companies and so, in 1996, the Federal Energy Regulatory Commission issued

Orders 888 and 889 which introduced open access to the transmission system and to transmission system information. These deregulatory changes at the national level provided the context for the crisis in California's energy, most notoriously in the period 1998 to 2001, which resulted from a disastrous attempt by the State Legislature to deregulate the energy system.

Energy deregulation in California

California is the most heavily populated state, with nearly 35 million inhabitants. Its economy is very powerful, regularly appearing in the top ten list of the largest economies in the world. It is based on technology industries, particularly in Silicon Valley, which are heavily dependent on a continuous supply of electricity. Before California deregulated its electricity industry in 1998, three large vertically integrated private sector utility companies provided 80 per cent of the electricity consumed in the state. These utilities produced, transmitted and sold power to consumers at rates set by the California Public Utilities Commission. Pacific Gas & Electric covered the northern half of the state, while Southern California Edison supplied electricity to most of the southern half, and San Diego Gas & Electric serviced that city. The exception to this private provision is the city of Los Angeles, which has been supplied with electricity for 100 years by the municipally owned Los Angeles Department of Water and Power.[38]

The impetus for deregulation of the integrated utilities in California originated with the state regulator, the Public Utilities Commission, whose membership by 1994 had been 'entirely appointed by successive right wing Republican Governors committed to removing government intervention in the economy'.[39] The commission was subject to intensive lobbying by companies such as the energy company Enron which 'hired lobbyists by the bushelful' and made substantial campaign contributions to Californian politicians. The commission was even treated to a personal appearance by Jeffrey Skilling, president and chief operating officer of Enron, who claimed that complete deregulation of the electricity industry would save the state precisely

US$8.9 billion per year.[40] In 1995, very soon after, the commission ordered the utilities to unpack their integrated systems so that the costs of their different sections, such as power generation and distribution, would be made transparent in preparation for possible dismemberment.

In 1996 the California State Legislature became the first in the country to pass a Bill which liberalised the electricity market. The integrated utility companies were forced to sell off their generating units and buy power in the open market. Further, although used to operating prudently on the basis of long-term contracts, the utilities were forbidden from entering into any significant long-term contracts and obliged to purchase power in the spot market on a daily basis. In what was to prove a fatal mixture of regulation and deregulation, retail prices to consumers were capped but there was no cap on the wholesale price of electricity.

In order to operate the new power market, the State Legislature created two new agencies. Firstly, the California Power Exchange was to set hourly prices for electricity through auctions, conducted the previous day and on the day of delivery, in which utilities were obliged to buy all their power. As wholesale prices were involved, the regulatory responsibility passed from the state to the Federal Energy Regulatory Commission which was required by law to ensure that prices were 'just and reasonable'. Secondly, the Independent System Operator, which also came within the oversight of the Federal Energy Regulatory Commission, was in charge of the maintenance of the network of transmission lines. It also conducted auctions of electricity in real time and which were 'supposed to correct last-minute supply-and-demand imbalances and ensure adequate reserves'.[41] Supporters of deregulation confidently predicted that electricity prices would fall by 20 per cent and that the supply of electricity would increase. The reality proved to be somewhat different.

The crisis develops

Deregulation was planned to begin on 1 March 1998 but, in a perfect metaphor for the disastrous experiment, the trading computers required to operate the markets were not yet operational. Thus, the start date was postponed for a month to April Fools Day, another portent of things to come.[42] Soon after, in June a combination of a heat-wave, some power plants being shut for maintenance and some (alleged) price manipulation by traders led to a sharp price spike. Wholesale electricity prices rose to as high as US$6000 per Megawatt hour (MWh), around 200 times the normal market price. Enron, the largest energy trader in the United States, was reported to have made at least US$50 million from the crisis.[43] Soon after, when the severity of the crisis led to some critics calling for the wholesale electricity market to be re-regulated, the wholesale electricity price returned to around US$30 per MWh. Supporters of deregulation felt vindicated.

This was to prove a dangerously complacent view however. In May 2000 the crisis returned after a warm spring increased demand for air conditioning and several power generators were taken off line for maintenance. Rolling blackouts affected 97 000 customers in the San Francisco Bay area on 14 June, and by the end of the month wholesale electricity prices at peak times were over ten times the average price in 1999. Rolling blackouts continued, with neighbourhood after neighbourhood in the most affluent nation in the world suffering power cuts on a rota basis. The wholesale price rises wiped out the profits of the two largest utilities, Pacific Gas & Electric and Southern California Edison, whose combined losses reached over US$10 billion by January 2001. Lacking long-term contracts, and unable to pass on the soaring wholesale prices to customers who had no financial motivation to conserve energy, the utilities 'were reduced to sending out pathetic press releases begging customers to 'turn off PCs, monitors, printers, copiers, and lights when not in use'.[44] The crisis not only affected California, but spread to many states and companies deriving power from the Western grid of the United States. Prices rose in a dozen states including Oregon, Utah and Idaho. In Montana, manufacturers announced temporary lay-offs because of power problems at the end of 2000, and many other companies predicted problems for the next year.[45] Unknown at the time, the problems experienced were greatly exacerbated by the illegal manipulation of the market by Enron.

Enron's role in the energy crisis

Enron was created in 1985 through a merger between natural gas companies Houston Natural Gas and InterNorth. In November of that year, Kenneth Lay was appointed chairman and chief executive of the new company. In 1988 the company made a major strategic shift and decided to pursue opportunities in unregulated energy markets alongside its regulated gas pipeline business. The Messianic belief which senior management had, both in themselves and in the opportunities available in free markets, was shown by the company's description of this crucial decision as the 'Come to Jesus' gathering.[46] Enron grew rapidly through the 1990s, particularly when it discovered the lucrative opportunities available in electricity. The company's reported revenue grew from US$13 billion in 1996 to US$100 billion by 2000, a spectacular growth of over 600 per cent which placed Enron at number seven in the *Fortune 500* list of the United States' largest companies in 2000. The company claimed publicly to have high ethical standards, and even featured prominently in several league tables for corporate social responsibility on the grounds of its extensive charitable donations and espousal of core values. In practice, both the company's revenue and its ethical standards were more apparent than real. One study argued that:

> The contrast between Enron's moral mantra and the behaviour of some Enron executives is bone-chilling. Indeed, the Enron saga teaches us the limitations of corporate codes of ethics: how empty and ineffectual they can be. Long touted as crucial accoutrements to moral rectitude, codes are useless when the words are hollow – when executives lack either the dedication to espoused virtues or the ability to make defensible ethical decisions.[47]

Much of Enron's increased revenue came from energy broking, where it arranged deals between buyers and sellers. Instead of recording only the company's commission on these deals, Enron executives boosted revenue hugely and deceptively by often showing the total value of the transaction in their accounts. Thus, out of the claimed revenue of US$100 billion for 2000, the company only made US$979 million in net profit. Even this profit figure was overstated, as a result of a complex web of special-purpose mechanisms established by Enron executives to keep losses out of the company's net profit calculation and to keep debt off its balance sheet.

Enron's relentless pursuit of revenue and profit by whatever means set the context for its illegal activities in California. Deregulating the power generators was supposed to increase the supply of electricity to the state, a state in which Enron did not own any generating capacity. Thus, its activities in the electricity market at best constituted speculation and at worst represented illegal market manipulation. Despite Enron having a vested interest in seeing the partial deregulation experiment in California succeed, since this would open up further lucrative opportunities as more states followed suit, from Kenneth Lay down, short-term profit-making took precedence over such wider considerations. Further, as California had not followed Enron's advice and gone for full deregulation, profit-making was combined with an element of revenge. As one of the senior executives put it, 'if they're going to put in place such a stupid system, it makes sense to try to game it'. Another executive summarised the amoral attitude which was expected from Enron's energy traders by commenting that 'it was the traders' job to make money, not to benefit the people of California'. The traders were only too happy to adopt such an approach. One former trader commented that 'the attitude was "play by your own rules". We all did it. We talked about it openly. It was the school yard we lived in. The energy markets were new, immature, unsupervised. We took pride in getting around the rules. It was a game.'[48]

One of the company's star traders, Tim Belden, rose to the challenge and took 'getting around the rules' to incredible extremes. He worked for many hours in order to learn the arcane rules of the Californian electricity market, and by May 1999 was ready with an experiment to game the system. On May 24 he submitted four bids to sell 2900 MW of electricity, using a transmission route called Silverspeak. There was just one problem, the chosen transmission lines could only handle 15 MW at a time. This created an emergency, which the Independent System Operator had to resolve by finding replacement supplies at the last minute, resulting in a price rise of over 70 per cent.

Exposure of Enron's actions led to a year-long investigation into Belden's experiment, the action being finally settled in April 2000 when Enron paid a risible fine of US$25 000 and was made to promise not to engage in 'substantially the same conduct'.[49] No changes were made to the market rules and such a small fine, together with an unregulated promise, was going to be no deterrent to a company like Enron. Kenneth Lay expressed his contempt both for regulators and the very concept of regulation, along with admiration for his traders, in a heated telephone conversation in 2000 with David Freeman, the head of the Los Angeles Department of Water and Power. Lay declared 'well, Dave, in the final analysis it doesn't matter what you crazy people in California do. I've got smart guys out there who can always figure out how to make money.'[50]

Following Belden's experiment and the reprimand, Enron continued to develop new ways to manipulate the energy market which meant that the company, in effect, earned a huge return on the very small fine it paid. Belden and his team of traders devised a range of largely illegal gaming strategies, under a variety of exotic code names which were often based on films. The 'Death Star' strategy, for example, involved filing some imaginary transmission schedules in order to receive up to US$750 per MWh in fees to relieve the non-existent 'congestion' on the lines. Another strategy called 'Get Shorty' entailed selling the power which the company did not have for use in reserve, while planning that the power would either never be needed or would be bought later at a cheaper price. Enron's trading strategies were so successful that executives appear to have been in a rare state of embarrassment at the size of the profits. In contrast to its standard behaviour of hiding losses, the company put as much as US$1.5 billion of the estimated US$2 billion in profits it made out of the energy crisis 'into undisclosed reserves, hiding massive profits while denying accusations that it generated excessive profits by price-gouging Californians'.[51]

Public intervention in the crisis

As wholesale electricity prices remained very high throughout 2000, both the utilities and the Californian authorities looked to the Federal government for support. On 10 August the Independent Service Operator issued a report blaming the crisis on the abuse of market power, and on 17 August the utility companies presented a list of alleged trading abuses to the Federal Energy Regulatory Commission. One commissioner, William Massey, was sympathetic to these complaints:

> It is no secret that I have been deeply concerned about the apocalypse
> occurring in California power markets. Prices have not been just
> and reasonable, and market power has been exercised ... As a result,
> the transfer of wealth from purchasers of power to sellers has been
> absolutely staggering and completely defies the public interest. No
> legitimate public purpose has been furthered by this regrettable
> spectacle. The State's two largest utilities are virtually bankrupt
> because the billions in wholesale power purchase costs vastly exceed
> the amounts they have been allowed by State policy to recover from
> their customers ... Meanwhile, virtually no new generation has been
> installed in California in over ten years ... In addition, substantial
> transmission additions are necessary to eliminate bottlenecks that
> prohibit cheaper power from reaching the consumers.[52]

Contrary to these scathing comments, the Federal Energy Regulatory Commission was generally unsympathetic to the complainants and strongly in favour of deregulation. On 23 August, the commission finally agreed to order an investigation into the wholesale prices in California's electricity markets. A month later, on 24 September 2000, representatives from the power traders met with the commission to defend their position. Enron sent a lawyer, Mary Hain, who blamed high prices on scarce supply and argued that the commission ought to be discouraged 'from taking any action that would hurt the vibrant wholesale market' in California and the West.[53]

The commission gave its investigators, who lacked the power to subpoena records, only three months to report. As a result, despite many accurate suspicions about the activities of Enron, no substantive evidence of market manipulation was discovered. Had subpoenas been used, it is likely that incriminating evidence could have been extracted from Enron. The company's head of litigation foresaw just how damaging the gaming strategy code names, such as 'Death Star', would prove in court: 'Can't you just call them Puppy Dog and Momma's Cooking?', he asked the electricity traders plaintively in October 2000.[54]

The commission's report published on 1 November 2000, which was both partial and incomplete, took a very feeble approach to Enron and other market manipulators, and focused instead on the flawed market structure and supply and demand imbalances:

> that the electric market structure and market rules for wholesale
> sales of electric energy in California are seriously flawed and that
> these structures and rules, in conjunction with an imbalance of
> supply and demand in California, have caused, and continue to have
> the potential to cause, unjust and unreasonable rates for short-term
> energy ... While this record does not support conclusions about
> the actions of individual sellers, there is clear evidence that the
> California market structure and rules provide the opportunity for
> sellers to exercise market power when supply is tight.[55]

The worsening electricity crisis in 2000 was not helped by the commission's complacent report. The Independent Service Operator had attempted to reduce wholesale prices by gradually lowering the price it would pay for power generated in California from US$750 per MWh to US$250 per MWh. In what was quite possibly a non-coincidental reaction to this move, in mid-November 2000 nearly one quarter of California's generating capacity was taken off line for maintenance or emergency repairs, almost three times the outage rate of the previous year. State-wide blackouts were only narrowly averted when Bill Richardson, Energy Secretary in the Federal Clinton administration, imposed a state of emergency and ordered suppliers in the whole Western region to sell power to California.

On 15 December, the commission rejected a request for a whole-sale electricity price cap which would cover California. Instead, it effectively abolished the temporary price caps imposed by the Independent Service Operator, with the result that prices rose to around US$1500 per MWh, compared to the average price of US$45 for the previous year. The rapidly escalating energy crisis was the focal point of the annual state address by the Democratic governor of California, Gray Davis, on 8 January 2001. He focused the blame on the flawed deregulation scheme which he had inherited, along with the companies manipulating the market and the complacent Federal Energy Regulatory Commission. In a powerful speech, seething with both anger and frustration, he declared that:

> In 1996 the Legislature and the Governor launched an untested
> restructuring of California's electricity market … I assume the
> proponents of deregulation really did envision lower energy costs
> and smaller electricity bills. They certainly didn't envision this
> mess. But we must face reality. California's deregulation scheme
> is a colossal and dangerous failure. It has not lowered consumer
> prices. And it has not increased supply. In fact, it has resulted in
> skyrocketing prices, price-gouging and an unreliable supply of
> electricity. In short, an energy nightmare … We have surrendered
> the decisions about where electricity is sold – and for how much – to
> private companies with only one objective: maximizing unheard-of
> profits.[56]

On 17 January 2001, more rolling blackouts spread throughout northern California, and Governor Davis declared a state of emergency which was to last two years. In February, the governor signed into law a provision allowing utilities to once again enter into long-term electricity contracts, and in March he authorised the state to spend US$40 billion buying electricity on behalf of its utilities at unfavourable open market prices. The state also raised consumer prices by up to 15 per cent and then commenced buying the transmission systems of the utilities. The staff of the Federal Energy Regulatory Commission now recommended that price caps were also urgently required. Vice

President Cheney, who chaired the National Energy Development Task Force, and was advised by Kenneth Lay, predictably was not persuaded, declaring that 'Price caps are not a help'.[57]

The crisis continued, and in April 2001 Pacific Gas & Electric filed for bankruptcy, with a loss of US$8.9 billion. In a bizarre coincidence, this was exactly the amount which Jeffrey Skilling had claimed could be saved annually if California completely deregulated its electricity industry. Finally, on 19 June the Federal Energy Regulatory Commissioners were persuaded by the gravity of the situation to reverse their previous stance and so imposed caps on wholesale electricity prices in California and ten neighbouring states in order to ensure that prices 'would fall within a zone of reasonableness'.[58] The California cap of US$92, combined with conservation measures and mild weather, brought down the average wholesale price of electricity from US$234 per MWh for the first five months of the year to US$43 by the end of June.

Enron had been quite correctly suspected of extensive market manipulation during the energy crisis, but no proof had been available. When in December 2001 the company filed for bankruptcy after the true position of its debts was revealed and its share price plummeted, its 'smart guys' fought all attempts by state and Federal authorities to gain access to its records. In May 2002, Enron's lawyers were finally compelled to provide internal memoranda detailing the California gaming strategies and their code names to the Federal Energy Regulatory Commission. The company still refused to release the audio and data tapes detailing its trading activities, until they were seized by the Justice Department for use in the criminal investigation of Enron. In March 2003, having finally acquired some evidence of Enron's illegal activities, the commission issued a report on price manipulation in the western United States energy markets. This not only reiterated the earlier supply–demand findings from the 2000 report, but went much further:

> Many trading strategies employed by Enron and other companies were undertaken in violation of antigaming provisions ... The Commission [should] initiate proceedings to require guilty companies to disgorge

profits associated with these tariff violations ... Enron [had] proprietary knowledge of market conditions not available to other market participants ... This created a false sense of market liquidity, which can cause artificial volatility and distort prices. Enron's informational trading advantage ... was lucrative; the company took large positions and was an active and successful speculator ... Prices in the California spot markets were affected by economic withholding and inflated bidding ... this violated the antigaming provisions.[59]

In June 2003, the commission brought orders against several of the smaller companies involved in market manipulation requiring them to 'disgorge' their illegal profits. Dynergy, for example, settled for US$3 million and Coral Power agreed to return US$7.7 million, but Enron continued its fight.[60] The Californian Attorney General, Bill Lockyer, who anxiously wanted to prosecute both Kenneth Lay and Enron but lacked evidence, expressed both his frustration and an awareness of the sordid reality of life for many in the American penal system in his sulphurous comments to the *Wall Street Journal*: 'I would love to personally escort Lay to an eight by ten cell that he could share with a tattooed dude who says, "Hi, my name is Spike, honey"'.[61] Both Kenneth Lay and Jeffrey Skilling were found guilty of fraud in 2006, with Skilling receiving 24 years in prison. Kenneth Lay was spared the interesting fate by a fatal heart attack. The fight to make Enron return its illegal profits continues. It was only in June 2007 that the Federal Energy Regulatory Commission finally obtained a judicial decision requiring the company to surrender its 'unjust profits' of US$1.6 billion, which represented around 80 per cent of the profits earned from the energy crisis.[62] Whether any of these profits will ever be returned is debatable. Enron's remaining business was taken over by Prisma Energy International Incorporated in 2003, which was then sold to Ashmore Energy Limited in 2006.

Although California suffered from a major economic disruption during the energy crisis, it is not the only state or country to have deregulated its electricity sector. While many electricity markets which have been deregulated 'have suffered problems, California clearly takes the prize as the worst of the lot'.[63] California provides

a case-study in how not to partially deregulate the electricity industry. The flawed partial deregulation combined with illegal manipula-
tive strategies of some predatory companies, and poor oversight at
Federal level, to produce a 'colossal' failure. The neoliberal market
ideology underlay both the attempted deregulation of electricity, and
also the inherently unstable and philosophically dubious position of
a key regulatory body, the Federal Energy Regulatory Commission,
whose commissioners were largely in favour of deregulation. Just as
the disastrous railway privatisation experiment in Britain, discussed
in chapter four, was only alleviated by stronger regulation and a large
increase in public subsidies, so the Californian crisis was only solved
by re-regulation at both state and Federal levels and by substantial
public expenditure.

The energy crisis is an event featuring many villains, but it is also
possible to identify an 'unexpected hero' in California, the Los Angeles municipal utility, the Department of Water and Power. Under the
leadership of David Freeman, who later advised Governor Davis on
the crisis, the department refused to take part in the deregulation
experiment. As a result of long-term planning and investment, it was
able to keep prices low, and even sell surplus power to other utilities
by bringing spare generating capacity back on line. Los Angeles did
not suffer any power shortages or blackouts during the energy crisis.
A *Los Angeles Times* article highlighted the advantages of this 'hero':

> Many believed the Department of Water and Power would have
> to be privatised to be competitive … By continuing to say 'no' to
> deregulation, the Department of Water and Power can ensure LA's
> future economic competitiveness. It and other public utilities are the
> State's lowest cost providers of electricity. They possess the reserves
> needed to provide ultrahigh reliability to an electricity-dependent
> economy.[64]

Thus, the Department of Water and Power at Los Angeles provided a
successful counter-example to the neoliberal dreams of the benefits to
be gained from deregulation in California. The success of the vertically
integrated, municipally-owned utility, which does not channel public

profits to the private sector, has been shown to provide a far better model for the state to follow.

Water privatisation in Britain

In the nineteenth century, British cities' water supplies were localised and initially relied upon private water companies, wells (often privately owned) and water carts. In Birmingham, for example, a private water company was established in 1826. This supplied some piped water to part of the population but the charges were too expensive for many and the water service was only provided on three days per week. Thus, half the population of 300 000 people 'drew its drinking water from surface-wells, most of them tainted, some horridly polluted, by percolating sewage'.[65] Not surprisingly, water-borne diseases such as cholera, typhus and typhoid were endemic in Britain in the early and mid-nineteenth century, arousing considerable public interest and concern, and eventually public health reform campaigns by social reformers such as Sir Edwin Chadwick. Eventually, in 1848, parliament passed the Public Health Act as a result of the efforts of reformers like Chadwick. The Act empowered a central Public Health Board to establish local boards with the duty to ensure that new houses had suitable drainage and that local water supplies were adequate. Thus, the principle of public sector involvement in water provision at both national and local levels had been established by the middle of the century.

Local government played an increasingly important role in the provision of a safe water supply as the nineteenth century progressed. Over 50 large towns, including Liverpool, Manchester, Plymouth and Glasgow, had municipal water authorities by the 1870s. So important was public ownership of water supply considered that the wealthy industrialist and Liberal Mayor of Birmingham, Joseph Chamberlain, attempted to purchase the town's private water company by agreement. While the company served the wealthier parts of Birmingham, the people living in the slum areas of central Birmingham had to choose between 'drawing water from open wells scarcely distinguishable from sewers and stealing it from the company's taps'.[66] After the private water company refused to co-operate with Chamberlain's plans, he made an impassioned speech to the Birmingham Council in 1874 advocating the compulsory purchase of the water company. His speech began by establishing a key principle of municipal government, which is given in the quotation at the start of this chapter, that regulated monopolies should be controlled by elected representatives rather than placed in the hands of 'private speculators'. He went on to highlight the problems caused by the private supply of water in Birmingham, both anticipating and brilliantly satirising the wilder fantasies of the free market ideologues:

> Many of the most experienced magistrates of this town have told me that of all their duties the saddest is that of registering convictions against poor people brought up at the instigation of the water company for stealing that which is one of the first necessities of life. They might almost as well be convicted for stealing air. I have sometimes wondered why the supply of air is not regulated by the Legislature and handed over to some company with a dividend limited to ten per cent.[67]

He went on to argue that it would be intolerable to close down the insanitary wells, if this merely resulted in 'enormously increasing the profits of a private company', and forcefully argued that the 'power of life and death' should not be the province of a private company. Chamberlain had previously proposed to take over the local gas company, which he argued should be run at a profit in order to help to finance local government. Water was different, argued Chamberlain, and so it 'should never be a source of profit; all profit should go in reduction of the price of water'.[68] The council, particularly impressed that such arguments emanated from a wealthy, successful businessman, endorsed Chamberlain's proposals unanimously. Birmingham sent its gas and water Bills to parliament, where they passed into law together, and Chamberlain gained a radical reputation as the mayor who brought 'gas and water socialism' to Birmingham. The municipal takeover of the water company in 1875 was followed by an extension of its water supply service and a reduction in charges. Sanitary inspectors closed many of the private wells, thereby benefiting the health of the city's population.

The twentieth century saw a gradual consolidation under municipal ownership of the many different organisations in the water industry. There were three main types of organisations: water undertakings, sewerage disposal authorities, and river authorities. Until the 1950s there were over 1000 separate water undertakings. Unlike other industries nationalised by the Attlee government, there was no need to nationalise the water industry as most of the water undertakings were already publicly owned by local governments. The desire to amalgamate to achieve economies of scale meant that by the early 1970s the number of these water undertakings, however, had fallen considerably to 198. Of these, 64 were run by individual local authorities, 101 were run by joint boards comprising more than one local authority, and 33 were privately owned water companies. There were also over 1300 sewerage disposal authorities run by individual local authorities or, as in the case of water undertakings, joint boards.[69] In addition, there were 29 river authorities, created in 1965, to take responsibility for such matters as water conservation and control of river pollution.

A major change to this situation occurred in 1973 when the Conservative government, with strong support from other parties, introduced the Water Act. This transferred responsibility for the water supply and sewerage disposal from local authorities to ten Regional Water Authorities, thus effectively nationalising them. These Water Authorities were owned and managed by boards which had been nominated jointly by central government and the local authorities. As the transfer of assets was internal to the public sector, no compensation for their loss was paid to the local authorities. (This later became very controversial when the water industry was privatised and all the proceeds went to central, rather than local, government.[70]) Until 1983, the ten Regional Water Authorities were run by boards with a majority of local authority members. This element of local democratic accountability was lost when the Thatcher government introduced the 1983 Water Act which provided for smaller boards, all of whose members were appointed by ministers sitting at Westminster. The smaller boards, which met in secret, were intended to bring a more commercial approach to the operation of water and sewerage disposal in preparation for privatisation.

The privatised water companies

Many doubts were raised in Britain about the privatisation of the ten regional water and sewerage organisations, first proposed by the Conservatives in 1984, because of their obvious importance as an essential utility. Doubts focused on the possible adverse consequences of water privatisation on both the price and the quality of service under profit-maximising companies. These concerns, which proved to be entirely justified, were contemptuously dismissed by Prime Minister Thatcher as 'emotive nonsense'. She even invoked the deity in her responses to the critics, arguing that the 'rain may come from the Almighty' but He did not 'send the pipes, plumbing and engineering to go with it'.[71] What the Almighty thought of this is not known, but there may have been some divine disapproval at the disingenuous nature of the Conservatives' arguments. Firstly, the argument that water prices would have to rise to pay for investment in the infrastructure elements such as pipes ignored the fact that a substantial share of the increased revenue of the privatised companies would have to go towards paying the shareholders' dividends. In addition, the Thatcher government, which had limited the borrowing powers of the ten Regional Water Authorities, had then attacked the consequences of this poor decision by criticising the authorities for their poor investment record.

Water privatisation was delayed because of public disquiet until after the 1987 general election and finally implemented in 1989. As in earlier privatisations, such as gas and electricity, the Conservative government argued that the water industry would be transformed by competitive market pressures and private sector management. The key transformation in many of the earlier privatisations resulted from making 'efficiency' savings at the expense of the workforce, in order to free up revenue to distribute dividends to shareholders. Indeed, there are strong parallels between the nationalised water and rail industries in that both had achieved large productivity gains in the 1980s by making substantial numbers of employees redundant. However, unlike rail, the water industry did not have a huge workforce to reduce. Nevertheless, the ten Regional Water Authorities, just like

British Rail, had made some substantial productivity gains in the 1980s by reducing the size of the workforce. Employment in water was reduced by 17 per cent between 1981 and 1985, and then by a further 11 per cent up to 1989. Thus, the workforce fell from over 70 000 workers in 1981 to just under 48 000 by 1989.[72]

Regulatory problems with the privatised water industry

The privatised industry required a complex and expensive regulatory system in order to regulate three key issues: the environmental impact of the industry, the quality of drinking water, and the economic performance of water companies. Thus, regulation was divided between three bodies. Environmental regulation is carried out by the Environment Agency, the quality of drinking water is monitored by the Drinking Water Inspectorate, while the economic regulation of the industry is operated by the Office of Water Services (OFWAT). OFWAT's key function – to ensure that the industry has sufficient revenue to carry out its activities – requires it to determine the price rises which can be implemented by the water companies. At privatisation, the water companies were granted generous licences which allowed them to operate for 25 years (that is until 2014). This generous treatment was supplemented by OFWAT's decision in 1991 that the companies deserved 10 years advance notice if their licences were to be terminated. This made it very difficult for a future British government to consider renationalising the water industry.

Given that the water industry, like rail, had to find substantial sums for investment in run-down infrastructure assets, there was an immediate conflict between the demands of shareholders for dividends and the longer-term needs of the industry and its consumers for investment. This dilemma was resolved at the very considerable expense of the consumers, for OFWAT permitted the companies substantial above-inflation rises in water prices to finance investment. Thus, in the first nine years after privatisation the water companies raised prices by an average of 46 per cent in real terms, and their turnover rose by 62 per cent. The increased revenue enabled the water companies to spend £13 billion on infrastructure repairs and investment, while also paying out £6.9 billion in dividends to shareholders.[73]

Despite the increased level of capital investment, serious questions have frequently been raised about the adequacy of the industry's infrastructure and of its regulatory body OFWAT. In 1998, the House of Commons Select Committee on Public Accounts published a very critical report on both. The committee emphasised that each of the water companies had local monopolies, which meant that there was 'a risk that customers may be exploited, through excessive prices, poor quality services, or both'.[74] The report highlighted four key points of concern.[75] Firstly, it was concerned that by 1994–95:

> 30 per cent of the water distributed by the companies was being lost through leaks. We are surprised that it has taken OFWAT so long to commence improving the arrangements they inherited in 1989 for monitoring the water companies' ability to provide a reliable supply of water.

Secondly, the committee argued that monopoly suppliers like the water companies need to be:

> continually challenged by their regulator to meet customers' reasonable expectations. We are not convinced that OFWAT's general reliance in the past on drawing comparisons between companies was a sufficient stimulant to securing improvements in each company's performance. Setting specific targets for each company can provide a more effective focus, and we look to OFWAT to monitor closely whether the companies meet the target OFWAT have now set them.

Additionally, the committee noted that 'Each year customers raise some 15 million queries about their bills. We look to OFWAT to complete urgently their investigation of the reasons for these queries and to ensure that, where they are the result of poor service, the companies take remedial action'.

Finally, the committee expressed concern that water companies:

> are currently achieving a rate of return of ten per cent, substantially above the level of around five to six per cent that OFWAT consider appropriate in the long term. This emphasises the importance of regulators pressing companies to provide a satisfactory quality of service for their customers in return for the prices charged … In our view it is right that regulators should be prepared to impose financial sanctions where persuasion and the setting of targets have failed to produce the improvements needed.

The Select Committee's report had been prompted both by problems relating to all of the water companies, such as the very high leakage rate, and by the specific problems experienced by the customers in Yorkshire. During the hot summer of 1995 the reservoirs in the West Yorkshire region of Britain ran dry, despite the fact that they had been full only months before after a very wet winter. The company's management blamed both the unusually dry summer and the consumers for their record demand for water. Critics, however, drew attention to the key fact that Yorkshire Water Services admitted to a loss of water through leakages of 26 per cent. As might be expected, management's preferred policy of blaming the customers did not mobilise public support. This was in marked contrast to the previous major drought in Britain in 1976 when the public responded to requests for restraint from the then publicly owned Regional Water Authorities and demand fell by over 20 per cent. This time, instead, a widespread program of emergency measures was introduced. Yorkshire Water obtained permission to increase its use of water from local rivers, non-essential water uses including garden watering and car washing were banned, and standpipes were erected to serve neighbourhoods. The western half of Yorkshire, a region inhabited by over four million people, came very close to a complete failure of its water supply.

Faced with a major public outcry, Yorkshire Water was forced to undertake a program of improvements to the infrastructure and to attempt to refill all the reservoirs. The latter operation required the use of over 700 tankers on a daily basis for a full five months. The end of the drought was only officially declared in November 1996. Yorkshire Water was then severely criticised for mismanagement in two independent reports, and fined £40 million by the regulator OFWAT for prioritising its dividends over the maintenance of the water supply to the consumers. The Yorkshire Water financial accounts provided ample evidence for this charge. Between the years 1989–90 and 1994–95, operating profit rose by 104 per cent to £193.3 million, dividends increased by 133 per cent to £27.6 million, but capital investment fell as a proportion of turnover from 15.7 to just 9.9 per cent.[76]

The reluctant investment by water companies eventually began to have an impact on the very high rate of leakages in the late 1990s. The total industry leakage fell from 5.1 million litres per day in 1994–95 to 3.55 million litres per day in 1998–99. This leakage reached its lowest point of 3.24 million litres per day in 2000–01, but then increased to a plateau of around 3.6 million litres per day between 2002 and 2006.[77] These later disturbing results were addressed in another critical report published by the Select Committee on Public Accounts in 2007. It singled out Thames Water, one of the largest companies, as the worst serial offender for missing its leakage reduction targets for six consecutive years since 2000. OFWAT, rather than fining the company up to 10 per cent of its turnover, accepted a legally binding undertaking to spend £150 million replacing 370 kilometres of water mains. The committee argued that 'by not imposing a fine, however, OFWAT risks sending a message to the industry that it will not readily use sanctions where appropriate'.[78] The report went on to highlight key problems both with the poor service provided by Thames Water and the reluctance of OFWAT to exercise its powers:

> Thames is one of the largest water companies and should be able to benefit from economies of scale, to the extent that they exist in the water industry. However, Thames has a range of problems in areas such as the serviceability of its infrastructure and its security of supply.
>
> OFWAT can refer a water company to the Competition Commission if it believes the merger is not in the interest of the consumer. Despite the ongoing problems at Thames Water, OFWAT

has never issued an enforcement order or fined the company. Nor has it used any sanctions or action that may encourage the company to change its corporate structure or to become more efficient.[79]

Also of some concern to the committee was the consequences of the size of the water companies following a number of takeovers and consolidations. It noted how:

> OFWAT considers that the size of the company may be responsible for its inefficiencies and the current poor quality of service ... but it is not clear whether OFWAT can promote a de-merger if a large company is performing poorly and not benefiting from economies of scale.[80]

The comments made concerning corporate structure are particularly pertinent for the water companies. After the Conservative government removed the ban on takeovers in 1995, the water companies, like the electricity companies, have been subject to an intensive wave of takeovers. Privatised water companies are very attractive pieces on the global capitalist chessboard because of their guaranteed cash flows. The heavily criticised Thames Water was purchased by the German energy group RWE for £4.3 billion in 2001, and then sold in 2006 to a consortium of funds led by Macquarie Bank of Australia for £8 billion. In just one month, October 2007, two of Britain's water companies changed hands. Royal Bank of Scotland, which together with the French company Veolia had purchased Southern Water for £2 billion in 2003, sold it for £4.2 billion to a consortium led by Australia's Challenger Investment Fund. South Staffordshire Water, which was purchased in 2004 for £245 million by Arcapita, the Bahrain-based investment group, was also then sold to the American fund Alinda for around £400 million. All these takeovers have occurred without a reference by OFWAT to the Competition Commission, a fact which, together with its extreme reluctance to apply sanctions, leads critics to argue that the organisation is suffering from 'regulatory capture' and is putting company interests before those of customers.

One interesting counter-example to the trend for water companies to be bought and sold in the interests of shareholders is that of Welsh

Water. In this case, the company, despite attempting to maintain share-holder value, finally accepted that it was not possible to reconcile the competing demands of shareholders with the need for infrastructure investment. Thus, in 2001 Welsh Water sold the assets that carried the operating licence to Glas Cymru, a not-for-profit company limited by guarantee similar to air traffic controller NavCanada. Glas Cymru was financed by debt capital in the form of a £1.9 billion bond issue which, it was estimated, would reduce its finance costs by £50 million per year. The financial surpluses it makes are no longer distributed to shareholders as dividends, but used to contribute to the financing of investment to ensure reliable, high-quality service to its customers.

The Sydney water treatment scandal

In the 1990s Australia followed, if not always as extravagantly, the policy of deregulation and privatisation in public utilities which had been adopted in Britain and New Zealand. In the early 1990s, the New South Wales state Liberal (conservative) government corporatised the Sydney water system. Sydney's water supply had been provided by a state-owned authority, the Sydney Water Board, which drew on good quality water by world standards. Sydney Water was corporatised in 1995 to become a profit-making government agency responsible for providing clean water to the 3 million inhabitants of Australia's largest city. Before the corporatisation preparations had been completed, contracts costing A$3 billion over 25 years had been signed with three consortia to build and operate four private water treatment plants. The Liberal Minister for Planning and Housing, RJ Webster, explained in detail the government's case for this in parliament in September 1992:

> Consistent with the Government's policy on private sector
> infrastructure provision, the use of private consortia will save overall
> costs, avoid or defer large capital spending and introduce technical and
> operational skills not currently available. The public interest will be
> protected by the normal environmental impact assessment for projects
> and appropriate controls in agreements ... The evaluation process by

which the winning consortium is being chosen is meticulous and is being carried out in accordance with approved guidelines.[81]

The role of the private water treatment centres soon came under close scrutiny after water quality alerts were issued in 1998. The Department of Health issued three separate 'boil water' alerts in July, August and September of that year after the city's main supply of water, the reservoir at the Warragamba Dam, had become infected with two very unpleasant and indeed potentially fatal parasites – giardia and cryptosporidium. The seriousness of this position was demonstrated by a similar cryptosporidium outbreak in the American city of Milwaukee in 1993 which had killed over 100 people and made many thousands ill.

Most of Sydney's water passed through the privately owned water treatment plant at Prospect in western Sydney, which was operated by Australian Water Services (AWS). AWS was a partnership of two organisations, a French global water supply company, Suez Lyonnaise des Eaux and the Australian real estate and finance company Lend Lease. (The privatised global market for water is dominated by two French transnational businesses, Suez Lyonnaise des Eaux and Veolia Environment, which between them own, or have control of, a range of water companies in over 120 countries across five continents.[82]) The New South Wales government had claimed that contracts for the water treatment centres would only be awarded after a 'meticulous' evaluation process. In reality, it turned out that AWS was the winning bidder for the Prospect plant because it had submitted the cheapest bid, not because it promised the highest quality service. During the tendering process, officials had 'expressed doubts about Australian Water's ability to operate the plant because it proposed using a single sand filter – as opposed to the dual filters other consortia bidding for the contract had proposed'.[83] Yet this was symptomatic of a selection process that:

> gave no weight to tenders that could offer superior quality. The overriding consideration appears to have been the capacity to meet Sydney Water's specified requirements at the minimum price.

The emphasis on price over quality has been one source of the recrimination that followed the contamination.[84]

The public outcry over the contaminated water, which was compounded by the state Labor government's ham-fisted attempt to withhold from public access the contracts with AWS on the grounds of commercial confidentiality, led to a major inquiry into the scandal. The McClellan inquiry, which took months to deliberate in 1998 and 1999, produced four separate reports totalling 850 pages. The inquiry found that the parasites which had contaminated the water were possibly present at the plant or passed through it without being treated, and then were released into the drinking water supply during 'operational difficulties'. The plant had:

> been operated by AWS within the terms of its contract, but it used the lowest possible chemical doses to remove contaminants from the water, used filter runs of up to 70 hours to conserve energy, and re-used filter-cleansing water in a way that might have allowed parasites to pass through the plant and into the city's drinking supplies.[85]

AWS refuted any suggestion that it was responsible for the polluted water, and even went so far as to dispute the evidence in the form of the contamination readings obtained by Sydney Water. Unsurprisingly, with the state government under great public pressure to find the culprit and to ensure that this unprecedented calamity would never recur, relations between Sydney Water Corporation and AWS became acrimonious, with the corporation at one point threatening 'to shut down or take over the Prospect plant'.[86] However, such a radical interference with the sacred right to make profits by following a contract to the letter, but not beyond, could not be seriously contemplated in a market state. Instead, it was the managing director and the chairman of Sydney Water, the government agency, who appeared to take responsibility for the scandal when they both resigned in 1999 after the publication of the final McClellan report. The fundamental organisational change which was recommended by McClellan, and accepted by the New South Wales government, was the creation of a new public authority, the Sydney Catchment Authority. This new authority was given the sole control over all reservoirs and the water supply, with clear and explicit health and environmental responsibilities.

———

Examination of key public utilities which might be natural monopolies has shown that in all cases privatisation and deregulation has led to substantial price increases for consumers and to huge profits for the owners of companies. This privatisation of public profit, which is always promoted in terms of the alleged benefits of the market and the greater opportunities to raise capital for infrastructure investment, has often been accompanied by a decline in service quality. In Britain, despite increased investment in the water infrastructure, there are still very substantial daily leakages from water pipes. In California, the flawed electricity deregulation experiment, far from attracting new investment in power generation, instead brought extortionate wholesale price rises but no additional generating capacity to the state.

A second major implication of the above cases is the extremes to which an amoral company will go in the obsessive pursuit of short-term profit-maximisation, irrespective of the consequences for the wider public interest. Enron's behaviour, both in its fraudulent accounting and in its illegal manipulation of the Californian electricity market, was so extreme as to verge on the suicidal. In New Zealand, Mercury Energy neglected its electricity cables, including the ones which had passed their replacement date, thus undermining its core business and bringing chaos to Auckland's central business district. In Sydney, by following its contract to the letter AWS was complicit in allowing dangerous parasites to pollute the city's water supply. Indeed, privatisation and deregulation offer many opportunities to companies to tender for work at low costs in the short term, with the long-term needs of customers then often neglected. In late 2007, after yet another series of large increases in the price of electricity to residential customers, British Energy denounced the extensive, injurious collusion between the six largest suppliers of domestic electricity and the refusal of the regulator Ofgem to intervene. The companies were so powerful that they were able to manipulate prices at will and to preclude the entry of new entrants to the market.[87]

Another important conclusion of the cases examined here is that, where deregulation and privatisation occur, strong regulatory bodies are needed. It is essential that such bodies are run by people who actually believe in the concept of regulation and exercise regulatory powers accordingly. The crisis in California could have been resolved much earlier had Enron been investigated using subpoena powers in 2000, and had price controls covering western states been introduced much earlier. The key underlying problem was that the Federal Energy Regulatory Commission was run by people who were constrained by their fundamentalist belief in deregulation. In Britain, OFWAT has extensive powers but very rarely uses them. None of the recent profit-driven takeovers of water companies has been referred to the Competition Commission, while action has only been taken against Thames Water, the worst offender in terms of water leakages, after it had missed its leakage reduction targets every year for six years.

For public policy, one last compelling implication of these critical failures of privatised utilities is to ensure that such privatisation and deregulation does not lead to disasters which then have to be remedied using a combination of stronger re-regulation and public money. This occurred in both the Californian electricity case and Sydney's water crisis, and again demonstrates the flimsiness of the liberal rhetoric which promoted such policies in the first place.

Prisoners to privatisation

In January 2002, Tyson Johnson was being held in Santa Fe County Jail. Tyson was awaiting trial for stalking and aggravated assault. Tyson Johnson asked to see a psychiatrist because he was suffering from severe anxiety, a condition that stemmed from his history of claustrophobia. Unfortunately the jail, run by Management and Training Corporation, didn't have a psychiatrist, a psychologist or a mental health nurse to attend to him. Tyson had told the jail's nurse that he felt suicidal. Ten minutes later Tyson was found hanging from a sprinkler head in a windowless isolation cell. He was just 27 and had no previous criminal record.

The Justice Department's investigation into his death suggested it was a direct consequence of cost-cutting within the prison sector, exacerbated by the push to run a profitable prison. It was discovered that the closest doctor on contract was a two-hour flight away from the jail and that he only visited every six weeks, seeing a few patients at a time. The nurse who had attended to Tyson Johnson that fateful night had an order in her file to spend no more than five minutes with each inmate patient. Although the jail met its requirements to have a mental health clinician on contract, in reality the doctor never assessed or evaluated any inmates at the prison. His employment merely ticked a contractual box, leaving both inmates and staff without essential medical support.

Tyson Johnson's death was easily preventable. Staff at the Management and Training Corporation were under extraordinary pressure to meet the company's performance criteria, and this required significant cost-cutting. This was not because the money wasn't there to support people like Tyson Johnson, but because a portion of funds that could have helped him was being retained in order to provide a substantial return to shareholders.

In essence, public funds were being used to build private profits at an extraordinary cost.

(Compiled from information in F Butterfield, 'Justice Department report shows trouble in private US jails preceded job fixing Iraq's', *New York Times*, 6 June 2004)

THE PRICE OF AN ORDERED SOCIETY: PRISONS

Scandals have had no effect on the demand for CCA [Corrections Corporation America] jails. The Third Way not only abdicates democratic control of law and order but does not presume to act as a mere regulator. CCA has flourished in this moral and political vacuum. Its value grew from $50 million in 1986 to $3.5 billion in 1996 – a record that has drawn admiring puns of 'crime pays' from financial analysts.

(N. Cohen, *Cruel Britannia*, 1999, p122)

For centuries, imprisoning people has been a popular solution to socially unacceptable behaviour. Three hundred years ago, all English prisons were self-financing endeavours limited only by the entrepreneurial skills of the gaoler. Then in the nineteenth century there was a move away from for-profit prisons. This was seen as a civilising initiative in which the state would provide gaols and prison guards to meet broader social policy objectives, thereby removing profiteering as a motive for incarceration. It was also hoped that universal standards of service could be developed throughout prisons, and that programs could be adopted and monitored to ensure that correctional centres would produce the kinds of socially acceptable outcomes required by government policy. More recently, private prisons have again become attractive as reformist governments across the globe have contracted out prison management, construction and maintenance to private companies. The resulting incarceration industry is now a highly profitable, global endeavour in a competitive, profit-driven sector of the economy which was once a primary function of the state.

Governments and private firms have proffered many reasons for the current push to privatise prisons. In particular, governments have promised that market competition will improve the quality of prison services, spur innovation, gain access to expertise and services unavailable to the public, reduce costs, help overcome state prison overcrowding, improve accountability and enable better risk management, and improve the efficiency and flexibility of the prison system. The privatisation of prisons was proposed as a solution to the perceived deterioration of public prisons, in part resulting from a steady increase in the use of prisons as a response to criminal behaviour and, with this, significant increases in the associated costs.[1] This chapter will consider just how far governments have been prepared to go in the outsourcing of prisons and correctional centres, and the impact that this has had on prison services and the society that sanctions them.

The changing prison

Incarceration has a variety of different public policy objectives and justifications, including deterrence, reform and incapacitation. Imprisonment also involves a number of unintended and highly damaging consequences, affecting those imprisoned in more ways than may have been always anticipated by the state. Prisons can be morally impoverished places, inflicting unintended damage on the very people prisons are attempting to correct, improve and socially rehabilitate. Apart from the most obvious loss of freedom, imprisonment results in the interruption of the individual's life path. Family and social relations become difficult to maintain, with the result that the prisoner's life can become lonely, idle and under-stimulated. Within prison there is a reduction in civil liberties such as privacy, and life must be lived in an atmosphere that is frequently charged with distrust and violence. These realities of prison life place an inescapable moral responsibility on society to ensure that there are clear objectives associated with incarceration, and that imprisonment meets broader social objectives by operating in a socially acceptable manner. Accordingly, operating a prison brings with it significant responsibilities.

The foremost responsibility in operating prisons is prisoner health, safety and dignity, all of which are prioritised in Australia under the *Standard Guidelines for Corrections in Australia 1996* and internationally in the *United Nations Standard Minimum Rules for Treatment of Prisoners*. Public prisons have been notoriously bad at providing safe and dignified conditions for their inmates, which has made it difficult to mount arguments suggesting that they are more able than private prisons to meet these qualitative outcomes. However, there is significant evidence to suggest that the pursuit of profit by private prison contractors has exaggerated the erosion of the quality of services and conditions being provided by public prisons to prisoners and to the community. A study conducted by Biles and Dalton found that the Australian privately run Port Phillip, Deer Park and Arthur Gorrie prisons all had higher death and suicide rates that the Australian average for public prisons.[2]

Although some of the findings are alarming, the significance of Biles and Dalton's report does not just lie in what it reveals about the performance of these prisons. Also important is the inability of a community to effect change, express outrage, demand greater scrutiny and ensure better outcomes for that community and the prison system as a whole. Internal papers from the British Prison Service leaked to the BBC in early 2008, which contained performance league tables ranking all prisons in England and Wales, showed private prisons were generally the worst for security and maintaining order. Ten of the eleven privately managed prisons were consistently in the bottom quartile. This again prompted the governors of the main public prisons to call for the abandonment of the experiment with the private management of prisons.

As imprisonment has struggled to maintain legitimacy as a form of punishment that has positive outcomes for the 'punished', and society in general, the introduction of the profit motive into this arena raises further concern.[3] It has also had a deleterious impact on public accountability arising from a systemic endeavour by governments to divorce economic and social policy, as though one can be justified through the other, rather than each being equally important components of social organisation. At the very least, in the case of prisons the accountability process should reveal whether the contracted private operators are fulfilling their contract and providing the services that have been agreed upon. However, after 15 years of privatisation throughout the world, government officials still have almost no reliable data to assess whether for-profit prisons are doing their job, let alone achieving the promised cost efficiencies.[4]

The decision to imprison a person involves a society holding a criminal accountable for their actions and, as such, the institutions entrusted with this power must also be accountable to society for the well-being of those imprisoned. With privatised prisons, accountability for these social responsibilities is now complicated by the opportunities that some private entities have to profit from incarceration, and that these entities have a vested interest in the maintenance, if not the expansion, of incarceration as a response to criminal behaviour. The possibility for tension between social and profit objectives in prison management has led some to ask again the question regarding privatisation which has recurred throughout this book: whether there are 'services that are "inherently governmental" and should thus be quarantined from the process?'[5]

A preference for the private provision of prison services relies on the assumption that the administration and allocation of punishment can be separated, and that the day-to-day operations of the prison are a contractible dimension of the state. New public managers who have pushed for prison privatisation have argued that a clear distinction can be drawn between sentencing, which should remain the responsibility of the state, and the administration of that sentence. However, such a distinction is not necessarily as easy or as desirable as this suggests. With the state having the power to deprive a person of their liberty, it is critical that the administration of sentences is subject to an appropriate standard of care, that human rights are observed, and that the actions of those vested with control over detainees should be closely scrutinised and monitored. The further this task moves away from the state the more difficult it is to monitor, and the state has more opportunity to retreat from its responsibility to ensure such conditions. Moyle has argued that 'It should be emphasised that prison regimes, and the powers exercised by those who manage them, involve a continuation of sovereign power' and that there is a need to identify 'the powers that may not be delegatable within a democracy'.[6] It is certainly important to consider whether the stated aims of privatisation can be supported by its outcomes and whether they are appropriate in a liberal democratic state.

The increasing preference of governments to purchase from private contractors the many peripheral services that are integral to the operation of a public prison – including employment advice or training, garbage collection, energy and water/sewerage services – blurs the boundaries between the public and the private sectors. This complicates accountability arrangements and makes it more difficult to justify the place of the public sector within such an environment. This situation has been capitalised upon by private operators, who argue they are just providing cheaper services, whilst distancing themselves from the significance of these services to the community. This contemporary transference of responsibility for prisons from the public to the private sector began in the United States 20 years ago and is now commonplace in Britain and Australia, with the latter holding about 17.8 per cent of its incarcerated population in privately owned and/or operated prisons.[7] This transformation has also signified changes in accountability relationships between the community, government and the private prison operator that are only beginning to be investigated.

It is now possible for a private, for-profit company to be accountable to the government for the delivery of prison services and facilities, and the government to be then accountable to the public (including prisoners) for the quality of these services. In so doing, distance is placed between the service provider and the community in a way that would present significant challenges to fulfilling any technical, let alone moral, accountability function. In an attempt to further reinforce this distancing, private prison operators overwhelmingly present largely technical, quantifiable accounts of their stewardship to fulfil their contractual requirement of accountability for the delivery of specified services of a certain quality against agreed performance indicators.[8] The government is then able to report on these in what appears to be a relatively objective manner and, thus, distance itself from direct responsibility. At the same time, questions about the ethical and moral responsibility of government and society to these citizens now under the supervision of a profit-seeking, private contractor are almost eradicated from debate. This is certainly evident in the opening story about Tyson Johnson.

The promise of private prisons: a global story

Since the early 1980s there has been a concerted, triumphant move back towards private prisons. This has been particularly apparent in the United States, Australia, Britain and Canada, where the privatisation of prisons has paralleled the privatisation of the broad range of other public services noted earlier. The corrections industry worldwide is now worth US$50 billion, thereby constituting an industry bigger than tobacco. The popularity of private prisons is no accident, but the consequence of a vigorous, relentless campaign aimed at influential politicians by the private sector. In the United States alone, the National Institute of State Money in Politics between 2000 and 2004 found that companies involved in the corrections sector gave US$3.3 million to political candidates and political parties.[9] In such an environment, the public and private motivations for incarceration are no longer clearly distinguishable.

The transformation of prisons took place throughout the 1980s and 1990s with little public scrutiny, despite the United States having approved 153 privately operated correctional facilities housing more than 119 000 prisoners by 2000.[10] This rise in privately held prisoners parallels a rise in prisoners more broadly. In 1980, the United States held 320 000 people in prison, but by 2002 this had grown to 1.4 million, an increase of more than 400 per cent.[11] This rapid rise in the prison population, but especially those in private hands, only emerged as a significant public issue around 2000 when groups within the wider community became aware of the increasingly large numbers of people who were being incarcerated. Not only did this raise justice and sentencing issues, but also questions about the quality of the services that were being provided by private contractors and the costs of these services.

So popular have private prisons become throughout the world that it seems that a day hardly passes without an announcement of yet another country and another corporation considering the benefits of a new private prison, immigration detention centre, or a new 'removal' centre as they are now called in Britain. The result is that private prisons and similar institutions are now found in France, Britain, the United States, Australia, Canada, Chile, Peru, Japan, Korea, the Czech Republic, Germany, South Africa, Israel and Belize. Where they do not yet operate, many nations such as Bulgaria, Costa Rica, Honduras, Hong Kong, Poland, Nigeria and Thailand are seriously considering some form of public/private arrangements for their prisons in the future. In August 2006 the declaration by the National Congress of Honduras that its overcrowded prison system was in a state of emergency paved the way for a private company to be commissioned to build and operate a new maximum security prison. Meanwhile, Israel's Noa Group has lobbied the Honduran government in the hope that it will be awarded a 30-year contract worth more than US$6 million a year to build and run a 2500-bed prison. In June 2006, a 20-strong delegation of government officials from Hong Kong visited Canada to explore the use of public-private partnerships for its prisons. This follows a similar visit by 28 Chinese officials to Britain in 2005.[12]

There are also several projects underway across the globe. In mid-2006, the state of Saxony-Anhalt in Germany signed a 25-year contract with the private construction firm Bilfinger Berger to finance, design, build and operate all non-sovereign services at a 650-bed prison to be built at Burg which is expected to open in 2009. The company has also won a 20-year contract from the state of Saxony, worth over €130 million, to design, finance, build and operate the Chemnitz Justice Centre which will include a municipal court and state attorney's offices. In Britain, the Scottish Prison Service has contracted Addiewell Prison Ltd, which is owned by Sodexo Investment Services Ltd, Royal Bank Project Investments and Interserve PFI Ltd, to finance, design, build and operate a new 700-bed prison in West Lothian.[13] The prison is Scotland's second private prison and is expected to be fully operational by 2009.

Since 1988, the private sector has played an expanding role also in the operation of Australia's correctional facilities. This move was led by the Kennedy Report for the Queensland Corrective Services Commission into correctional reform, which recommended that a private operator under contract to the commission should develop one prison.[14] This was based on its findings that problems within the existing state-run system could be solved through privatisation, creating a market for corrective institutions which would allow for increased flexibility in correctional arrangements and develop competition in order to have something against which to test the performance and costs of state prisons.

It is widely accepted within the literature on private prisons that the fundamental motivations for prison privatisation have been the belief that private prisons will reduce operating costs, largely through reduced labour costs, provide faster and cheaper prison capacity as a result of the removal of barriers to financing and construction, and improve the quality of the service through innovation.[15] Although these arguments have been presented as neutral, technical representations of the issues, they are not devoid of political intent. Indeed, it is clear that ideological assumptions underpinned the Kennedy Report, most significantly the appeal to 'the market' to solve persistent employment 'failures' within the prison sector. It argued that financial problems – said to be caused by the unionised workforce which was 'difficult' and 'problematic' for refusing to accept further compromised work conditions – could be overcome by the 'flexibility' supposedly allowed by private contracting. However, the Kennedy Report ignored that this would come at the cost to working conditions and, therefore, would have an effect on quality or performance. In addition, there is the presumption that competition will enable performance to be measured more accurately on the basis of cost. This, however, diverts attention from attempts to develop other ways of evaluating and improving punishment and prison services,[16] suggesting that the Queensland decision to privatise prisons was a highly politicised move emanating from a need by government to disassociate itself from the myriad, seemingly intractable problems within prisons.

Although the possibility of political motivations was raised within the Australian media at the time that prison privatisation was proposed and concern voiced about the Queensland government's approach, the findings and recommendations of the Kennedy Report were quickly accepted. This led the Queensland Corrective Services Commission to call for tenders to manage and operate Borallon Correctional Centre, a 240-bed medium-security prison near Brisbane. Eventually, Corrections Corporation Australia (CCA) was awarded this contract in 1989 and, under a three-year contract, the first private prison in Australia was opened in 1991 at a cost of A\$22 million with a contract fee of A\$9.7 million to manage the prison for the 1991 financial year.[17]

This contract was awarded partly as a result of the lobbying efforts of senior executives from CCA who travelled throughout Australia 'informing' state governments of the benefits of private prisons. Subsequently, contracts have been awarded to private prison operators throughout the country with the result that, today, Australia has seven privately operated adult prisons operating in five states. These are run by three companies, all of which are foreign-owned: Australian Integrated Management Services, a wholly owned subsidiary of the French-American company Sodexo Alliance; GEO Group, previously known as Australian Correctional Management; Management and Training Corporation, whose corporate headquarters are in Utah, and GSL Custodial Services, formerly Group 4 Falck. From the Kennedy Report onwards the possibility that private companies could play a role in the provision of correctional institutions throughout Australia was firmly entrenched.

Countries that are yet to contract out any prisons are none-the-less showing mounting interest. In Ireland, for example, the *Third Annual Report* (2004–05) of the Inspector of Prisons and Places of Detention recommended that the Irish government should 'open at least one prison to private companies'.[18] In 2004, a British White Paper issued by the Blair Labour government titled *Reducing Crime – Changing Lives* proposed a new willingness to work with the private sector in building much-needed prisons. The former Home Secretary, David Blunkett, described it as a 'progressive agenda for the future'. Referring to the 139 prisons in Britain, of which ten are being run by private companies, the White Paper argued for a deepening of the relationship between government and private providers.

Elsewhere, in 2005 the Czech Republic conducted a feasibility study into the development of some form of private prison, while the Economy Ministry in Russia is also considering prison privatisation. Although the Russian Justice Minister, Yury Chalka, has expressed his opposition to prison privatisation, he has acknowledged that the prison system needs a US$9 billion investment in order to modernise and meet future demand – money which is unlikely to be available from public funds.

The challenges of prison overcrowding which many countries are experiencing, and which have made private prisons more attractive, are in part a result of population growth. They are, however, more easily explained by the 'tough on crime' election campaigns and policy strategies of conservative and other right-leaning governments, despite there being little evidence that crime is on the increase. On the contrary, in the United States, Canada and Australia violent crime has been decreasing on a per capita basis. This has not stopped politicians like Canada's prime minister Stephen Harper, for example, launching what he calls 'a battle with criminals' involved in gangs, guns and drugs. Consequently, Canada's judges are now required to issue a mandatory minimum sentence for violent and repeat offenders, while for other criminals conditional sentences and house arrests are expected to 'keep criminals in jail for the duration of their sentences'. A similar response has occurred in Australia, with state governments running political campaigns which pander to perceived public anxiety about their safety, in which a toughened stance on crime is advocated.

The resulting increase in mandatory minimum sentences that this has produced has lead to a large increase in the level of incarceration.

Although extra prisons have been the preferred solution to a rising prisoner population in most countries, some are considering alternative possibilities which do not involve incarceration yet are both cost effective and of a high quality. In Belgium, for example, its 33 prisons, mostly built over a hundred years ago, can no longer meet current correctional needs, thus compelling the government to look for alternatives. These have included attempting to reduce the number of prisoners on remand by providing magistrates with sentencing discretion, and considering the use of electronic tagging as an alternative to custody.

Scandinavian countries have adopted an approach to incarceration that is substantially different to that of the rest of the world. Penal policy in Sweden, Norway and Finland is run largely on a principle of mutual respect and personal responsibility, rather than the punitive/correctional approach that is prevalent elsewhere. One striking difference is the commitment to education that dominates all prisons in these countries. As a result, their prisons may cost more in the shorter term but they have significantly lower rates of incarceration (62 per 100 000 people compared to 600 per 100 000 in the United States), lower levels of recidivism and, on average, the sentences are shorter.[19] Unfortunately, in the present political climate there is little scope in Anglo-American jurisdictions for creatively re-imagining prisons or responses to criminal behaviour when both corporations and governments have become increasingly invested in the privatised prison solution.

The unravelling of order: private prisons in practice

Although prison privatisation has promised a great deal, from the many spectacular failures that have occurred in many countries it is clear that the results of the contracting out of this unique sector have fallen far short of its many promises. Nowhere is this more clearly seen than with the staffing of private prisons. Among the more persuasive arguments in favour of private prisons, it has been suggested that private prisons will be able to attract and retain higher quality staff than has been the case with public prisons, and that the staff will be used more efficiently and effectively than the largely unionised public prison employees. Unfortunately, throughout countries which have succumbed to private alternatives, serious staff shortages, debilitating high levels of staff turnover and the recurring poor quality of staff have continued to plague both private and public approaches to prison delivery, despite vigorous assurances to the contrary. In 2006, the state of Colorado found that Corrections Corporation of America (CCA) was running two prisons, Kit Carson and Crowley County, without the correct number of prison guards. It penalised CCA, even if only symbolically, by withholding US$126 000 of its performance bonus. It had been found, contrary to their contract, that the staff-to-prisoner ratio was a fraction of the ratio operating in state prisons at the time. Far from being novel or new, this problem had been exposed earlier by the Colorado State Auditor who had found, when he investigated a prison riot at Crowley County in 2004, that there had been only 33 prison wardens guarding 1122 prisoners, approximately a seventh of the number of staff in an equivalent state-run prison.[20]

The risible size of the penalty for CCA's failure in 2006 could only encourage astute investors to conclude that it makes good business sense to understaff prisons, since it was obvious that employing the correct number would certainly cost a great deal more than any fines which might be imposed. During this time CCA's share price rose from US$11 in September of 2003 to US$27 in September 2007.

Too often the situation in Colorado has been mirrored in other prisons across the globe, where attracting and keeping good prison staff is made especially difficult by the poor pay, difficult workplace and where the conditions of employment are constantly under review in order to meet the financial performance objectives of prison management. Among the little research to date into the impact of pay on prison staff in private and public prisons, a report produced by Britain's Prison Service Pay Review Board in 2004 suggests that the differences are substantial. It found that custodial staff in private prisons earned 43 per cent less in terms of base hourly wages than those working in a public prison, which would help to explain the perceived cost-effectiveness of the private prison and the subsequent service delivery challenges they experience.[21]

In Scotland, Kimarnock prison, run by Premier Prisons, has also come under scrutiny for staffing deficiencies. Former employees have claimed that the prison was understaffed, that it operated with poor security, and that drug abuse was endemic. Although these problems exist within the entire prison sector, it has been claimed they were exacerbated in this private prison because of the especially difficult conditions imposed on the operation of the prison by the private operator. Many of these and other accusations were made public through a series of BBC documentaries and investigative reports.[22] In one case in 2005, the BBC's investigative journalist, Steve Allen, applied for a job with Premier Prisons. The fact that his resume was a complete fiction went unnoticed by a facility where the personal and work history of staff should be a crucial qualification for employment. Within ten weeks he was left alone to be responsible for 80 prisoners, some on suicide watch. The reporter kept a hidden camera with him for the entire 16 weeks he was working in the prison and yet no-one noticed, not even the airport-style metal detectors that were supposed to ensure nothing hazardous entered the prison.

In the course of his undercover exposé, Allen observed that many of the problems associated with the management of the prison were a direct result of poor staffing levels, inadequate pay and working conditions. These all ensured the poor quality of the staff, whose primary responsibility appeared to be to save their employer money. One effective way to do this was not to report incidents, as required by the contract, because they incurred a financial penalty for the private contractor. At Kilmarnock, the performance incentives perversely resulted in no incentive to report incidents. In his training course, Allen was told that a positive drug test would cost the prison £3000, and a physical assault of a prisoner or staff member would lead to a fine of £16 000. Although the compliance trainer was clear that all incidents should be reported, the reality was quite different. According to Allen's report, when guards found 'hooch' – home-brew produced by the prisoners – they threw it away rather than report it.

Prison guards also turned a blind eye to contraband such as mobile phones and drugs to avoid the prison being fined when reported. More seriously, priority tasks such as suicide watches were not conducted properly, with documents recording the watches often falsified. By not reporting offences and helping to minimise fines, staff hoped that this would lead to a pay rise.

Allen's investigation prompted a major inquiry and in January 2007 the Director of Detention Services appointed a private company to carry out an audit of race relations and the treatment of detainees at several private and public detention centres, known in Britain as the 'removal estate'.[23] Although instances of poor management practices and racial abuse were reported in public detention centres, the auditors' report was especially critical of those operated by private contractors. With one exception, private firms were ranked the poorest. At several of the private centres the auditors found poor living conditions and an atmosphere that was 'distressing'. In the case of Colnbrook Immigration Removal Centre, run by the private contractor Serco, detainees described the facility as 'worse than a prison'. Bullying and racial abuse were said to be common at facilities such as Colnbrook. At roll call and meal times, detainees were often taunted with 'Animals, lock-up time' and 'Animals, come get your food'. At Harmondsworth, Britain's largest immigration detention centre and the site of a major outbreak of violence in November 2006, detainees reported being regularly verbally abused and intimidated by staff. Particularly worrying for the investigators was the way in which this behaviour was accepted as a normal part of the management of detainees.

In contrast, the investigators found that government controlled centres, such as Dover Immigration Removal Centre or the Haslar Immigration Removal Centre and Lindholme, were professionally managed and the relationship between staff and detainees was very good. At the Haslar facility, the investigators found that the officers enjoyed their work, were highly motivated to provide a friendly and efficient service and to ensure that the detainees were actively and productively engaged each day: 'This is all done with a firm and yet compassionate understanding of the issues that accompany detention'. These qualities of service delivery are those which are expected of public services. At the privately operated Oakington and Yarls Wook Immigration Reception Centres, management could not have been more different. There was little attempt to provide the detainees with fulfilling activities or to engage with them beyond the very basic requirements of everyday living. This caused the detainees to feel frustrated and neglected.

In Australia, the ABC program 'Four Corners' investigated the privately run immigration detention centre at Woomera after a series of high-profile events in 2003 drew attention to its operations. Especially disturbing were the images of detainees who had sewn their lips together as a protest to attract attention to their plight. At the time, 189 people were on a hunger strike, of whom 55 men, two women and five children had sewn their lips together to protest the conditions in which they were expected to live and their debilitating frustrations with the Immigration Department. Many people, including children, were held for years in the facility which was run by the private corporation Australian Correctional Management (ACM). Although the uncertainty under which they were expected to live was hard enough to endure, the people in the Woomera detention centre also had to suffer a centre managed by a company ill-equipped to provide for the needs of the growing number of refugees.

The centre had been initially designed to house 400 people, but within weeks of opening nearly 1000 people had been sent to Woomera. There were not enough toilets and people were housed in temporary buildings without adequate cooling – in a facility which was located in one of the most barren and hottest parts of Australia. In addition, there were only two nurses to assess the condition of the refugees, three officers to process the new arrivals, no interpreters and no clear procedures as to how the centre was to be managed and the welfare of those held was to be assured. Despite these gross inadequacies, by April 2000 Woomera had 1500 detainees with still only three washing machines and five toilets. Even though it is estimated that from late 1999 to 2003 Woomera had cost the Australian government more than A$170 million in contract payments to ACM, the contract has never been made public, thereby allowing for the possibility that it may well have been perfectly acceptable, at least in technical contractual terms, to run a detention centre on this basis.

The deficiencies in ACM's operation at Woomera have been neither unique to this one site nor an isolated occurrence in privately managed institutions of incarceration. In Britain, the Chief Inspector of Prisons found in 2005 that Doncaster Prison, which is privately managed by Serco, previously Premier Prison Services, was not performing well against three of four 'healthy prison' tests, and that conditions inside the prison had deteriorated over the time of the contract with Premier Prison Services. The inspector found that the physical conditions of prisoners were well below a level normally deemed acceptable, with prisoners living without pillows, adequate mattresses, toilet seats and storage facilities. This had impacted on the level of general respect for prison officers by prisoners and, as a consequence, prison safety. The inspector also found that the prison had not addressed concerns about the treatment of new prisoners, who are acknowledged to be most vulnerable, and that the prison management, although operating for ten years, still had no clear strategies for dealing with the detoxification and bullying issues that affected these prisoners. Further, it was reported that there was little productive activity with which to fill the prisoners' days and that this had serious implications for the prison's ability to limit re-offending. In her report, the chief inspector said:

> It is noticeable that the deficits we found are all in areas not
> specifically mandated by the contract under which the prison is run.
> There remains a concern that, focusing on meeting their contractual
> obligations prison managers had allowed important areas to slip below
> what was safe and decent; and indeed may have sought savings in
> precisely those areas.[24]

After experiencing not dissimilar problems to those of Britain, in April 2006 the government of Ontario, Canada, made the difficult decision to transfer the operation of the Central North Correctional Centre back to the public sector. The provincial government's community and correctional services carried out a study in 2001 to compare prison performance over five years to determine if there were any advantages of privatisation. It compared the private prison to an identical, publicly run institution, the Central East Correctional Centre (CECC), and found that the CECC performed better in key areas such as security, health care and reducing re-offending rates. Although the private prison was found to be slightly less expensive to operate, and had complied with the specific terms of its contract, all non-cost-related performance criteria, as in the Doncaster example above, had been systematically and purposefully neglected.[25]

Of all the criteria which could be a clear measure of the success of private prisons, recidivism has been used consistently to justify them, especially given that rates of recidivism in all prisons are high and the issue of re-offending is a significant public policy concern. In the state of Florida, although legislation stipulates that private prisons are to operate more effectively and more efficiently than public sector prisons, new research has found that for Florida's prisoners there is 'no empirical justification for the policy argument that private prisons reduce recidivism rates better than public prisons'.[26] Governments have promised, and were promised by private companies, a great deal in their experiment with prison privatisation and private companies. Yet, although the scope for prison privatisation is growing globally, there are increasingly grave doubts, recognised in the Florida study, about the ability of these experiments to deliver high-quality, low-cost prisons. Communities are also beginning to question the legitimacy of punishment by firms seeking profits, while there are growing questions about the impact this is having on the level of public accountability provided to citizens, prisoners and the families of those incarcerated.

Accountability and quality issues

Apart from the inability to determine convincingly the cost benefits of privatisation, there have also been difficulties in ensuring access to information relating to the quality of service provision. The monitoring of contracts, that are supposed to clearly set out the operators' performance criteria, has been decidedly flawed. There is significant evidence to suggest that private prison operators are not providing government with even the most basic, contractually required information within the defined time frames. Under these arrangements, it is very difficult for either the government or members of the broader community to scrutinise the activities of the prison operators.

It is also possible that such contracts may be used by the private firm to ensure that information about its performance does not enter the public domain. Governments and private contractors have an interest in ensuring that private prisons project an image and a reality devoid of imperfections and which can be used as a means to justify further privatisations. A report on the Kilmarnock private prison by Scotland's Chief Inspector of Prisons had to be stopped and copies were destroyed because the private operator, Premier Prisons, threatened legal action on the basis of commercial confidentiality if staffing levels, which were 30–50 per cent lower than public sector prisons, were made public.[27]

In Australia, access to information related to prison privatisation has also been kept from public scrutiny under the guise of 'commercial confidentiality', stalling many attempts to investigate the operations of both state and private prisons.[28] In mid-2004, after much agitation and changes in governments, contracts for private prisons in Victoria and Western Australia were finally made public, but not the financial information they contained. Although in Australia some information about private prisons has been made available through freedom of information claims, this is costly, time consuming and often vital information is censored before release.[29] Some public information on privately managed prisons has been provided through audit reports by auditors-general and official investigations into prison operations, such as the Victorian government's *Audit Review of Government Contracts* in 2000 and the Australian Productivity Commission's *Annual Report on Government Services*. Especially informative have been two commissioned reports by Victorian Correctional Service, including its *Report on the Metropolitan Women's Correctional Centre's Compliance with Contractual Obligations and Prison Services Agreement* and the *Report of the Independent Investigation into the Management and Operations of Victoria's Private Prisons*.[30] Although these are certainly of considerable value, they are characteristically limited in scope, focused on efficiency improvements, emphasise financial expenditures which are used to test performance against set measures, and they are constrained by the framework in which they operate, thereby reinforcing the current arrangements. Appraisals that adopt a broader evaluative stance are not commonplace and are more likely to result from investigative journalism rather than any officially sanctioned system of accountability.[31]

The legitimacy of concerns about the information upon which accountability is dependent was convincingly demonstrated with the Victorian government's privately operated Metropolitan Women's Correctional Centre (MWCC). Managed by Corrections Corporation Australia (CCA), the prison was the first private women's prison outside the United States when it was opened in 1996. The project promised substantial savings, correctional innovation and quality improvements, attributes which were virtually impossible to assess. Compounding this problem, the Victorian government legislated to prevent parliamentary scrutiny of the prison by designating the contracts as 'commercial in confidence', thereby allowing CCA to operate without any substantive independent external assessments of its performance.

In spite of this, it became apparent that CCA was not performing adequately and that the innovations that CCA introduced had transformed the prison in unacceptable ways. Many found it particularly objectionable that tear gas was used against women in prison for the first time in Australia. Further, designating 25 per cent of the women in the prison as 'protected' – which required that they were separated from the other women in the prison for fear of physical violence to them – was well above the norm. In New South Wales this figure was approximately 3 per cent. Problems within the prison's management were reflected in the high staff turnover, with nine different general managers appointed in four years, and the need to subcontract the medical centre to three different firms over four years. Possibly most worrying, 95 per cent of prisoners were on prescribed medication.[32]

Despite these alarming features of the MWCC's management, limits placed on access to the information that would reveal the internal operations of the prison contrived to ensure that they came to light only long after the event. Many of the default notices issued to the contractor related to the management decision not to report required information in a timely manner. Given that any meaningful system of accountability requires the exchange of information, these breaches undermined the ability of the government to ensure the private contractor was held accountable. They also undermined the ability of the public to hold the government accountable for its actions. The Auditor General of Victoria's Report on Ministerial Portfolios in 2001 identified a number of key issues that related to Victoria's private prison operators failing to report information. He found that significant incidents were not 'immediately reported' and many incidents were 'not declared at the earliest opportunity', undermining the most basic dimension of accountability.[33]

The problems associated with access to information were highlighted in the Correctional Services Commissioner's report in 2000 on the MWCC's compliance with its contractual obligations and prison services agreement.[34] Many of the issues it raised had not been in the CCA's reports required under the contract and were only made apparent through additional detailed investigations, and not through the standard accountability arrangements. For example, the contract required that the prison operator report drug related incidents to the commissioner, and that no more than 8.26 per cent of prisoners test positive for non-prescribed drug use.[35] Achieving these targets accounted for 20 per cent of the CCA's performance-related fee: should this target not be reached, then the fee would be reduced by a proportion established within the contract.[36] Ideally, the emphasis placed on these kinds of performance outcomes should improve the performance of the service. However, the emphasis can also mean that operators take steps to ensure that the outcomes are met 'technically' without actually improving performance. As an example of how the measurement criteria can be manipulated in order to meet contractual requirements, the commissioner's investigation found that:

> for the last 3 months, prisoner 'E' has been tested on 13 occasions between 4:00 am and 5:20 am. The MWCC Manager Health Services has advised [that] there is no medical reason as to why prisoner 'E' has to be tested at these times. The testing of prisoner 'E' at these times

is of significant concern as the predictability of testing enables the prisoner to use drugs with a decreased likelihood of being detected.[37]

Such distortions of 'success' are inevitable when the criteria for measurement are as limited as measures such as the number of positive drug tests. Rather than the contracts ensuring that private contractors perform well, at a minimum according to the terms of the contract, these examples suggest that there is a large incentive to ensure that the private contractor merely *appears* to be performing well. Information about the quality of the services has often been limited to that which is easily counted, such as the number of escape attempts, positive drug tests, or 'incidents'. Important as this may be, it is questionable whether such data can adequately shed light on the quality of the service being provided. Shichor has argued that difficulties in evaluating private prison performance are further accentuated because 'of the paucity of benchmark data to forecast future developments', the 'problems of access to the records of private companies', and the difficulty of evaluating private operators when 'there is already an assumption that they are doing a better job than state run prisons'.[38]

Although some state audits and special investigations by parliament into private prisons have provided insight into the management of the private prisons, this has been limited by a number of factors that are unique to the new private arrangements. For example, for traditional accountability purposes prisoners' accounts to outsiders have been a good source of information about what is occurring within a prison.[39] This is no longer applicable to the same degree with private prisons. While criminal lawyers have regularly complained about the difficulties of working with prisoners in prisons operated by government, the situation has been shown to be noticeably exacerbated when a prison is managed privately.

De Kretser, of the Federation of Community Legal Services in Victoria, has reported that in a private prison it typically takes around three to ten days for a lawyer to be put on a prisoner's 'phone list' – enabling the prisoner to call the lawyer – and that the prisoner, who may earn as little as A$13 per week, must then pay for the costly long-distance calls. Lawyers can make calls to their client, but must provide significant advance notice. Accordingly, if a prisoner wanted to talk to a lawyer about prison conditions, as opposed to their criminal case, this is made very difficult. Face-to-face visits are possible but these also require considerable notice and take exceptionally long periods of time to organise because of the security requirements of the prison. At Port Phillip, one of Victoria's privately operated prisons, documents cannot be directly exchanged between a client and a lawyer, they must be administered by the prison, thereby making it almost impossible for a prisoner to confidentially complain about prison treatment. Often mail between lawyers and prisoners is opened.[40]

The overall result of these almost petty impediments is that a prisoner's capacity to interact with the public is limited. Further, calling the media is banned and all phone calls are recorded. This has meant that there has been a marked decrease in the amount of information about what happens inside prisons from the prisoners. The report into MWCC by the Victorian Auditor-General concluded that communication problems for prisoners were further exacerbated when inadequate staffing led to excessively long lock-down periods, thereby making it impossible for prisoners to access telephones or meet with family and friends for extended periods.[41]

The cost of order: Monitoring the contract

Despite the impediments outlined above, monitoring private prison contracts is essential to ensure that operators provide the service that has been defined in the contract and paid for. The secluded environments in which all prisons operate mean that outside parties are forced to rely substantially on the records of activities that are kept by prison operators and the reports provided to the public by government-appointed monitors. With the private prison rewarded financially if its records show that it has managed to meet its performance criteria, significant pressures are created to ensure that the performance reports demonstrate compliance.

From a purely technical point of view, the contract with the private prison needs to ensure access for official visitors, protection of the government's right to oversee the operations, parliamentary scrutiny, and that the provisions of freedom of information legislation are not thwarted. Although the contracts that are being monitored need to be available, in many cases either parts of the final contracts or the contracts entirely are treated as being 'commercial in confidence' – even to the monitors.[42]

Herein lies the threat of regulatory capture by the private prison operators. In one compelling case at Junee prison in New South Wales, where a major riot broke out in 2003, the prison regulator had abdicated its responsibilities, preferring instead to rely upon the assurances of the contractor that they were meeting the conditions of their agreement. The Correction Services of New South Wales, which has the responsibility to directly monitor the implementation of private prison contracts, had not persisted with the employment of an on-site, full-time monitor provided for in the contract. Instead, they had withdrawn their monitor, leaving Junee prison without a representative of the regulator to monitor the operations. Another example of this 'capture' is the Borallon prison in Queensland, which was supposed to have a monitor employed by the prisons regulator, the Queensland Corrective Services Commission. When interviewed only a year after the opening of the prison, the monitor was spending just one day per week at the site, the other days spent monitoring another four sites.[43] It has been suggested that if the contract is sound, it can provide strict safeguards by specifying standards and providing default, penalty, termination and step-in clauses. However, according to Harding, a 'loose contract will tend to have loose accountability; a tighter one should facilitate accountability'.[44] As the Borallon and Junee examples suggest, contracted and actual accountability may be significantly different.

In order to properly oversee and monitor the performance of a private prison, the state must retain some organisational knowledge of that system. However, as noted above, the process of privatisation means that the quality of knowledge is significantly diluted. Governments may find it increasingly difficult to gain access to information which would allow them to properly analyse how the private system is working, and whether the service is improving or getting worse under the private arrangements. This is particularly true if the prison has been privately operated over a number of years.

Profits and performance

A recent New South Wales parliamentary inquiry into the *Value for Money for NSW Correctional Centres* found that no meaningful comparison and, thus, no definitive conclusion could be drawn as to the cost-effectiveness of private prisons because each prison varies according to its size, mixture of prisoners, level of responsibility, its expectations, the building design, its geographical location and the level of services required.[45] In another analysis of the costs pertaining to private prisons, the Victorian Auditor-General, while unable to release the contracted benchmarks for government operating costs, was at least able to conclude that all contracts incorporated performance levels which were less than the government's own benchmarks.[46] Still, he was unsure about the cost savings because of the inability to incorporate less quantifiable considerations such as long-term social costs, societal risks and monitoring cost 'realities'. In terms of accountability, the contracts that are available provide little information about how much of the total contract fee would be reduced in the case of breaches, information which is essential in order to understand how the contractor is encouraged to comply with the contract. There is also minimal information about how the contractor can make a profit and what actions they can take to do so.

Generally, the fees associated with a prison contract have been divided into three parts: an accommodation service charge, which is for the provision of physical facilities; a correctional services fee, for the day-to-day operations of the prison; and a performance-linked fee, representing the investment reward or profit. It is the last that distinguishes the private operator from the government. It is a fee that should encourage quality service delivery by enabling the operator to make a profit. However, the performance-linked fee has often led to an erosion of reporting quality rather than an improvement in service. The following section will offer some examples of how this fee structure has not enhanced the accountability framework of private prisons, either financially or in terms of service quality.

The accommodation service charge, which appears to be a simple fee for service payment, has proven to be especially controversial. In one notorious case, the Australian Broadcasting Corporation reported in 2000 that ACM had been using charities to clothe its prisoners.[47] ACM's contract requires it to ensure that there is adequate clothing for the detainees and prisoners, but it puts no limits on how they can source and finance these needs. According to the report, ACM initially sourced clothes from the religious charity St Vincent de Paul, which agreed to provide them at A$5 per kilogram – a charge which ACM had negotiated down from the already usual low rate of A$8 per kilogram. Even this was not sufficient for ACM which, it was discovered, later managed to source the clothes from another section of St Vincent de Paul for free. Upon being exposed, ACM agreed to pay A$21 000 for 2000 kilograms of clothes for which they had originally negotiated a rate of A$5 per kilogram.

When commercial relations between St Vincent de Paul and ACM broke down, it went to another charity, the Uniting Church, and asked for clothes and basic housing items. According to the Uniting Church there was no suggestion that ACM would pay for these. When the Uniting Church realised that 'the government is actually, on behalf of the Australian people, paying ACM to provide those things ... we decided then not to go ahead with it'.[48] Deficiencies in the private prisons contracts had allowed the private operator the opportunity to exploit charitable organisations and still fulfil its requirements, in an attempt to maximise its profits. This is but one example among many which has exposed the way in which private operators can provide the services more cost effectively. More seriously, the situation exposed the inability of government to hold the private operator accountable for the standard of service which they provided.

The second component of ACM's contract payments, the correctional services fee, also initially appeared to be a straightforward payment, but instead it has proven to be very contentious. For example, in January 2003 prison guards at the Arthur Gorrie Correctional Centre were in dispute with ACM over a plan to use prison labour to increase prison profits.[49] The proposal involved replacing those prison staff performing non-custodial functions in areas such as the kitchen with inmates. Although ACM was paid a fee to provide for this day-to-day management of the centre, this proposal did not appear to contravene the contract as it had not defined how the kitchen services should be provided. After protracted and strained negotiations with the unions, the proposal was finally dropped. This attempt by ACM to reduce costs presented a similar dilemma to that outlined previously where the mode of delivery is left out of the contract to enable 'flexibility'. The reality is that, instead, this imprecision could be interpreted as allowing the company access to exploitative practices to maximise returns with, unlike publicly provided services, no formal process that allowed the government and the community to hold the provider accountable.

The third element of the fee paid to private prison contractors, the performance-linked fee, was designed to enable the company to make a profit above the costs of the operation, as long as it met certain specified standards. Unfortunately, as noted earlier, this performance incentive has often led to under-reporting of incidents, rather than excellence in service quality. For instance the Woomera Detention Centre has provided particularly graphic examples of how far corrections corporations will go to in order to be 'cost effective' and maximise their profits by failing to report 'incidents' that would have had a negative impact upon their performance evaluation. One incident that received considerable media attention in 2000 occurred when ACM failed to report an alleged rape of a 12-year-old boy in its Woomera facility. It was also widely reported that the company was reluctant to disclose this information because it would lead to a financial penalty of around A\$20 000. Even though this incident occurred within a facility managed entirely by a private contractor, which the public believed would be held accountable, it was left to the government to answer any accusations and criticisms when the Minister for Immigration and Multicultural Affairs was forced to defend the processes at Woomera. On the ABC's 7:30 Report, anchor Kerry O'Brien observed with some exasperation that 'we did approach Australasian Correctional Management who run the detention centre at Woomera, but they referred all enquiries to Immigration Minister Phillip Ruddock'.[50]

Thus, the glaring reality of this kind of marketisation, as so often demonstrated throughout this book, is that when there is a crisis it is usual for the private company to make little public comment and for a representative of a government department to front the controversy. For the state to maintain its ability to enforce accountability, ultimately it must maintain the infrastructure needed so that it can step in and take over a failing organisation. Therefore, it must maintain a pool of prison guards, administrators, medical service experts and others who are able to retrieve the situation should it be necessary.

Despite the lack of detailed information that might help to understand how the profit motive is affecting the provision of prison services, a considerable amount of the research that has been conducted into the cost-efficiencies of private prisons has found that, if there are any immediate costs savings, they are predominantly a result of the lower staff salaries associated with the individual employment contracts preferred by private contractors. There are also strong incentives to hire poorly trained and poorly educated guards and to invest less in staff training programs. The consequences of these cost-related staffing pressures have been felt throughout the private prison sector and in almost all countries that operate them.

Contract awarding, renewal and termination

The process of awarding, renewing and terminating contracts must enable the government to hold the contractor accountable for its actions and also should allow the community to have some input into the arrangement.[51] Unfortunately in Australia this has proven difficult, as the tendering and renewal process has not encouraged sufficient competition. This is particularly true in the case of contract renewal, where many of the contracts allow the current operating company the right to renew the contract over other operators in the industry. In the United States, many states do not impose time limits on their contracts for prisons, with others explicitly allowing for long-term contracts. This removes the opportunity for regular government oversight in the form of a contested contract process. Another consequence is that these long contract terms decrease the opportunities for new entrants into the market, thereby entrenching the small number of service providers that currently exist. This lack of competition undermines a significant part of the privatisation rationale which relies heavily on the notion of competitive innovation stimulated by the market. The effect of this advantage differs according to the extent to which prison operations are privatised.

There are many ways prisons can be privatised. Currently in Australia, the prisons at Borallon, Arthur Gorrie and Mt Gambier are 'management only' contracts, whereas Woodford and Junee are 'design, construct and management' contracts. The only fully privatised prisons are Victoria's Deer Park, Fulham and Port Phillip. For the most part, Australia has adopted a model whereby private contractors, or their financiers, have paid for and own the prison structure itself, with the government repaying the capital and the borrowing costs over time. At the expiry of this contract period, the private contractor continues to own the structure and has a further 20-year lease of the land. Most of these contracts also come with initial five-year management contracts with three-year renewal periods. If part of the push to privatise is founded on the argument that competition will lead to better services at a lower cost, it is questionable whether this can occur when the owner/operator is in such a powerful position to bid for the continuance of the initial contract. Losing the management contract to a competitive bidder is unlikely.

If a government elects to allow full privatisation of the prison buildings and land, it may make it difficult to take back the administration of prison services if the company breaches its contract. Given that this is an integral part of the public accountability process, these ownership and control issues have the ability to erode any real accountability mechanisms. Indeed, there are many examples of state governments failing to step in when companies have breached their contracts. For example, after the Inspector General of Corrective Services for New South Wales criticised ACM's management of the Junee Correctional Centre when he found that there were a number of unresolved service delivery issues, the Corrective Services Department continued to find that the contractor had satisfactorily met its contractual obligations.[52]

On another occasion in May 2003, a pistol, ammunition, drugs, mobile phones and a digital camera were found in prison cells during a lock-down in the Port Phillip prison, operated by Group 4. When the government did not step in and confront Group 4 about the deficiencies in its management, preferring instead to deflect objectors to the private contractor, there was considerable public criticism. The minister responsible, Andre Haermeyer, in response to community concern about the imbalance of power in the contracts between the government and Victoria's two private prison operators, said that 'we have contractual obligations and it is only when there is a serious and repeated material default against the contract that we can actually step in'. Asked whether a loaded gun constituted such a breach, he replied 'well, no, it isn't, under the contract, no'.[53]

So inconsequential were these incidents deemed to be that the contracts with Group 4 for this prison and Fulham were renewed in October 2004, with what the government described as 'tighter performance measures'. However, this was not part of a competitive re-tendering process, because the initial contract gave the existing operators first rights to new contracts. Part of a government's reluctance to revoke an agreement with a contractor may also be related to the not insignificant financial and political costs that it faces in re-establishing the service under government control or finding another private contractor at short notice.

When a private prison fails, such as the MWCC in Victoria, the costs associated with resuming control are considerable. Even though the situation at the MWCC was only revealed in 2000, the reluctant decision to terminate the contract was the culmination of four years of repeated serious breaches of contract and failure to meet the service delivery requirements. In 2000 alone: gatehouse officers failed to stop police officers from carrying their firearms into the prison; five prisoners forced their way past staff into a section of the prison reserved for protected prisoners; the keys for the management section of the prison went missing, taking 33 hours for their disappearance to be reported; syringes and needles went missing from a medical bag after it was left in a prisoner's cell; classified internal documents relating to a prisoner were obtained by an ex-prisoner; prisoners rioted over cigarette restrictions; and a representative of Correctional Services was allowed to enter the prison without being processed by the gatehouse officer.

As serious as these failures were, there was little precedence for revocations of contracts, and as a result the conditions for the dismissal of the private contractor were complicated and negotiations protracted. In the end, the state of Victoria was forced to purchase the building from the contractor and the government took back ownership and management of the prison in November 2000 at a cost of A$20.2 million, A$17.8 million of which was for the building, infrastructure and chattels, and A$2.4 million for the costs of terminating the loan on the facility that had been taken out by the private operator. The state's auditor general noted that A$1.2 million of these costs were specifically related to the step-in and administration of the facility – costs not considered when privatising and indicative of the ideologically driven cost data that is used to justify such decisions.[54] The problems with the MWCC contract provided a compelling caution of how, as a result of the complexities of the contracting process, it is hard to hold either the government or the private operator accountable for their actions.

Private order: The quasi-judicial powers of prisons

Accountability within the prison sector also has important ethical dimensions, with the removal of a person's right to participate in society a significant state power because of its moral intent. This intent can not be discharged by a 'check the box' style accountability arrangement, for whenever punishment and denial of liberty are involved the moral responsibilities of the state, the community, the prison provider and the criminal are more substantive than any immediate, measurable outcomes would lead us to believe. To give the appearance of addressing these issues of moral responsibility and prison management, the outsourcing of prisons has been justified by claims that the sentence and the administration of that sentence can be clearly separated.[55] However, there are a number of problems with this, particularly in regard to 'quasi-legal' decisions that are made within prisons to discipline prisoners, in some cases without outside arbitration or scrutiny. This means that prison management does have the ability to affect the way that the sentence is administered, and has some opportunity to significantly change the experience of that sentence as a result of internal decisions, particularly in the case of alleged breaches of prison discipline. In these cases, the hearing and review process often occurs entirely within a correctional centre, drawing into question the ability of private sector management to make credible, disinterested decisions about the treatment of prisoners.[56]

The lack of scrutiny of internal hearings is illustrated in the transcripts taken by Moyle, who attended a number at Borallon and Lotus Glen private prisons in Queensland. On one such occasion, the manager of operations at the Borallon prison is reported to have said that it was acceptable to breach inmates' rights if they were a 'problem at the centre'. The manager clarified the meaning of 'problem at the centre' as 'protecting CCA's business name'.[57] This is far from being an isolated incident in the context of private prisons. In Queensland, ACM runs the reception centre at Arthur Gorrie, where all the decisions about a new prisoner's classification as a maximum/medium/minimum security inmate are made. These decisions determine the movement of a prisoner through the correctional system and, although there are regulations that guide this decision, there is, in practice, extensive discretion to be exercised on behalf of the private contractor's classification staff. When Moyle interviewed an officer at ACM in 1997, he heard of the classification a serious sex offender:

We have to look at presentation, appearance, behaviour, mood, what he is thinking and his employment history. We should get a psychologist to do this but because of a shortage we have a teacher doing it. I shouldn't tell you that. The recommendation should not be made by a teacher ... We know it's not their place.[58]

Moyle has argued that the ability of the private facility to make these decisions has meant that it is also able to choose 'profitable' or 'cheap' prisoners.[59]

Private prison management can also exercise quasi-judicial powers by placing a prisoner in solitary confinement, a practice that amounts to punishment but which does not have to be sanctioned directly by the state. At the Acacia prison in Western Australia, the contractor AIMS Corporation came under criticism from the state's inspector, Richard Harding, when he discovered that there was evidence that 'some inmates had been locked in their cell, with the electricity off as a form of punishment'.[60] These internal disciplinary regimes, in effect, involve an extension of state authority which has not been explicitly sanctioned. In addition, private prisons can directly affect remission, parole and disciplinary decisions, and can thus increase the length of sentence of an inmate with some of these matters not subject to review or appeal.[61] The potential for prisoners to be left at the uncertain mercy of the private contractors, whose motives are heavily influenced by self-interest, is only too obvious.

The fact that private companies, primarily answerable to their shareholders, can make decisions about prisoners that go beyond administration, undermines the argument by governments that a prison sentence can be managed by a private entity. In Tennessee in the United States, CCA guards have reported that they are encouraged to send troublesome inmates into administrative segregation (solitary confinement), thereby adding 30 days to an inmate's sentence and earning the company an extra US$1000. The potential conflicts of interest are magnified by CCA also encouraging guards to buy company stock, thereby ensuring that they have a personal financial stake in how profitably the company is being operated. The New Mexico Corrections Department found in a 1999 report that CCA inmates lost 'good time' credits eight times more frequently than those at public institutions.[62] It is obvious from these examples how the quasi-judicial powers of prison management impinge on the state's ultimate responsibility to determine the punishment of the person. It also complicates the public accountability process, as the punisher is further removed from the society in whose name the punishment is being carried out.

Order, profit and punishment

Punishment is a complex social, ideological and cultural terrain which will never be characterised as an entirely rational execution of orders with clear objectives and controllable outcomes. This complexity is magnified under private control, where there are further and competing aims with innumerable unintended consequences. Garland has argued that 'The failure of modern punishment is in part the inevitable outcome of an over rationalized conception of its functions'.[63] Prisons enable a society to separate and classify those who it deems to be 'criminal', a process which is accentuated by the introduction of less accountable private prisons which further separate criminals. In light of this, the ability of a private corporation to profit from nuanced state and social objectives acted out on the body of a citizen could be considered unreasonable and morally repugnant. While cost may be an obvious consideration in the delivery of any public sector function, and by no means is it surprising that corporations will act to minimise costs, the centrality of cost and the possibility of profit for the private contractor in prison management are particularly problematic. Prisons and penal policy should be focused on broader social objectives and questions that lead to better outcomes for all members of a society, including prisoners. Within the current accountability arrangements, as has been shown, these concerns are denied the importance that they demand.

Imprisonment has an undeniable moral component. Punishment imposes deprivation and suffering on a citizen as a result of breaking the law. According to Ryan and Ward, it should be remembered that punishment represents the 'organized use of force in liberal democratic states', which means there is great scope for abuse by both private and public agencies.[64] This would suggest that there are profound ethical and ideological issues surrounding the privatisation of prisons, yet these have been ignored largely in favour of discussions regarding cost-effectiveness, comparative costs and value for money – all strong indicators of the current policy drivers of reformist, neoliberal governments.[65] It is also possible that the rewards available from private prisons may create a 'prison industrial complex' in which there is a vested interest in prison expansion and, hence, incarceration as a source of profit.[66]

The boundaries between the allocation and administration of punishment are also complicated within a private prison system when the prison operator has many discretionary powers that can affect the length and type of incarceration that the prisoner experiences.[67] This is also true of public prisons, but when a corporation which is ultimately bound by corporation law to maximise returns to shareholders is responsible for such decision-making, keeping prison beds filled and the industry growing are essential to the growth potential of the company. This may lead to a situation, of which there is already substantial evidence within the corrections industry, in which 'doing well beats doing good'.[68] The Western Australian inspector general's report on the Acacia prison in 2003 highlighted this when he discovered that 'quantities of food seemed to have diminished as population increased, as if the same sized cake were being divided more times'.[69]

Instead of communities demanding a form of accountability that highlights their elected officials' efforts to address the root *causes* of crime, and information about a government's efforts to reduce behaviour that is deemed to be socially inappropriate, we are left with accounts of how governments are reducing the *costs* of crime through privatisation. This is a view supported by Hallet, who claimed that privatising aspects of the corrections system has solved the problems of overcrowded and costly prisons but left 'the fountain of all profits – large populations of disenfranchised surplus population trapped in the inner city to be incarcerated for non-violent drug crime – conveniently intact'.[70] This is obviously in the interests of those who profit from imprisonment because, if government began to address root causes, the number of people going to prison would decrease, and private corrections companies' share prices would fall.

Overall, connecting profits to punishment means that there will be less incentive to reduce rates of incarceration and enormous private resources will be mobilised to ensure that prison policy does not deviate from a policy that continues to enrich private interests.[71] For Shichor, even the potential 'for conflict between the social interests to reduce prison population, and the financial interests of private correctional corporations to increase it' is too much. He warns that 'The logic and nature of corporations further the consistent drive toward expansion and they will build a growth factor into the correctional system'.[72]

———

The prevailing logic of neoliberalism has left little of public life unaffected. As this chapter has shown, there has been an extraordinary experiment with prison privatisation across the globe. It is a process that has benefited both corporations and governments, but it is questionable whether these benefits extend to the community more broadly and to the outcomes of incarceration more precisely. Communities worldwide have been promised the possibility of cheap, high-quality solutions to incarceration through privatisation, but the outcomes have fallen well short. The privatisation of prisons connects punishment with profit, and although many argue that the sentence and the administration of that sentence can be separated, this is a problematic assumption not supported by verifiable evidence.

In particular, the idea that profits can be derived from punishment presents our society with a considerable ethical dilemma. Those opposed to such a relationship have often couched this opposition in terms of the superiority of the state over the private sector. The difficulty with this argument is that public prison systems are also riddled with problems and, thus, a debate that centres on the provider can fail to analyse the role of prisons and punishment within society. Raising the issue of 'ethical accountability' creates a level of complexity that can be confusing and messy, but considering such issues can lead to deeper considerations of the inequities that operate within our societies and the impact these have on criminality. Ethical accountability also highlights the prejudices that are institutionalised and the effect this has on how we define deviance and illegality, the alienation experienced within post-industrial society, and the ways that power operates to define the parameters of the acceptable and unacceptable. It is in this way that punishment is both a social expression and an instrument of social control, wherein discussions about the role of the state in sentence administration can be a distraction from the deeper issues of economic, political and social influence. Unfortunately, this experiment with privatisation appears to have provided a vehicle for such distraction.

The expeditions of private capital into areas that have been off limits, such as prisons, are indicative of the crises that face the expansionist imperative of capitalism in economies that are no longer industrially oriented. As capital looks for places to grow, public sector services are a logical focus, with prisons not left out of this process. What we do know is that, although cost and quality are important, the motivation to produce profits from prison services has been more of a problem than an innovation. If there is enough money to provide a mental health worker to a prison such as the Santa Fe County Jail, why would we choose instead to give this public money to a private shareholder? If we do choose this in the hope that it will create cost-effective and high-quality prisons, we need to remember the Tyson Johnsons of this world and just how different things may have been had public money been spent on public need.

LAST THOUGHTS, PRIMARY RESPONSIBILITIES

The proper role of government is to create certainty in the market and maintain a clear distinction between compulsory regulation and voluntary action.

(Director General of the Confederation of British Industry, *The Guardian*, 27 Aug 2008)

Although there may be many examples of critical, highly costly market failures which might seem to justify Western governments rolling back the marketisation of public services, there is no evidence that these governments are preparing to return to a form of governing which had been regarded as conclusively discredited. The resilience of the market discourse and its political appeal to parties show few signs of abating. This was confirmed yet again by the election of Nicolas Sarkozy as president of France in 2007 on a platform of neoliberal reform, and the New South Wales government's attempts in 2007 and 2008 to privatise parts of the state-owned electricity industry.

Globalisation, as a willing accomplice, can only but accentuate and sustain this political urge which has become a maxim of government. The growing demand for public services places governments under ever greater political pressure to find quick solutions, which the private sector has shown itself to be especially adept at providing. Thus, the overcrowding of existing gaols in most Western states has, and will, make private provision of these services ever more attractive to governments. In Britain, where prison numbers have grown faster than any other period in recent years, the Justice Secretary Jack Straw announced in 2007 the building with private involvement of three 'super prisons' which would house another 7500 prisoners, allowing British prisons to accommodate 96 000 prisoners by 2014.

In the absence of either a catastrophic economic or political crisis that threatens the future of all, it is unlikely that governments will revoke their commitment to, and faith in, markets, no matter the problems encountered in the meantime. However many market failures may occur, of themselves, either individually or as a mounting body of evidence, it is unlikely that they will be sufficient to dislodge the hold that markets have on many governments. The ideological intransigence of government was notable for Margaret Cook who, reviewing Allyson Pollock's highly critical study of the increasing private sector involvement in Britain's National Health Service, observed how with further privatisation:

> New Labour leaders know that they are defying evidence and sense in
> their obsessive commitment to market policies. Why else would they
> go to such lengths to falsify evidence, use manipulative techniques
> and, when all else fails, to threaten and intimidate to carry their will?[1]

For some observers, the crisis with the necessary severity to shake government confidence in market solutions arrived with the collapse of the American sub-prime mortgage market in 2007 and the subsequent financial fall-out which rapidly spread across the globe. Jonathan Freedland believes that this has fully and fatally exposed the weakness of the neoliberal mission and the barrenness of its philosophy of unlimited selfish gain, surely leaving supposedly non-conservative governments no alternative but to turn away and regain their senses.[2] Martin Wolf in Britain's *Financial Times* feared that the weaknesses which were being exposed in the financial system, not the least of which was the ability of a small privileged group of insiders to gain huge rewards without any apparent constraints, would threaten 'the political legitimacy of the market economy'.[3] If the market economy was in serious trouble, Freedland concluded, then the ideology upon which it depended for its influence 'should be on life support'.[4]

Keynes and his state-derived prescriptions for economic and social well-being may not have been as misguided as economists and their fellow travellers have resolutely and impatiently maintained. Even the usually ultra-liberal International Monetary Fund has recently advocated that governments be more proactive in the use of fiscal rather than monetary policy, and be less obsessed with balancing their budgets. The dramatic and confronting nature of this apparently softened view of the role of the state at this time of economic crisis was further reinforced in January 2008 when President Bush called upon Congress to provide US$150 billion to energise and reassure the American economy.

Despite the opportunity for a comprehensive crisis in confidence in market solutions which the sub-prime crisis has presented, there have been few signs that a tectonic shift in government policies will occur. The political costs of moving away from the market as the authoritative arbiter of what is good and in the public interest now have become too high, especially for non-conservative governments which, in an endeavour to shift to the centre and gain power, have felt compelled to adopt conservative remedies and market philosophies. Adopting some of the policies of the conservative side of politics both confuses the conservative opposition and broadens electoral appeal by signalling centrist intentions. Most famously, the British Labour Party cut its ties with its socialist past and refashioned itself as New Labour to achieve government after 18 years out of office. This was symbolised in the party's revocation in 1995, two years before they came to power, of clause IV of its constitution, which demanded the common ownership of the main means of production and which many in the party saw as the reason why it had been kept out of government for so long. The market reform credentials of New Labour were greatly enhanced once in office when it gave the Bank of England its independence, thereby allowing it to regulate interest rates free from overt, direct political control. The Hawke and Keating Labor governments in Australia were noted for a similar break from their party's left-leaning past, often using privatisation as the means to re-define the role and expectations of government, even though the newly found market priorities of these governments were bitterly opposed within their own party.

The historical difficulties of non-conservative political parties in gaining office means that once in government they will, if necessary, avoid whenever possible any intimation that their commitment to dominant market values and disciplines may be faltering, whether this be a tendency to intrude in the affairs of private businesses or to support the disadvantaged too readily. Governments are fearful of the impact on their political credibility of any signals that might infer that neoliberalism's attractions may have lost their appeal. Prime Minister Gordon Brown, decries Polly Toynbee, will not proclaim his supposed strong attachment to social justice, choking on the words 'as if they would cause his political death'. There is a 'deliberate refusal to be defined'.[5]

Conservative governments have no such political insecurities, having always represented those whose interests are most closely identified with and advanced by an unfettered market. Without the need continually to justify themselves and convince others in a market society of their commitment to minimal government and market values, conservatives are able to use the supposedly discredited priorities and allegiances of their opponent's past as ideological cudgels to ensure that political debates and priorities remain fixed on the very principles which define and favour conservative politics. The delay of the Brown government, until mid-February 2008, in announcing the inevitable nationalisation of the troubled bank Northern Rock was widely seen as a recognition by the government that their Conservative opponents would use this to try and destroy Labour's market credentials. 'After years of crying wolf', reminded *The Daily Telegraph*, the Conservatives 'will now be hoping that the charge sticks', that Labour after all were not to be trusted with the economy.[6]

For political parties to do other than confirm their commitment to market values may jeopardise their political futures by implying that they are seeking the return of discredited and failed rivals. The British Conservative leader David Cameron made it very clear in the first days of 2008 that his party's allegiances were still primarily with the market by promising to introduce greater choice and private sector 'rigour' into Britain's National Health Service.[7] While strongly supporting its importance to Britain and his party's commitment to preserving its role, he rejected the presumption that doctors and nurses should be motivated by a public sector ethos rather than by the values of the market.

Market hegemony has become so securely embedded in political and social identities that any attempt to undermine this nexus is perceived as threatening the well-being of both individuals and the social collective, and a fatuous, ignorant rejection of beliefs that have become for the most part beyond question. Unlike the welfare state after World War II which has increasingly come to be seen as an historical aberration rather than a natural historical consequence of the evolution of modern society, the market state has successfully been projected as founded on an eternal and unvarying set of principles which can innately, reliably and profitably adapt to any new circumstances and demands. Albeit with contemporary fine-tunings, neoliberals feel emboldened in their claims that history has consistently proven that society gains the most from new challenges when it places its full confidence in the market, when individuals are allowed to do what they believe is best for them without denying others the same opportunities. They refer to societies which have been the most developed and the most enduring as those which have been heavily reliant upon trade and traders – that is the market. Into the twenty-first century this symbiosis between prosperity and political power, between the market and economic development, if not immediately social well-being, is for the neoliberal again irrefutably demonstrated by the meteoric rise of China and India, despite their very different political forms.

With both sides of politics committed to the market either by fundamental, historical conviction or more recent political necessity, there is little chance in normal circumstances of any threat appearing to market hegemony. Of course this does not mean that the priorities and programs of both sides of politics will remain rigidly determined by present circumstances. Any change that is likely to occur, however, will be contained by the political necessity of remaining faithful to the precepts of the market state. The resilience of the attractions of the market values of neoliberalism, despite a growing sense of gloom about the state of the world economy, was dramatically attested in 2007 in the most unlikely place, Sweden, which has otherwise epitomised the avowed social and economic benefits of a strong and generous welfare state. In 2006, the Social Democratic Party, after governing for 61 of the previous 70 years, was removed from office by the right-leaning four-party Alliance for Sweden. The 'smaller government' policies of the Alliance party are intended to bring about the shrinking of the welfare state and a reduction in the high income taxes for which Sweden had been famous, and upon which their welfare, consensus, social democratic state had depended.

To address the current high rates of unemployment in Sweden, the new Alliance government will provide incentives for employers to create jobs while unemployment benefits are to be drastically reduced from the long-standing level of 80 per cent of former income to compel the able-bodied to seek work. Business taxes will also be reduced and employers will be no longer expected to contribute directly to sickness benefits. Most controversially, the new government is also to embark on a concerted program of privatising Sweden's 57 state enterprises. Starting with six of the largest state companies, the government is to sell Nordea (Sweden's largest bank), Telia (a telecommunications company), and Vasacronan (a property company). These are to be followed, though not finally, by Vin & Sprit (the highly profitable maker of the iconic Absolut vodka) and OMX (the owner of the Swedish stock exchange). The Swedish airline, SAS, however, has proven to be a privatisation too sensitive for the present. Apart from the immediate financial gains from privatisation, its supporters have also referred to the uncompetitive impediments under which these companies have been forced to operate, not the least of which were their more stringent public accountability requirements. For those who vigorously oppose these privatisations, the government is betraying the Swedish state model by imperilling the very foundation of its cohesive and fair society.

In the final stages of writing this book, the New South Wales Labor government in Australia has also shown itself prepared to embrace the more contentious aspects of neoliberalism by deciding to privatise electricity distribution. Fully aware of the controversy that their decision would provoke, and that it had been considered and refused by a previous conservative, pro-market government, the Labor government promoted its privatisation plans in December 2007 as a means by which additional energy resources would be provided without any cost to the taxpayer. While key electricity generation assets, and others, are to be retained by the state, electricity generators owned by the government will be leased to private operators. Customers will be protected, at least until 2013, by regulated prices until the government can be assured that competitive markets are operating and jobs will be preserved in the public sector electricity generation sector of the economy. As this book has demonstrated, the reasons given to justify this change in policy have been shown on many previous occasions to be either convincingly discredited or exposed as flagrant and irresponsible exaggerations of more moderate expectations. Past failures, however, are no impediment to the market plans of the next government.

As several of the case studies in this book have shown, should a market failure occur in services that have been relinquished to the private sector, rather than allowing this to question the underlying principle of private delivery the most usual response is to blame the way in which the change was implemented. Done differently, it is argued, the problems that arose could be avoided. The result is to deflect attention and criticism from the practice or principle to the reform process, and to provide the opportunity for another private sector provider to enter, if they can be found, to redeem the situation. However, with past failures still fresh in mind, with the government possibly shaken by the ever-mounting financial cost of failure and on the brink of resuming the service, and traumatised by the spectre of a political denouement, this time a new provider may only be obtained by the government providing additional, highly lucrative and far more expensive inducements. The few large companies who may be the only possible contenders to assume the responsibilities of a failed private sector service provider will be aware of the government's plight, and be able to negotiate terms which ensure that concern for the public interest will be sacrificed to the possibility of great gain for many years to come.

Not only will potential suitors require considerable financial rewards but, wherever possible, they will insist that government legislates to protect their income stream. Operating protections and guarantees are especially attractive to prospective entrants. In the case of Metronet, the private company which had been contracted to refurbish part of the London Underground, the taxpayer was to provide £17 billion of guaranteed funding over a period of 30 years. Protections in the form of guaranteed minimal levels of revenue are a favourite ploy of the private firms in Australia who build and operate new toll motorways. Protections provided by government for private sector service providers could take also the form of very large, ongoing subsidies, as with the British railways and its nuclear power industry, which may eventually far outstrip the costs that were one of the original reasons for privatisation.

The case of the nuclear power industry in Britain is perhaps the epitome of how far governments are prepared to allow the public to be held hostage to both a government's political beliefs and to the unlimited self-interest of private corporations which have demanded that government assume all liabilities for decommissioning and associated costs. The important thing for governments is that the largesse shown toward private partners allows them to keep their ideological integrity intact and to avoid resuming responsibility for the service. To be seen to retreat in one case of failure, irrespective of the financial and social costs of persisting, may be sufficient to allow political opponents to question convincingly the government's commitment to reform and to market values and that, after all, in the case of non-conservative governments the espoused conversion to the market was indeed a sham.

From the market society to the good society?

At the commencement of this work, we mentioned concerns expressed about the social consequences of the marketisation of the state, in particular the mounting apprehension about the perceived breakdown in social institutions and civil values leading to greater violence, uncertainty and fear. These concerns have been increasingly expressed both within government, leading to new legislation, and by opposition parties possibly sensing a changing mood amongst voters. The British Conservative Party in 2007 referred to Britain as a 'broken society', a society in which gun crime was becoming endemic, drug and alcohol abuse widespread and the youth alienated from society.[8] For the American historian and social commentator Gertrude Himmelfarb:

> it is not enough to say that if only the failed welfare policies are abandoned and the resources of the free market released, economic growth and incentives will break the cycle of dependency and produce stable families. There is an element of truth in this view, but not the entire truth, for it underestimates the moral and cultural dimension of the problem ... such an economy does not automatically produce the moral and social goods that they value.[9]

The market society has brought improved material well-being to many, but it may have come at the expense of the 'good society' in which all citizens are able to live their lives pursuing their own best interests, but never at the expense of the well-being of the social collective. The ideal of the good life requires each to give to others in order to be able to live fully. A society which regards itself as fair, just and civilised, warn Davidson and Davidson, cannot be sustained if the well-being of some sectors is protected by denying others a share in the economic gains, for to 'base social prosperity on the hardship of others is a barbaric philosophy of government'.[10] As prominent British

Labour politicians Cruddas and Trickett observe, while certainly the economy and its health is very important:

> a tendency to prioritise the market inverts the principal point of social democracy – to ensure society is the master and that social justice and cohesion are our objectives. Left uncontrolled, the market leads to the growth of inequality and social recession across all classes.[11]

Such a need to reinvigorate the social sphere, to mitigate some of the excesses of market values, was harnessed by the Australian Labor Party while in opposition prior to the federal elections in 2007, by the Conservative Party in Britain in the same period as it sought to destabilise the New Labour prime minister, and by the Democratic Party in the United States seeking to capture the presidency in 2008. Changes in policy direction which the new British prime minister, Gordon Brown, began to signal in 2007 were for Cruddas and Trickett a sign that the government was 'stepping away from the failed policy of marketisation of public services' and seeking instead to develop policies that which will lead to the 'Good Society'.[12]

Irrespective of this optimism, prompted as it is by a litany of startling failures which might have forced governments to have second thoughts about their primary responsibilities, there is no sign that this will ever return public sector involvement in service delivery to previous levels in the foreseeable future. Indeed, even when the market may seem to falter and disappoint, the long periods of relentless gains in some areas and the strong, undiminished upward historical economic trajectory of advanced and emerging states are sufficient for fervent neoliberals to remind doubters that governments will always be of secondary importance when compared to the contributions of markets.

Democratic deficit in the market state

The commodification of the democratic rights of individuals associated with the rise of the market state in major liberal democracies is a paradox of increasing concern. Individual citizens have been assured that they must not fear the opportunity to exercise their greater freedom of choice which the marketisation of state has made possible. However, this greater choice has come with conditions: all are to be watched and controlled as they exercise this choice. The unfettered behaviour which the robust individualism of the market state seeks cannot be allowed to provide some individuals or organisations with the ability to endanger the freedoms of others.

As each individual exercises invigorated opportunities to pursue their own interests, Robert Putnam observed, there is the tendency to become more suspicious of similarly selfish others and, in the process, to become increasingly socially isolated and disengaged.[13] This has been greatly exacerbated by the culture of fear that Australian, American and British governments, amongst many, have methodically created in response to the attack of September 2001. Many of the rights of citizens, and even their representatives, have been significantly eroded, often without the opportunity for citizens to affect the process. Professing their only interest to be the welfare of individual citizens, governments have assumed powers in their 'war on terror' which have never been permitted outside times of war. As a consequence, the right of individuals to enjoy, without the fear of an intimidating state presence, the liberty which the democratic state is meant to preserve and protect has been one of the first casualties of the culture of fear which now pervades much of Western societies. If individuals can no longer depend on their fellow citizens to come unconditionally to their aid when in need or to behave in a manner which does not preclude a concern for others as a primary motive for their behaviour, then apprehensive, anxious citizens will be more willing to allow their governments greater powers to step into the social void. Hence, the explosion of surveillance and security checks in public places, with Britain providing an especially extreme example of the extent to which this might be taken.

Saturated surveillance of everyday life in Britain through the promiscuous use of CCTV and authorised phone tapping is now so extensive and accepted in public and private spaces that Britain is now referred to as the 'surveillance society', a term normally associated with totalitarian regimes. In 2005 a Home Office report found that there were over four million public and privately operated sur-veillance cameras in Britain, more than any other country.[14] Grow-ing concern about the possibility that information collected could be networked and centralised to be used by the state prompted a further investigation, this time by the House of Commons Home Affairs Committee which reported in 2008.[15] So extensive has this intrusion become in the lives of the ordinary citizen in Britain and America that many fear that both countries risk becoming police states, that indeed the pre-conditions for this are already in place. A report by the British Interception of Communications Commis-sioner noted that, on average, more than 1000 applications were made each day throughout 2006 to allow government agencies at all levels to intercept private communications.[16] This level of intru-sion represented a very significant increase on previous years. The leader of the British Liberal Democratic Party, Nick Clegg, warned in parliament that with this level of monitoring and with '1 million innocent people on the Government's DNA database; and 5000 schools now fingerprinting our children at school' the government 'have turned the British public into the most spied upon on the planet ... The Prime Minister seems to see no limits. He is creating a surveillance state.'[17]

In reply, Prime Minister Gordon Brown, relying on the potency of the terrorist image, reminded his opponents that they also 'support CCTV. I take it that they support the intercept action that is taken when it is necessary for national security.' Mindful of mounting con-cerns about the level of surreptitious state intrusion, he argued that the people 'in this country are reassured by the presence of CCTV ... That is one very important part of the investigatory and surveil-lance powers that we give the police to carry out their work.' He then gave the passing, and none-too-convincing, assurance that 'We are taking the steps to protect the liberties of the citizens'.

In his support for ever-greater levels of electronic monitoring, Brown still felt the need to recognise that no matter how much gov-ernments may refer to their citizens as consumers in other contexts and allude to the importance of efficiency and the contributions of the market to the well-being of individuals and society, the limits of a government's responsibilities to its citizens are far more extensive than delivery performance. Those who seek to soften the selfish drive of markets and the intolerant preoccupation of markets with economic values emphasise equity in dealings with their government derived from the rights of citizenship rather than from economic capability and aptitude.

However, as suggested in Brown's responses to concerns over the creation of the 'surveillance state', in a world where the self rules it is possible for democratic processes to become almost irrelevant to the common good and for this to be promoted as a necessary, indeed, essential condition. Without this feature, argues Krugman, the hegemonic success of the neo-conservatives in the United States since the Reagan presidency would not have been possible: 'Movement conservatism has been antidemocratic, with an attraction to authoritarianism, from the beginning ... The antidemocratic, authoritarian attitude has never gone away.'[18]

Thus, with Friedrich Hayek opposed to anything which might deflect the operation and intentions of the market, it is possibly not surprising that he is highly suspicious of the benefits of majority decision making in democracies. Indeed, Hayek believes that modern democracies are weakened by the flawed process of consultation, deliberation and negotiation upon which democracy itself depends. Instead, this openness militates against 'good' law.[19] Hayek prefers a 'democracy' which provides for considered responses by those best qualified to make decisions on behalf of others – that is a select group who do not have to be elected.[20] Of course for the resulting legislation to be regarded as worthwhile it must be entirely informed by the needs of the free market. To ensure that legislation results from a long gestation period of mature reflection free from partisan political pressures, Hayek further advocates both restricting voting eligibility and establishing an elite legislature which remains in power for periods of up to 15 years. This would provide its members with the freedom they needed to respond more to their consciences and less to the interest groups, for whom market values are not everything, bent on capture.[21] Not only does this iconoclasm betray an authoritarian naivety common to many neoliberal theorists, its prescription for government contains the seeds of the very form of society which Hayek and others set out to supplant with market relationships.

The public choice theorist Gordon Tullock takes the need to refashion society along undemocratic lines even further by using the coercive powers of government to suggest, in order to reduce the supposedly deleterious consequences of bureaucratic self-interest, that public bureaucrats should not be entitled to vote.[22] This strategy of disenfranchisement and contempt for participative democracy, which Tullock concedes will make him a target of ridicule, has the professed advantage of reducing the ability of public servants to influence resource allocation decisions which favour them at the expense of the public whom they are meant to serve. Perversely, to disenfranchise them is a statement of the sanctity of the public interest. Suggestions such as these could be discounted easily as the harmless musings of a disaffected or scorned theorist if it were not that public choice theory, developed by Tullock with Buchanan and Hayek's ideas, has been so influential. This darker side of neoliberalism has yet to be fully appreciated.

———

That partnerships between governments and the private sector can be of great value cannot be doubted. Governments have rightly recognised that there is much that markets can do better, and should be allowed to do so. The discipline, initiative, innovation and commitment which are the sources of success for businesses can also be harnessed to the public benefit in the delivery of public services. What is now much less certain is that the private sector will *always* be best, that the presumption should always be in favour of the market.

The more extreme supporters of the market refuse to acknowledge that there will ever be a public service for which markets are not the best means of provision. They continue to seek to intrude markets and the private sector wherever a profitable advantage might be obtained. Indeed, as the options for privatisation have shrunk from state-owned corporations to the core or essential services which have figured prominently in this book, many of which are natural monopolies, the private sector sees even greater opportunity for profit. Perversely, serious past problems are construed as an advantage for those promoting further privatisations.

Thus, irrespective of the many serious privatisation failures, the Adam Smith Institute, a right-wing think-tank, has advocated that it is now time, after learning from these experiences, for government and the business sector to 'revive' the momentum for privatisation in core public services.[23] Apparently, with the problems of the past out of the way, the future can only be bright for privatisation. The lessons learnt from past problems will ensure that any future privatisations will be far more successful and, accordingly, that there is no reason now to quarantine services previously seen as beyond private control.

If governments are able to resist these more extreme demands for absolute private sector control of core public services, they can still take advantage of the many valuable contributions of the private sector in the delivery of even the most critical public services. But this must be in a close working relationship with government, with all the consequent accountabilities to government and to the public. This will allow the public to benefit from the significant combined strengths of private and public participants and to be reassured that while the profit motive may save tax-payers' money, this would never be at the cost of the public interest.

NOTES

Preface

1 Feigenbaum et al 1999, p 2.
2 See 'Power brokers', *The Australian*, 2 June 2008.
3 See eg Cahill and Beder 2005, pp 5–22; Argy 1998.

1 The state under siege

1 Hutton 1995, p 12.
2 Hutton 2002, p 12.
3 Cruddas and Trickett, *The Guardian*, 30 October 2007, p 30.
4 *The Guardian*, 22 January 2008, p 28.
5 *Daily Mail*, 24 August 2007, p 6.
6 Hutton 2002.
7 Hibou 2004, p vii.
8 See eg Harvey 2007.
9 Francis Fukuyama, 'Bring back the state', *The Observer*, 4 July 2004.
10 Kain 1996–97, p 5.
11 HV Evatt Research Centre 1988, p 16.
12 Crowley 1973, p 432.
13 See Lucio et al 1997 for an examination of public concern which influenced the British government's decision to abandon their first attempt at the privatisation of the Royal Mail in 1994.

14 Greenaway 1996, p 20.
15 Reserve Bank of Australia 1997, p 9.
16 Reserve Bank 1997, pp 8–9.
17 National Commission of Audit 1996, p v.
18 Victorian Public Accounts and Estimates Committee 2006, p 19.
19 See eg John Howard, Commonwealth Parliamentary Debates, House of Representatives, 13 April 1989 and the House of Commons Select Committee on Transport 1995, 'Second Report of the Transport Committee on the Privatisation of National Air Traffic Services'.
20 See eg *The Guardian*, 27 July 2007, p 31; 12 September 2007, p 30.
21 Savas 1982, p 118.
22 Offe, quoted in Giddens 2000, p 56.
23 Bank of England, speech by Governor Mervyn King to the British Bankers Association, 10 June 2008, p 2.
24 Peters 1998, p 55.
25 *The Times*, 30 August 2007, p 33.
26 See eg *The Guardian*, 30 May 2007, 'Society guardian', p 3.
27 See eg the House of Commons Select Committee on Transport 1995.
28 House of Commons Select Committee on Transport 1995, p xv (emphasis in original).
29 See eg the Victorian Public Accounts and Estimates Committee 2006.
30 Giddens 2000, p 51.
31 Whitfield 1992, p 3.
32 Hayek 1979, p 63.
33 Tullock 1970, p 30.
34 Jones 1989, p 9; Brown 1993, p 111.
35 Friedman 1962; Hayek 1945.
36 Hutton 1995, preface and p 18.
37 UNICEF 2007.
38 *The Guardian*, 14 February 2007, p 1.
39 *The Guardian*, 14 February 2007, pp 1–2.
40 *The Daily Telegraph*, 12 February 2007, p 1.
41 See eg the House of Commons Select Committee on Transport 1995.
42 *The Guardian*, 13 October 2006, p 37.
43 Hutton 1997; Hobsbawm, quoted in Emy 1998, p 31.
44 Giddens 2000, p 36.
45 Clarke and Pitelis 1993, pp 5, 6.
46 Jackson and Price 1994, p 16.
47 See eg the House of Commons Select Committee on Transport 1995.
48 *The Guardian*, 6 December 2006, p 10.
49 NSW Auditor-General 1994; see also Chesterfield-Evans, NSW Parliamentary Debates, Legislative Council, 20 October 2005.
50 Burnie Port Authority v General Jones Pty Ltd (1994), 179 CLR 520 at 551.
51 Peters 1998, p 52.
52 Klein 2007, pp 295–98.
53 Feigenbaum 1999, p 82 and note p 85.

54 Pierson 1996, p 110.

2 'The benevolence of the butcher': self-interest vs public interest

1   Buchan 2007, p 90.
2   Greenspan, quoted in Buchan 2007, p 2.
3   Klein 2007, p 117.
4   Brereton and Temple 1999, p 458.
5   Dilley 1992, pp 21–22.
6   Smith 1966, pt 2, section 2, chapter 2.
7   Mill 1982, p 72.
8   Hayek 1960, p 20.
9   See Buchanan, in Finn 2006, p 17.
10 Mill 1942, p 18.
11 See Arblaster 1984, p 239; Dewey 1963, pp 7, 8.
12 Smith, quoted in O'Driscoll 1979, p 28.
13 Tucker, quoted in Hayek 1969, p 7.
14 De Mandeville 1724, vol xlvi, *The Grumbling Hive*.
15 Tully 1993, pp 75–76; see also Hayek 1969, p 4.
16 Hayek 1973, p 3.
17 Hayek 1976, pp 12, 13.
18 See eg Hayek 1979, p 132; 1960, pp 11, 20; 1969, pp 16–17; Friedman 1962, p 4.
19 Proponents of the market have been less forthcoming about the tendency of economic power to concentrate and the effects of this, including the increased political access this economic power affords.
20 Butler 1985.
21 Mill 1891, p 570 (emphasis added).
22 Hobhouse 1919; Milton and Rose Friedman 1980, p 2.
23 Friedman, quoted in Finn 2006, p 15.
24 Friedman 1962, p 3; although neoliberals insist on the amorality of the market they are prone to use arguments of morality, such as favoured by Friedman, to support their case.
25 Spencer, quoted in Girvetz 1963, p 76.
26 Buchanan, quoted in Finn 2006, p 16.
27 Jackson and Price 1994, pp 2 and 4.
28 De Mandeville 1724, vol xlvi, *The Grumbling Hive*.
29 Keynes 1972, pp 284 and 288.
30 Friedman 1980, p 5.
31 Nevile 1998, p 175.
32 Hayek 1979, p 46.
33 Clarke and Pitelis 1993, pp 1 and 6.
34 Jackson and Price 1994, p 16; Hutton 1995, p 12.
35 See Veljanovski 1988, p 29.

36   *The Sunday Times Magazine*, 4 November 2007, p 51.

37   *The Times*, 20 October 2007, p 37.

38   *The Guardian*, 14 and 16 October 2007.

39   *The Sunday Times*, 11 November 2007, News Review, p 10.

40   Child 1998, p 246; Finn 2006, p 62.

41   Monbiot, *The Guardian*, 23 October 2007, p 31.

42   Arrow 1993, p 260.

43   Latham 1998, p 38.

44   Smith 1966, bk 1, ch 10, pt 2.

45   *The Guardian*, 29 November 2007, p 26.

46   See *The Daily Telegraph*, 8 September 2007, p 8.

47   See Smith in Buchan 2007, p 94.

48   Smith 1900, bk 1, ch 11, pt 3.

49   Smith 1900, bk 4, pt 2, ch 9.

50   Friedman and Friedman 1975, pp 28 and 120; see also Hayek 1979, p 83.

51   Vebleen, quoted in Miliband 1969, p 70.

52   Harvey 2007.

53   Harvey 2007, pp 16 and 19.

54   Cahill and Beder 2005, pp 5–22.

55   Spencer 1970, p 146.

56   *Financial Times*, 2 February 2008, p 4.

57   House of Lords Science and Technology Committee 2007, p 7.

58   House of Lords Science and Technology Committee 2007, p 7.

59   On the effects of the US legislation on UK gaming companies see *The Guardian*, 30 August, 2007.

60   See Arblaster 1984, p 14; Brown 1993, p 109.

61   Friedman and Friedman 1975, p 1.

62   Paine 1969, p 90.

63   Smith 1900, pt 2, section 2, ch 3.

64   Buchanan, quoted in Marginson 1992, p 47.

65   Buchanan, quoted in Zafirovsky 2001, p 671.

66   Aquinas, quoted in O'Toole 2006, p 21.

67   Fukuyama 2000, p 6.

68   Gordon Brown, speech, 25 October 2007, University of Westminster, <www.number-10.gov.uk>.

69   Hobhouse 1960, pp 27 and 29.

70   Quoted in Lane 1996, p 37.

71   Fukuyama 1995, p 150; Emy 1998, p 28; Rawls 1972, p 73.

72   See Dewey in Ryn 1978, p 17.

73   Ryn 1978, pp 82–83.

74   Sandel 1996, pp 11–14 and 16.

75   Aquinas, quoted in D'Entreves 1967, p 223.

76   Bentham 1871, p 95.

77   See Hobhouse 1960, p 61; Chapman and Hunt 1987, p 24.

78   Hobhouse 1960, p 133.

79   Giddens 2000, p 33.

80 Marginson 1992, p 3.
81 Saul 1993, p 335.
82 O'Toole 2006, p 2.
83 Smith 1900, pt 2, section 2, ch 2.
84 Smith 1900, pt 1, section 1, ch 1.
85 Fukuyama 2000, p 14; Chomsky 1999, p 11.
86 Barber 1983, p 102.
87 *The Guardian*, 22 August 2007, p 12.
88 Okun 1975, p 13.
89 Hutton 1995, pp xii and 15.
90 See eg Drucker 1969, p 205; Smith 1998, p 52; Dunleavy 1991, p 154; Barberis 1998, p 454.
91 Zafirovski 2001, p 669.
92 Buchanan and Musgrave 2000, p 217.
93 Tullock et al 2000, p 11 (emphasis added).
94 Downs 1967; see also Dunleavy 1991, pp 148–50.
95 Zafirovsky 2001, p 683.
96 Quoted in Zafirovsky 2001, p 677.
97 Kettl 1988, p 13; see also Stretton and Orchard 1994, ch 5.
98 March and Olsen 1995, p 5.
99 Plato, quoted in O'Toole 2006, p 3.
100 Brereton and Temple 1999, p 456.
101 House of Commons Public Administration Select Committee 2002, p 5.
102 House of Commons Public Administration Select Committee 2002, p 13.
103 Godwin 1971, p 14.
104 Fukuyama 1995, p 270; Rousseau 1930, p 17.
105 *The Guardian*, 30 April 2007, p 27.
106 O'Toole 2006, p 9.
107 Kemp 1998, pp 7 and 9.
108 See eg Australia's Financial Management and Accountability Act (Cwth), section 44.
109 O'Faircheallaigh et al 1999, p 153.
110 Walsh 1995, p 199.
111 See eg Hutton 1995, p 5.
112 Grimshaw et al 2002, p 480.
113 Cook and Levy 1990, p 2.
114 Saul 1993, p 407.
115 See the Report of the Royal Commission of Australian Government Administration 1976; Wilenski 1977; O'Faircheallaigh et al 1999, p 23.

3 The 'proper' ends of government

1 Mill 1909, p 796.
2 Rousseau 1930, p 73.
3 Ofgem, press pelease, 25 January 2008; Ofgem, *Debt and Disconnection Best*

Practice Review, 25 January 2008.

4   Constitution of the Commonwealth of Australia, section 51.

5   Paine, quoted in Bramsted and Melhuish 1978, p 195.

6   Dunleavy and O'Leary 1987, p 1.

7   Mill 1942, p 5.

8   Quoted in Vincent 1994, p 80.

9   This view of constitutions informed much of AV Dicey's work.

10 British legislation included the Education Acts of 1870 and 1880; Public Health Acts of 1866, 1872 and 1875; the Disease Prevention Act of 1883; Joint Stock Companies Act of 1844; Companies Clauses Consolidation Act of 1845; Limited Liability Acts of 1855 and 1856; and the Joint Stock Companies Act of 1862.

11 The term 'invisible hand' appears only three times in *The Wealth of Nations*.

12 HV Evatt Research Centre 1988, pp 17–18.

13 The line was completed in 1917: Crowley 1973, p 192.

14 Crowley 1973, pp 376–77.

15 Cited by Crowley 1973, p 181.

16 Fukuyama 1992.

17 See eg senior Australian Labor politician Lindsay Tanner, National Press Club, Canberra, 8 August 2007.

18 *The Daily Telegraph*, 8 May 2007, p 5.

19 Hayek 1979, p 125; 1969, p 11.

20 Locke 1884, bk 5, ch 1, pt 2.

21 Ryan 1993, p 293; Marginson 1992, p 56; Tully 1993, p 76.

22 Spencer 1969, p 18.

23 Jefferson, quoted in Friedman and Friedman 1980, p 4.

24 Mill 1909, p 947.

25 Mill 1909, p 804.

26 Spencer 1970, p 311.

27 Nozick 1974, p ix; 1993, p 285; For observations by Chamberlain see Crabtree and Thirlwell 1993, p 57.

28 Soros 2000; Bank of England, speech by Governor Mervyn King to the British Bankers Association, 10 June 2008, p 2.

29 Wolf, *Financial Times*, 15 January 2008, 'Regulators should intervene in bankers' pay'.

30 *The Guardian*, 11 August 2007, p 36; also 10 August 2007, p 29; *Daily Telegraph*, 21 August 2007, p B7.

31 *The Guardian*, 23 October 2007, p 31.

32 Crabtree and Thirlwell 1993, p 52; Buchanan and Wagner 1977, pp 69 and 73.

33 Friedman 1980, p 29.

34 Mill 1891, pp 479–80; Girvetz 1963, p 72.

35 Skidelsky 2003, p 367; Keynes 1972, p 291.

36 Mill 1909, p 796; and see p 800 for the essential functions of government.

37 Galbraith 1963, p 28.

38 Tony Blair, quoted in *The Guardian*, 'Leader', 24 June 2004.

39 Mill 1891, pp 482 and 590.

40 *The Guardian*, 10 September 2007, p 7.

41 Contracting out, where the service is owned by the state but provided by a private contractor, was commended by Mill 1909, p 963 who advocated this for canals and railways.

42 *The Canberra Times*, 1 August 1998; 1 November 1998.

43 NSW Auditor General 2002.

44 HM Treasury, *PFI: Meeting the Investment Challenge*, July 2003, p 19.

45 Victorian Public Accounts and Estimates Committee 2006, pp 30 and 39.

46 Victorian Public Accounts and Estimates Committee 2006, p 13; and 2003, p 7.

47 Victorian Public Accounts and Estimates Committee 2006, pp 43–44.

48 UNISON 2001.

49 Victorian Public Accounts and Estimates Committee 2006, p 18.

50 Monbiot, *The Guardian*, 4 September 2007, p 29.

51 See eg Chesterfield-Evans, NSW Parliament, Legislative Council, 20 October 2005.

52 Kayee Griffin, NSW Parliament, Legislative Council, 20 October 2005; Christine Robertson, 13 October 2005.

53 Grimshaw et al 2002.

54 Monbiot, *The Guardian*, 30 November 2004.

55 National Audit Office 2008b.

56 Victorian Public Accounts Committee and Estimates Committee 2006, p 20.

57 Weber 1947, p 186.

58 Rawls 1995, p 73.

59 Prior et al 1995, pp 48–49; Moe 1994, p 114.

60 House of Commons Home Affairs Committee 2008, p 38.

61 Johnston 1995, p 14.

62 Monbiot, *The Guardian*, 23 October 2007, p 31.

63 Monbiot, *The Guardian*, 23 October 2007, p 31.

64 Hayek 1945, p 29.

65 Smith 1900, bk 5, ch 1, pt 3, article 1–2; also bk 4, ch 9; Mill 1891, p 482.

66 See Polsby 1998, p 221.

67 Galbraith 1958, p 44.

68 Galbraith 1996, pp 30 and 76.

69 Galbraith 1996, pp 26–27.

70 Hayek 1976, pp 89–90.

71 *The Daily Telegraph*, 9 May 2007, p 4.

72 Arrow 1993, p 260; see also Rawls 1972, p 6.

73 See *The Daily Telegraph*, 8 May 2007, p 5.

74 Tullock et al 2000, p 16.

75 *The Guardian*, 1 August 2007, p 9; also Scahill 2007.

76 The administration of justice was for Smith the second duty of 'the sovereign': 1900, bk 5, ch 1, pt 2, p 555.

77 Hogan nd, pp 1 and 2.

78 Hogan nd, p 3.

79 See eg *The Daily Telegraph*, 26 September 2007, 'Business', p 1.

80 Treasury White Paper on Banking Supervision, December 1985, cmd 9695.

81 *The Guardian*, 21 September 2007, 'Financial', p 30.

82 *The Guardian*, 24 September 2007, p 10.

83 *The Daily Telegraph*, 21 September 2007, 'Business', p 1.

84 *The Daily Telegraph*, 19 September 2007, 'Business', p 6.

85 US Federal Reserve, Board of Governors, press releases, 7 and 10 March 2008.

86 <www.treasury.gov/press/releases/hp1079.htm>; testimony of Henry Paulson, secretary to the US Treasury Department Office of Public Affairs, before the Senate Banking Committee, 15 July 2008, <banking.senate.gov/public/_files/071508PaulsonHMPTestimony.pdf>.

87 Andrew Clark, *The Guardian Unlimited*, 15 July 2008.

88 *The Guardian*, 16 July 2008, p 23.

89 Spencer 1970, p 373.

90 Hayek 1979, p 44.

91 See eg Downs 1967, p 34.

92 *The Daily Telegraph*, 27 July 2007.

93 *The Guardian*, 10 August 2007, 'Financial', p 31.

94 Hayek 1976, p 28.

95 *The Guardian*, 30 May 2007; *The Daily Telegraph*, 30 May 2007.

96 *The Times*, 4 May 2007, p 37.

97 See eg Mill 1909, bk 5; also the final chapter in his *Principles of Political Economy*.

98 Kirkpatrick et al 2001, p 50.

99 Grimshaw et al 2002, p 496.

100 Kirkpatrick et al 2001, p 60.

101 Kirkpatrick et al 2001, p 60.

102 House of Commons Select Committee on Public Accounts 2007a, pp 3 and 5.

103 National Audit Office 2008b; Edward Leigh, statement by the chairman of the Select Committee on Public Accounts, 17 January 2008.

104 Thompson, in Petrie and Wilson 1999, p 183.

105 Smith 1900, bk 5, ch 1, pt 3.

106 Amongst the myriad government regulators created in Britain after the privatisation of a public utility are: OFTEL, established by the Telecom Act 1984; OFGAS, established by the Gas Act 1986; OFFER, which accompanied the Electricity Act 1989; and OFWAT, following the Water Act 1991.

4 Structural failure: Brtitish transport infrastructure

1 Shaoul 1997, p 500.

2 Shaoul 2004, p 30.

3 Harris and Godward 1997, p 52.

4 Gourvish 1992, pp 374–83.

5 Gourvish 1992, pp 291–94.

6   Department of Transport 1992.
7   Department of Transport 1992, para 19.
8   Department of Transport 1992, para 21.
9   Department of Transport 1992, para 1.
10 Department of Transport 1992, para 3.
11 Crompton and Jupe 2003a, p 620.
12 Giddens 2002, p 59.
13 Wolmar 2005, p 64.
14 Foster 1994, p 3.
15 Murray 2001, p 11.
16 Jupe and Crompton 2006, p 1038.
17 Chadwick 1859, p 381.
18 Jupe and Crompton 2006, p 1039.
19 Veljanovski 1991, p 3.
20 Crompton and Jupe 2003b, p 403.
21 Department of Transport 1992, para 60.
22 Department of Transport 1992, para 19.
23 Foster 1994, p 23.
24 Harris and Godward 1997, p 107.
25 Crompton and Jupe 2003a, p 630.
26 Department of Transport 1992, para 43.
27 Wolmar 2005, p 170.
28 National Audit Office 2000, p 8.
29 Crompton and Jupe 2003b, p 407.
30 Crompton and Jupe 2003a, p 633.
31 Murray 2001, p 57.
32 Wolmar 2005, pp 100–101.
33 Murray 2001, p 57.
34 Department of Transport 1992, para 76.
35 Department of Transport 1992, para 77.
36 Wolmar 2005, p 97.
37 Harman 1993, p 22.
38 House of Commons Select Committee on Transport 1993, para 474 and 475.
39 Murray 2001, p 58.
40 Murray 2001, p 71.
41 House of Commons Select Committee on Transport 1996, para 35.
42 Uff 2000, pp 168, 87 and 145.
43 Cullen 2001, pp 114 and 61.
44 Wolmar 2005, p 150.
45 Wolmar 2005, p 156.
46 Wolmar 2005, p 157.
47 Wolmar 2005, p 182.
48 Health and Safety Executive 2003, p 6.
49 Giddens 1998, pp 99–100.
50 Department of Transport 2004.
51 House of Commons Select Committee on Environment, Transport and

Regional Affairs 2000, paras 25 and 27.
52 House of Commons Select Committee on Environment, Transport and Regional Affairs 2000, para 83.
53 Department of Transport 2000, paras 2 and 5.
54 Department of Transport 2000, paras 32 and 30.
55 Shaoul 2003, p 191.
56 House of Commons Select Committee on Transport, Local Government and the Regions 2002, paras 19 and 23.
57 House of Commons Select Committee on Transport, Local Government and the Regions 2002, para 87.
58 Department of Transport, Local Government and the Regions 2002, para 23.
59 Department of Transport, Local Government and the Regions 2002, paras 26, 30 and 59.
60 House of Commons Select Committee on Transport 2008.
61 *The Observer* 2008, p 4.

5 The privatisation of public profits: utilities

1 Hannah 1979, p 4.
2 Hannah 1979, p 8.
3 Thatcher 1993, p 682.
4 Lawson 1993, p 169.
5 Newbery and Pollitt 1997, p 282.
6 Newbery and Pollitt 1997, p 270.
7 Newbery and Pollitt 1997, pp 271 and 296.
8 Domah and Pollitt 2001, pp 113 and 139.
9 Domah and Pollitt 2001, p 128.
10 Parker and Surrey 1992, p 58.
11 Lawson 1993, p 168.
12 Thatcher 1993, p 377.
13 Kelf-Cohen 1973, pp 25–26.
14 Thatcher 1993, p 344.
15 Milne 2004, p ix.
16 Lawson 1993, pp 160–61.
17 Milne 2004, p 376.
18 Milne 2004, p 388.
19 Bennett, Benyon and Hudson 2000.
20 Press release 2000, p 2.
21 House of Commons Select Committee on Trade and Industry 1998, para 116.
22 House of Commons Select Committee on Trade and Industry 1998, paras 117 and 119.
23 House of Commons Select Committee on Public Accounts 1999, paras 6 and 10.
24 House of Commons Select Committee on Public Accounts 1999, para 6.
25 Hewlett 2005, p 2294.

26 National Audit Office 2008a, p 7.
27 House of Commons Select Committee on Public Accounts 2007c, p 5.
28 House of Commons Select Committee on Public Accounts 2007c, p 6.
29 Dalziel and Lattimore 2004.
30 Rosenberg and Kelsey 1999, p 9.
31 Rosenberg and Kelsey 1999, p 10.
32 Rosenberg and Kelsey 1999, p 7.
33 Rosenberg and Kelsey 1999, p 11.
34 Rennie 1998, p 13.
35 Rennie 1998, pp 15–16.
36 Rennie 1998, pp 16 and 17.
37 Rosenberg and Kelsey 1999, pp 16–20.
38 Weinstein and Hall 2001, pp 4–5.
39 Weinstein and Hall 2001, p 7.
40 McLean and Elkind 2004, p 265.
41 McLean and Elkind 2004, p 266.
42 Weinstein and Hall 2002, p 8.
43 Fox 2003, p 197.
44 McLean and Elkind 2004, p 277.
45 Weinstein and Hall 2001, p 16.
46 Fox 2003, p vii.
47 Salbu, foreword, in Cruver 2003.
48 McLean and Elkind 2004, pp 267–68 and 275.
49 McLean and Elkind 2004, p 269.
50 McLean and Elkind 2004, p 281.
51 Fox 2003, p 220.
52 Federal Energy Regulatory Commission 2000, appendix pp 88–89.
53 McLean and Elkind 2004, p 273.
54 McLean and Elkind 2004, p 274.
55 Federal Energy Regulatory Commission 2005, pp 2–3.
56 Davis, State of State address, 2001, pp 1–2.
57 McLean and Elkind 2004, p 280.
58 Federal Energy Regulatory Commission 2005, p 6.
59 Federal Energy Regulatory Commission 2003, pp ES 1–2.
60 Federal Energy Regulatory Commission 2005, p 10.
61 McLean and Elkind 2004, pp 281–82.
62 Federal Energy Regulatory Commission 2007, p 4.
63 Bushnell 2004, p 8.
64 Erie and Phillips 2000, p 6.
65 Garvin 1932, p 191.
66 Marsh 1994, p 89.
67 Garvin 1932, p 192.
68 Garvin 1932, p 193.
69 Vickers and Yarrow 1988, pp 389–90.
70 Vickers and Yarrow 1988, p 391.
71 Thatcher 1993, p 682.

72 Shaoul 1997, p 491.
73 Shaoul 1998, p 244.
74 House of Commons Select Committee on Public Accounts 1998, para 1.
75 House of Commons Select Committee on Public Accounts 1998, para 3.
76 Letza and Smallman 2001, p 68.
77 OFWAT 2006, p 36.
78 House of Commons Select Committee on Public Accounts 2007b, para 27.
79 House of Commons Select Committee on Public Accounts 2007b, paras 29–30.
80 House of Commons Select Committee on Public Accounts 2007b, paras 29–30.
81 Webster 1992, p 1.
82 Barlow 2002, p 2.
83 McKay 2003, p 287.
84 Chapman and Cuthbertson 1999, p 2.
85 McKay 2003, p 287.
86 McKay 2003, p 288.
87 *Sunday Times*, 20 January 2008, p 2.

6 The price of an ordered society: prisons

1   John Howard Society of Alberta 2002.
2   Biles and Dalton 1999.
3   Cavise 1998, pp 20–23.
4   Bates 1999, pp 22–23.
5   Schombee 1997, p 141.
6   Moyle 1999.
7   This is the highest in the world on a percentage basis: Roth 2004.
8   Robinson 2003.
9   Bender and Casey 2006.
10 Ryan and Ward 1989.
11 Alfred 2005, p 511.
12 Nathan 2006.
13 Nathan 2006.
14 Kennedy 1988.
15 Shichor 1995; Calabrese 1993; Logan 1990.
16 Chan 1999.
17 Harding 1992, pp 1–8.
18 Irish Penal Reform Trust 2005.
19 Bondeson 2005.
20 Associated Press (US), 28 June 2006, 'Two private prisons fined for staffing shortages'.
21 DLA MCG Consulting 2004.
22 BBC ONE 2005, p 57.
23 Focus Consultancy 2007.

24   HM Chief Inspector of Prisons 2006.
25   Nathan 2006.
26   Bales et al 2005, p. 57..
27   Gender 2002.
28   Harding 1998, pp 1–6.
29   Under the Freedom of Information Act, you may be denied right of access to information where there is a legitimate need for confidentiality or where another person's privacy may be invaded. Under the legislation the business affairs of another person or business are often exempt from claims.
30   Armytage 2000; Kirby et al 2000.
31   Australian Broadcasting Corporation, 22 November 2000, 'Government announces inquiry into Woomera allegations', *7:30 Report*, <www.abc.net.au/7.30/stories/s215531.htm>.
32   George 2000.
33   Auditor-General of Victoria 2001, ss 3.4.39 and 3.4.40.
34   Armytage 2000.
35   Contract for the Management of Metropolitan Women's Correctional Centre, 1995, <www.contracts.vic.gov.au/major/49/Prison1.pdf>.
36   Armytage 2000.
37   Armytage 2000, p 37.
38   Shichor 1998, p 89.
39   Maguire et al 1985.
40   De Kretser 2007, p 30.
41   Armytage 2000.
42   Harding 1992.
43   Moyle 1994.
44   Harding 1998, p 80.
45   NSW Public Accounts Committee 2005.
46   Auditor-General of Victoria 1999.
47   Mares 2000.
48   Mares 2000.
49   Private Prison Report International 2003, no 55.
50   ABC, 'Government announces inquiry into Woomera allegations', 2000.
51   Scott 1997; Schoombee 1997.
52   Private Prison Report International 2003, no 56.
53   Private Prison Report International 2003, no 56.
54   Auditor-General of Victoria 2001.
55   Harding 1992.
56   Moyle 1999.
57   Moyle 1999, p 166.
58   Moyle 1999, p 169.
59   Moyle 1999; Harding 1998, pp 1–6, also outlines this possibility.
60   Private Prison Report International 2003, no 55.
61   Russell 1997, pp 7–9.
62   Alfred 2005.
63   Garland 1990, p 12.

64   Ryan and Ward 1989, p 70.
65   See Calabrese 1993; Logan 1990.
66   Stern 1998.
67   Ryan and Ward 1989; Moyle 1999.
68   Smith 1993.
69   Private Prison Report International 2003, no 55.
70   Hallett 2002, p 389.
71   Chomsky 1999.
72   Shichor 1998, p 84.

7 Last thoughts, primary responsibilities

1   Cook, 'In sickness and in health', *Guardian Unlimited*, 2 October 2004.
2   Freedland, *The Guardian*, 23 January 2008, p 29.
3   Wolf, *Financial Times*, 15 January 2008.
4   Freedland, *The Guardian*, 23 January 2008, p 29.
5   Toynbee, *The Guardian,* 9 Novemer 2007, p 33.
6   *The Daily Telegraph*, 18 February 2008, p 4.
7   See Pollock 2004.
8   *The Daily Telegraph,* 12 November 2007, p 1.
9   Himmelfarb 1994, p 73.
10   Davidson and Davidson 1996, p 6.
11   Cruddas and Trickett, *The Guardian*, 30 October 2007, p 30.
12   Cruddas and Trickett, *The Guardian*, 30 October 2007, p 30.
13   Putnam 2000.
14   Home Office 2005.
15   House of Commons Home Affairs Committee 2008.
16   *Report of the Interception of Communications Commissioner for 2006*, HC 252, 2008-9.
17   House of Commons Hansard, 6 February 2008, col 951.
18   Krugman, 2007, p 267.
19   Hayek 1960, p 104.
20   Ryn 1978, p 93; Mill 1952.
21   Crowley 1987, p 99.
22   Tullock 1970, p 127.
23   Hawkins 2008.

REFERENCES

ABC (2000), 'Government announces inquiry into Woomera', *7.30 Report*, <www. abc.net.au/7.30/stories/s215531.htm>

Albo, G (2002), 'Neoliberalism, the state, and the left: a Canadian perspective', *Monthly Review*, 54(1): 51

Alfred, CA Jnr (2005), 'Privatization, prisons, democracy, and human rights: the need to extend the province of administrative law', *Indiana Journal of Global Legal Studies*, 12(2): 511

Arblaster A (1984), *The Rise and Fall of Western Liberalism*, Oxford, Blackwell

—— (1987), *Democracy*, Milton Keynes, Open University Press

Argy, F (1998), *Australia at the Crossroads: Radical Free Market or a Progressive Liberalism*, St Leonards, Allen and Unwin

Armytage, P (2000), *Correctional Services Commissioner's Report on Metropolitan Women's Correctional Centre's Compliance with its Contractual Obligations and Prison Services Agreement*, Melbourne, Victorian Government Printer

Arrow, K (1993), 'Social responsibility and economic efficiency', in Donaldson and Werhane (1993)

Auditor-General of Victoria (1999), *Victoria's Prison System: Community Protection and Prisoner Welfare*, special report no 60, Victoria, Victorian Government Printer

Auditor-General of Victoria (2001), *Report on Ministerial Portfolio's: Part 3 4 Justice*, Victoria, <www.audit.vic.gov.au/reports_mp_psa/mp01just.html>

Aulich, C and J O'Flynn (2007), 'John Howard: the great privatiser?', *Australian Journal of Political Science*, 42(2): 365–81

Bales, WD, DT Ensley, GP Holley and ST Quinn (2005), 'Recidivism of public and private state prison inmates in Florida', *Criminology & Public Policy*, 4(1): 57–82

Barber, B (1983), *The Logic and Limits of Trust*, New Brunswick, Rutgers University Press

Barberis, P (1998), 'The new public management and a new accountability', *Public Administration*, vol 76, Autumn, pp 451–70

Barlow, M (2002), *The Water Privateers*, International Forum on Globalisation, <www.thirdworldtraveler.com>

Bates, E (1999), 'CCA the Sequel', *The Nation*, vol 268, pp 22–23

Bawden, N (2005), *Dear Austen*, London, Aurum Press

Bender, E and L Casey (2006), 'Private prison industry targets its campaign giving', *National Institute on Money In State Politics*, <www.followthemoney.org/Newsroom/index.phtml?r=256>

Bennett, K, H Benyon and R Hudson (2000), *Coalfields Regeneration: Dealing with the Consequences of Industrial Decline*, Abingdon, The Policy Press for Joseph Rowntree Foundation

Bentham, J (1871), *The Theory of Legislation*, London, Trubner

Bentley, M (1996), 'Boundaries in theoretical language about the British state', in E Paul, F Miller and J Paul (1998), *Problems of Market Liberalism*, Cambridge, Cambridge University Press

Biles, D and V Dalton (1999), *Deaths in Private Prisons 1990–99: A Comparative Study*, Australian Institute of Criminology

Bondeson, UV (2005), *Crime and Justice in Scandinavia*, Lossalg

Bowman, GW, S Hakim and P Seidenstat (eds) (1993), *Privatizing Correctional Institutions*, pp 175–91, Transactions Publishers

Bramsted, E and M Melhuish (1978), *Western Liberalism: A History in Documents from Locke to Croce*, London, Longmans

Brereton, M and M Temple (1999), 'The new public service ethos: an ethical environment for governance', *Public Administration*, 77(3): 455–74

Brown, R (1993), 'The contribution of sociology', in Goodin R and Pettit P (1993)

Buchan, J (2007), *Adam Smith and the Pursuit of Perfect Liberty*, London, Profile Books

Buchanan, J (1975), *The Limits of Liberty: Between Anarchy and Leviathan*, Chicago, University of Chicago Press

—— (1986), *Liberty, Market and the State: Political Economy in the 1980s*, Brighton, Harvester Press

Buchanan, J and R Musgrave (2000), *Public Finance and Public Choice: Two Contrasting Visions of the State*, Cambridge (Mass), MIT Press

Buchanan, J and R Wagner (1977), *Democracy in Deficit: The Political Legacy of Lord Keynes*, New York, Academic Press

Bushnell, J (2004), 'California's electricity crisis: a market apart?', *Energy Policy*, 32(9): 1045–52

Butler, E (1985), *Milton Friedman: A Guide to His Economic Thought*, Aldershot, Gower Publishing

Butterfield, F (2004), 'Justice Department report shows trouble in private US jails preceded job fixing Iraq's', *New York Times*, 6 June

Cahill, D and S Beder (2005), 'Regulating the power shift', *Journal of Australian Political Economy*, 55, June, pp 5–22

Calabrese, WH (1993), 'Low cost, high quality, good fit: why not privatization?', in Bowman et al (eds) (1993), pp 175–91

Cavise, LL (1998), 'Prisons for profit', *UNESCO Courier*, June, pp 20–23

Cecil, D (1955), *Melbourne*, London, Reprint Society

Chadwick, E (1859), 'Results of different principles of legislation and administration in Europe; of competition for the field, as compared with the competition within the field of service', *Journal of Royal Statistical Society*, vol 22, pp 381–420

Chan, JBL (1999), 'The privatisation of punishment: a review of the key issues', in P Moyle (1999), pp 37–62

Chapman, R and M Hunt (1987), *Open Government*, London, Routledge

Chapman, R and S Cuthbertson (1999), 'Sydney's water: a suitable case for private treatment?', *Public Policy for the Private Sector*, no 80, April, pp 1–7

Child, J (1998), 'Profit: The concept and its moral features', in Paul et al (1998)

Chomsky, N (1999), *Profit Over People: Neoliberalism and Global Order*, New York, Seven Stories Press

Clarke, T and C Pitelis (1993), *The Political Economy of Privatisation*, London, Routledge

Cohen, N (1999), *Cruel Britannia: Reports on the Sinister and the Preposterous*, London, Verso

Conway, M (ed) (1967), *The Writings of Thomas Paine*, New York: AMS Press

Cook, K and M Levi (eds) (1990), *The Limits of Rationality*, Chicago, University of Chicago Press

Cooper, C and P Williams (2005), 'Independently verified reductionism: prison privatisation in Scotland', *Human Relations*, 58(4): 497–522

Crabtree, D and A Thirlwall (1993), *Keynes and the Role of the State*, Houndsmill, St Martin's Press

Crabtree, L and A Thirlwall (1978), *Keynes and Laissez-faire*, London, Macmillan

Crompton, G and R Jupe (2003a), ' "Such a silly scheme": The privatisation of Britain's railways 1992–2002', *Critical Perspectives on Accounting*, 14(6): 617–45

—— (2003b), ' "A lot of friction at the interfaces": The regulation of Britain's privatised railway system', *Financial Accountability & Management*, 19(4): 397–418

Crowley, F (1973), *Modern Australia in Documents, 1901–1939*, vol 1, Melbourne, Wren Publishing

Crowley, B (1987), *The Self, the Individual, and the Community*, Oxford, Clarendon Press

Cruver, B (2003), *Enron: Anatomy of Greed*, London, Arrow Books

Cullen, L (2001), *The Ladbroke Grove Rail Inquiry Part 1 Report*, Suffolk, HSE Books

D'Entreves, A (1967), *The Notion of the State: An Introduction to Political Theory*, Oxford, Clarendon Press

Dalziel, P and R Lattimore (2004), *The New Zealand Macro-Economy: Striving for Sustainable Growth with Equity*, Melbourne, Oxford University Press

Davidson, G and P Davidson (1996), *Economics for a Civilized Society*, London, Macmillan

Davis, G (2001), 'State of the state address', January 8, <video.dot.ca.gov/state>

Dean, M and B Hindness (1998), *Governing Australia: Studies in Contemporary Rationalities of Government*, Cambridge,, Cambridge University Press

Department of Transport [UK] (1992), *New Opportunities for the Railways: The Privatisation of BR*, London, HMSO

—— (2000), *A Public Private Partnership for National Air Traffic Services Ltd (response)*, cm 4702, London, The Stationery Office Ltd

—— (2004), *The Future of Rail*, cm 6233, London, The Stationery Office Ltd

Department of Transport, Local Government and the Regions [UK] (2002), *The Government's Response to Two Reports on London Underground of the Transport, Local Government and Regional Affairs Committee,* cm 5486, London, The Stationery Office Ltd

Dewey, J (1963), *Liberalism and Social Action*, NY, Capricorn Books

Dilley, R (1992), *Contesting Markets: Analyses of Ideology, Discourse and Practice*, Edinburgh, Edinburgh University Press

DLA MCG Consulting (2004), Privately Managed Custodial Services Liverpool, Prison Service Pay Review Body

Domah, PD and MG Pollitt, (2001), 'The restructuring and privatisation of the regional electricity companies in England and Wales: A social cost-benefit analysis', *Fiscal Studies*, 22(1): 107–46

Donaldson, T and P Werhane (1993), *Ethical Issues in Business: A Philosophical Approach*, New Jersey, Prentice Hall

Dowdle, M (2006), *Public Accountability: Designs, Dilemmas and Experiences*, Cambridge, Cambridge University Press

Downs, A (1967), *Inside Bureaucracy*, Boston, Little, Brown and Company

Drucker, P (1969), *The Age of Discontinuity: Guidelines to Our Changing Society*, London, Heineman

Dunleavy, P (1991), *Democracy, Bureaucracy and Public Choice*, New York, Harvester Wheatsheaf

Dunleavy, P and B O'Leary (1987), *Theories of the State: The Politics of Liberal Democracy*, Basingstoke, Macmillan Education

Emy, H (1998), *States, Markets and the Global dimension*, in Smyth and Cass (1998)

Erie, SP and RV Phillips (2000), 'The state: the unexpected hero in a deregulated electricity market', *Los Angeles Times*, September 10, p 6

Federal Energy Regulatory Commission (2000), *Order Directing Remedies for California Wholesale Electric Markets*, doc 61 294, <www.ferc.gov>

—— (2003), *Final Report on Price Manipulation in Western Markets*, docket no PA02-2-000, <www.ferc.gov>

—— (2005), *The Western Energy Crisis, the Enron Bankruptcy, and FERC's Response*, <www.ferc.gov>

—— (2007), *Initial Decision on Enron Gaming*, docket no EL03-180-000, <www.ferc.gov>

Feigenbaum, H, J Henig and C Hamnett (1999), *Shrinking the State: The Political Underpinnings of Privatization*, Cambridge, Cambridge University Press

Field, F (1998), 'Inside the whale: redrawing the line between state and government',

Political Quarterly, pp 252–57

Finn, D (2006), *The Moral Economy of Markets*, Cambridge, Cambridge University Press

Focus Consultancy (2007), *Report on an Announced Race Relations Audit of The Border and Immigration Agency Detention Estate*, July

Foster, C (1994), *The Economics of Rail Privatisation*, London/Bath, Centre for the Study of Regulated Industries

Fox, L (2003), *Enron: The Rise and Fall*, New Jersey, John Wiley & Sons

Freeman, D (2002), *Testimony on California Energy Crisis*, Subcommittee on Consumer Affairs, Foreign Commerce and Tourism of the Senate Committee on Commerce, Science and Transportation, April 11, <comerce.senate.gov/hearings/>

Friedman, M (1962), *Capitalism and Freedom*, Chicago, University of Chicago Press

Friedman, M and R Friedman (1975), *Capitalism and Freedom*, Chicago, University of Chicago Press

—— (1980), *Free to Choose*, London, Secker and Warburg

Fukuyama, F (1992), 'Capitalism and democracy: the missing link', *Journal of Democracy*, 3(3): 100–110

—— (1995), *Trust: The Social Virtues and the Creation of Prosperity*, London, Hamish Hamilton

—— (2000), *The Great Disruption: Human Nature and the Reconstitution of Social Order*, London, Profile

Gaebler, T (1996), 'Reinventing government', in Weller and Davis (eds) (1996)

Galbraith, JK (1958), *The Affluent Society,* London, Hamish Hamilton

—— (1963), *The Liberal Hour,* Harmondsworth, Penguin Books

—— (1996), *The Good Society: The Humane Agenda,* Boston, Houghton Mifflin Company

Gamble, A (1988), *The Free Economy and the Strong State: The Politics of Thatcherism*, London, Macmillan

Garland, D (1990), *Punishment and Modern Society: A Study in Social Theory*, Oxford, Clarendon Press

Garvin, JL (1932), *The Life of Joseph Chamberlain*, vol 1, London, Macmillan Press Ltd

Gender, E (2002) 'Legitimacy, accountability and private prisons', *Punishment Society*, 4: 282–303

George, A (2000), 'Women prisoners as customers: counting the costs of the privately managed metropolitan women's prisons', <www.aic.gov.au/conferences/womencorrections/george.pdf>

Giddens, A (1998), *The Third Way: The Renewal of Social Democracy*, Cambridge, Polity Press

—— (2000), *The Third Way and Its Critics*, Cambridge, Polity Press

—— (2002), *Where Now for New Labour?*, Cambridge, Polity Press

Girvetz, H (1963), *Democracy and Elitism: Two Essays with Selected Readings*, New York, Scribner

Godwin, W (1971), *Enquiry Concerning Political Justice*, Oxford, Clarendon Press

Goodin, R and P Pettit (1993), *A Companion to Contemporary Political Philosophy*, Oxford, Blackwell

Gourvish, T (1992), *British Rail 1974–1997: From Integration to Privatisation*, Oxford, Oxford University Press

Gray, J (1993), *Beyond the New Right: Markets, Government and the Common Environment*, London, Routledge

Green, S and R Whiting (1996), *The Boundaries of the State in Modern Britain*, Cambridge, Cambridge University Press

Greenaway, J (1996), 'At your service: Victoria's privatisation program', *Eureka Street*, vol 6, January/February, pp 20–24

Grimshaw, D, S Vincent and H Willmott (2002), 'Going privately: partnership and outsourcing in UK public services', *Public Administration*, 80(3): 475–502

Hallett, MA (2002), 'Race, crime and for-profit imprisonment: social disorganization as market opportunity', *Punishment and Society*, 4(3): 369–93

Hannah, L (1979), *Electricity before Nationalisation*, London, Macmillan Press Ltd

Harding, R (1992), 'Private prisons in Australia', Trends and Issues: Australian Institute of Criminology, no 36, pp 1–8

—— (1998), 'Private prisons in Australia: the second phase', Trends and Issues: Australian Institute of Criminology, no 84, pp 1–6

Harman, R (1993), 'Rail privatization: Does it bring new opportunities?', *Public Money & Management*, 13(1): 19–25

Harrington, C and Z Umet Turem (2006), 'Accounting for accountability in neoliberal regulatory regimes', in Dowdle (2006)

Harris, J (1998), 'Political thought and the state', in Paul et al (1998)

Harris, NG and E Godward (1997), *The Privatisation of British Rail*, London, Railway Consultancy Press

Harvey, D (2007), *A Brief History of Neoliberalism*, Oxford, Oxford University Press

Hawkins, N (2008), *Privatization: Reviving the Momentum*, London, Adam Smith Institute

Hayek, F (1945), *The Road to Serfdom*, London, George Rutledge and Sons

—— (1960), *The Constitution of Liberty*, London, Routledge & Kegan Paul,

—— (1969), *Individualism and Economic Order*, Chicago, University of Chicago Press

—— (1973), *Economic Freedom and Representative Government*, London, Institute of Economic Affairs

—— (1976), *Economic Freedom and Representative Government*, London, Institute of Economic Affairs, occasional paper 39

—— (1978), *New Studies in Philosophy, Politics, Economics and the History of Ideas*, London

—— (1979), *New Studies in Philosophy, Politics, Economics and the History of Ideas*, London, Routledge and Kegan Paul

Health and Safety Executive (2003), *Train Derailment at Potters Bar 10 May 2002: Third Progress Report*, London, HSE

Hewlett, JG (2005), 'De-regulated electric power markets and operating nuclear power plants: The case of British Energy', *Energy Policy*, 33(18): 2293–97

Hibou, B (2004), *Privatising the State*, London, Hurst and Co

Himmelfarb, G (1994), 'A de-moralized society: the British/American experience', *Public Interest*, Fall, pp 57–80

HM Chief Inspector of Prisons (2006), *Report on an Announced Inspection of HMP & YOI Doncaster*, <www.inspectorates.homeoffice.gov.uk/hmiprisons/inspect_reports/hmp-yoi-inspections.html/Doncaster.pdf>, viewed 3 Dec 2007

HM Treasury, *PFI: Meeting the Investment Challenge*, July 2003

Hobhouse, LT (1919), *The Metaphysical Theory of the State*, London, Allen and Unwin

Hogan, C (nd), *Privatising Prisons: The Moral Case*, London, Adam Smith Institute

Home Office (2005), *Public Attitudes towards CCTV: Results from the Pre-Intervention Public Attitude Survey Carried out in Areas Implementing CCTV*, Home Office Online Report, 10 May

House of Commons Select Committee on Environment, Transport and Regional Affairs (2000), *The Proposed Public-Private Partnership for National Air Traffic Services Limited*, HC35 of session 1999–2000, London, The Stationery Office Ltd

House of Commons Select Committee on Home Affairs (2008), *A Surveillance Society?*, fifth report of session 2007–08, vol 1, HC58-1, London, the Stationery Office Limited

House of Commons Select Committee on Public Accounts (1998), *The Water Industry in England and Wales: Regulating the Quality of Services to Customers*, HC 483 of Session 1997–1998, London, HMSO

—— (1999), *The Sale of British Energy*, HC242 of session 1998–1999, London, HMSO

—— (2007a), *HM Treasury: Tendering and Benchmarking in PFI*, HC754, 2006–2007, London, The Stationery Office Limited

—— (2007b), *OFWAT: Meeting the Demand for Water*, HC286 of session 2006–2007, London, The Stationery Office Limited

—— (2007c), *The Restructuring of British Energy*, HC 892 of session 2006–2007, London, The Stationery Office Limited

—— (2002), *The Public Sector Ethos*, seventh report for session 2001–2002, vol 1, HC263-I, London, The Stationery Office Limited

House of Commons Select Committee on Trade and Industry (1998), *Energy Policy*, vol 1, HC471-I of Session 1997–1998, London, The Stationery Office Limited

House of Commons Select Committee on Transport (1993), *The Future of the Railways in the light of the Government's White Paper Proposals*, HC 246-I of Session 1992-1993, London, HMSO

——— (1995), *Privatisation of National Air Traffic Services*, vol 1, second report and minutes of proceedings, session 1994–1995, 36-1, London, MHSO

—— (1996), *Railway Safety*, HC 301-I of session 1995–1996, London, HMSO

—— (2008), *The London Underground and the Public-Private Partnership Agreements*, HC45 of session 2007–2008, London, The Stationery Office Limited

House of Commons Select Committee on Transport, Local Government and the Regions (2002), *London Underground*, HC680 of session 2001–2002, London, HMSO

House of Lords Select Committee on Science and Technology (2007), *Personal*

Internet Security, fifth report, 10 August, HL165-I, London, The Stationery Office Limited

Hume, L (1981), *Bentham and Bureaucracy*, Cambridge, Cambridge University Press

Hutton, W (1995), *The State We're In*, London, Jonathan Cape

—— (2002), *The World We're In*, London, Little Brown

HV Evatt Research Centre (1988), *The Capital Funding of Public Enterprise in Australia*, Sydney, Evatt Foundation

Irish Penal Reform Trust (2005), *Inspecting Private Prisons: An Evidence-Based Critique of the Prison Inspector's Call to Introduce Private Prisons in Ireland*, <www.iprt.ie/iprt/1466>, viewed 3 Dec 2007

Jackson, P and C Price (1994), *Privatisation and Regulation: A Review of the Issues*, London, Longman

John Howard Society of Alberta (2002), *Private Prisons*, <www.johnhoward.ab.ca/PUB/respaper/privpr02.htm>, viewed 2 Nov 2007

Johnson, P and C Price (1994), *Privatisation and Regulation: A Review of the Issues*, London, Longman

Johnston, V (1995), 'Caveat emptor: customers v citizens', *Public Manager New Bureaucrat*, 24(3): 11–15

Jones, P (1989), 'The ideal of the neutral state', in Goodin and Reeve (1989)

Jupe, R and G Crompton (2006), ' "A deficient performance": The regulation of the train operating companies in Britain's privatised railway system', *Critical Perspectives on Accounting*, 17(8): 1035–65

Kain, J (1996–97), *International Privatisation Perspectives: 1995–96*, background paper 3, Economics, Commerce and Industrial Relations Group, Department of the Parliamentary Library

Kelf-Cohen, R (1973), *British Nationalisation 1945–1973*, London, Macmillan Press Ltd

Kennedy, JJ (1998), *Final Report of the Commission of Review into Corrective Services in Queensland*, Brisbane, State Government Printer

Kettl, D (1988), *Government by Proxy: (Mis?)Management of Federal Programs*, Washington DC, Congressional Quarterly Press

Keynes, JM (1972), *The Collected Writings*, vol 9, *Essays in Persuasion*, London, Macmillan

Kirby, P, V Roche and B Greaves (2000), *Report on the Independent Investigation into the Management and Operations of Victoria's Private Prisons*, Melbourne, Private Prisons Investigation Panel

Kirkpatrick, I, M Kitcher and R Whipp (2001), 'Out of sight, out of mind: assessing the impact of markets for children's residential care', *Public Administration*, 79(1): 49–71

Klein, N (2007), *The Shock Doctrine: The Rise of Disaster Capitalism*, London, Allen Lane

Kretser, H de (2007) 'Prison litigation: barriers to justice', *Precedent*, 81: 29–33

Krugman, P (2007), *The Conscience of a Liberal: Reclaiming America from the Right*, London, Allen Lane

Lane, J (1996), *Constitutions and Political Theory*, Manchester, Manchester University Press

Laski, H (1925), *A Grammar of Politics,* London, George Allen and Unwin

Latham, M (1998), *Civilising Global Capital: New Thinking for Australian Labor,* Sydney, Allen & Unwin

Lawson, N (1993), *The View From No 11: Memoirs of a Tory Radical,* London, Corgi Books

Letza, S and C Smallman (2001), 'In pure water there is a pleasure begrudged by none: on ownership, accountability and control in a privatized utility', *Critical Perspectives on Accounting,* 12(1): 65–85

Liberal and National Party (1988), *Future Directions: It's Time for Plain Thinking,* Canberra

Locke, J (1884)[1689], *Two Treatises of Civil Government,* London, George Routledge and Sons

Logan, CH (1990), *Private Prisons: Cons and Pros,* Oxford, Oxford University Press

Lucio, M, M Noon and S Jenkins (1997), 'Constructing the market: commercialization and privatization in the Royal Mail', *Public Administration,* 75, Summer, pp 267–82

McKay, J (2003), *Public Private Partnerships in the Australian Water Industry Pre-COAG and Early COAG: Straining the Corporate Model,* Washington, Inter-American Development Bank

McLean, B and P Elkind (2004), *The Smartest Guys in the Room: The Amazing Rise and Scandalous Fall of Enron,* London, Penguin Books

Maesschalck, J (2004), 'The impact of new public management reforms on public servants' ethics: towards a theory', *Public Administration,* 82(2): 465–89

Maguire, M, J Vagg and R Morgan (1985), *Accountability and Prisons: Opening Up a Closed World,* New York, Tavistock Publications

Mandeville, B de (1724), *The Fable of the Bees: or, Private Vices, Publick Benefits,* London, J Tomson

March, J and J Olsen (1995), *Democratic Governance,* New York, Free Press

Mares, P (2000), 'ACM takes advantage of good nature', ABC Radio, 'PM', <www.abc.net.au/pm/s215482.htm>

Marginson, S (1992), *The Free Market: A Study of Hayek, Friedman and Buchanan and their Effects on the Public Good,* Public Sector Research Centre, University of New South Wales

Marsh, PT (1994), *Joseph Chamberlain,* New Haven and London, Yale University Press

Miliband, R (1969), *The State in Capitalist Society,* London, Weidenfeld & Nicolson

Mill, JS (1891), *Principles of Political Economy with Some of their Applications to Social Philosophy,* London, Longmans, Green and co

—— (1909), *Principles of Political Economy,* London, Longmans, Green and Co

—— (1942), *On Liberty,* London, Oxford University Press

—— [1859](1952), *On Liberty,* Great Books of the Western World, vol 43, pp 267–323, Chicago, Encyclopaedia Britannica

Milne, S (2004), *The Enemy Within: The Secret War Against the Miners,* London, Verso

Misztal, B (1996), *Trust in Modern Societies: The Search for the Bases of Social Order,* Cambridge (Mass), Polity Press

Moe, R (1994), 'The "reinventing government" exercise: misinterpreting the problem, misjudging the consequences', *Public Administrative Review,* 54(2): 111–22

Morris, C (2002), *An Essay on the Modern State,* Cambridge, Cambridge University Press

Moyle, P (1999), 'Separating the allocation of punishment from its administration: theoretical and empirical observations', *Current Issues in Criminal Justice,* 11(2,): 153–76

Moyle, P (ed) (1994), *Private Prisons and Police: Recent Trends in Australia,* Sydney, Pluto Press

Murray, A (2001), *Off the Rails,* London, Verso

Murray, M (1997), *An Inner Voice for Public Administration,* Westpart, Connecticut, Praeger

Nathan, S (2006) *Prison Privatisation Report International,* <www.psiru.org/justice/ PPRI7172.htm>, viewed 3 Dec 2007

National Audit Office [UK] (2000), *Ensuring that Railtrack Maintain and Renew the Railway Network,* HC397, London, The Stationery Office Ltd

—— (2008a), *The Nuclear Decommissioning Authority: Taking Forward Decommissioning,* HC 230, session 2007–2008, 30 January, The Stationery Office Ltd

—— (2008b), *Making Changes in Operational PFI Projects,* HC205, session 2007– 2008, 17 January, The Stationery Office Ltd

National Commission of Audit (1996), *Report to the Commonwealth Government,* Canberra, AGPS

Needham, C (2006), 'Customer care and the public service ethos', *Public Administration,* 84(4): 845–60

Nevile, J (1998), 'Economic rationalism: social philosophy masquerading as economic science', in Smyth and Cass (1998)

Newbery, DM and MG Pollitt (1997), 'The restructuring and privatisation of Britain's CEGB: Was it Worth it?', *The Journal of Industrial Economics,* 45(3): 263–303

NSW Auditor General (1994), *Private Participation in the Provision of Public Infrastructure*

—— (2002), *Outsourcing Information Technology in the NSW Public Sector,* performance report

NSW Pubic Accounts Committee (2005), *Value for Money from NSW Correction Centres,* report no 13/53

Nozick, R (1974), *Anarchy, State and Utopia,* Oxford, Basil Blackwell

O'Driscoll, G (1979), *Adam Smith and Modern Political Economy,* Ames, Iowa State University Press

O'Faircheallaigh C, J Warna and P Weller (1999), *Public Sector Management in Australia,* South Yarra, MacMillan

O'Toole, B (2006), *The Ideal of Public Service,* London, Routledge

Office of Water Services [UK] (2006), *Security of Supply, Leakage and Water Efficiency 2005–06 Report,* London, OFWAT

Okun, A (1975), *Equality and Efficiency: The Big Tradeoff,* Brookings Institution

Paine, T [1791] (1969), *The Rights of Man,* Middlesex, Penguin Books

Parker, M and J Surrey (1992), *Unequal Treatment: British Policies for Coal and Nuclear Power 1979–92*, no SR12, Science & Technology Policy Research Unit, University of Sussex

Paul, E, F Miller and J Paul (1998), *Problems of Market Liberalism*, Cambridge, Cambridge University Press

Peters, G (1998), *Comparative Politics: Theory and Methods*, Basingstoke, Macmillan

Petrie, S and K Wilson (1999), 'Towards the disintegration of child welfare services', *Social Policy and Administration*, 33(2): 181–96

Pierson, C (1996), *The Modern State*, London, Routledge

Pollock, A (2004), *NHS Plc: The Privatisation of Our Health Care*, London, Verso

Polsby, D (1998), 'Regulation of foods and drugs and libertarian ideals: perspectives of a fellow-traveller', in Paul et al (1998)

Prior, D, J Stewart and K Walsh (1995), *Citizenship: Rights, Community and Participation*, London, Pitman

Private Prison Report International, *Report No 55*, May 2003, <www.psiru.org/justice/PPRI55.1.htm>

—— , *Report No 56*, June 2003, <www.psiru.org/justice/PPRI56.asp>

Putnam, R (2000), *Bowling Alone: The Collapse and Revival of American Community*, New York, Simon and Schuster

Rawls, J (1972), *A Theory of Justice*, London, Oxford University Press

—— (1995), 'Distributive justice' in Ryan (1995)

Rennie, H (1998), *A Report of the Ministerial Inquiry into the Auckland Power Supply Failure*, Wellington, Ministry of Commerce of New Zealand

Reserve Bank of Australia (1997), 'Privatisation in Australia', *Reserve Bank of Australia Bulletin*, December

Robinson, P (2003), 'Government accountability and performance measurement', *Critical Perspectives on Accounting*, vol 14, pp 171–86

Rosenber, N (1979), 'Adam Smith and laissez-faire revisited', in O'Driscoll (1979)

Rosenberg, B and J Kelsey (1999), 'The privatisation of New Zealand's electricity services', paper to The Impact of Privatization of the Electricity Sector at the Global Level, 20–27 September, Mexico City

Roth, L (2004) 'Privatisation of prisons: background paper 3/2004', Parliament of NSW, Sydney

Rousseau, J-J (1930), *The Social Contract and Discourses*, Introduction by CDH Cole, London, JM Dent

Russell, S (1997), 'Private prisons for private profit', *Alternative Law Journal*, 22(1): 7–9

Ryan, A (1993), 'Liberalism', in Goodin and Pettit (1993)

—— (1995), *Justice*, Oxford, Oxford University Press

Ryan, M and T Ward (1989), *Privatization and the Penal System: The American Experience and the Debate in Britain*, London, Open University Press

Ryn, C (1978), *Democracy and the Ethical Life: A Philosophy of Politics and Community*, Baton Rouge, Louisiana State University Press

Sandel, M (1996), *Democracy's Discontent*, Cambridge (Mass), Harvard University Press

Saul, J (1993), *Voltaire's Bastards: The Dictatorship of Reason in the West*, Toronto, Penguin Books

Savas, E (1982), *Privatizing the Public Sector: How to Shrink Government*, Chatham, Chatham House Publishers

Scahill, J (2007), *Blackwater: The Rise of the Worlds Most Powerful Mercenary Army*, Serpent's Tail

Schoombee, H (1997), 'Privatisation and contracting out: Where are we going?', in McMillan (1997), pp 135–51

Shaoul, J (1997), 'A critical financial analysis of the performance of privatised industries: the case of the water industry in England and Wales', *Critical Perspectives on Accounting*, 8(5): 479–505

—— (1998), 'Critical financial analysis and accounting for stakeholders', *Critical Perspectives on Accounting*, 9(2): 235–49

—— (2003), 'A financial analysis of the National Air Traffic Services PPP', *Public Money & Management*, 23(3): 185–94

—— (2004), '*Railpolitik*: the financial realities of operating Britain's national railways', *Public Money & Management*, 24(1): 27–36

Shichor, D (1995), *Punishment for Profit: Private Prisons/Public Concerns*, New York, SAGE Publications

—— (1998), 'Private prisons in perspective: some conceptual issues', *The Howard Journal*, 37(1): 82–100

Skidelsky, R (2003), *John Maynard Keynes 1883–1946*, London, Pan Books

Smith, A (1900) [1776], *An Inquiry into the Nature and Causes of the Wealth of Nations*, London, George Rutledge and Son

—— (1966) [1759], *The Theory of Moral Sentiments*, New York, Augustus M Kelley

Smith, M (1998), 'Reconceptualizing the British state: theoretical and empirical challenges to central government', *Public Administration*, vol 76, Spring, pp 45–72

Smith, P (1993), 'Private prisons: profits of crime', *Covert Action Quarterly*, <www.mediafilter.org/MFF/prison.html>

Smyth, P and B Cass (1998), *Contesting the Australian Way*, Cambridge, Cambridge University Press

Spencer, H (1969), *Man Versus the State,* Harmondsworth, Penguin

—— (1970), *Social Statics*, Gregg

State Government of Victoria (2000), *Audit Review of Government Contracts: Contracting, Privatisation, Probity and Disclosure in Victoria 1992–1999*, Melbourne, Victorian Government Publisher

Steinberger, P (2004), *The Idea of the State,* Cambridge, Cambridge University Press

Stern, V (1998), *A Sin Against the Future: Imprisonment in the World*, Boston, Northeastern University Press

Stretton, H and L Orchard (1994), *Public Goods, Public Enterprise, Public Choice: Theoretical Foundations of the Contemporary Attack on Government*, London, Macmillan

Thatcher, M (1993), *The Downing Street Years*, New York, HarperCollins Publishers

Thompson, G (1990), *The Political Economy of the New Right*, London, Printer Publishers

in government we trust

Toynbee, P (2008), 'The new politics of welfare is the same old sabre-rattling', *The Guardian*, 29 January, p 31

Tullock, G (1970), *Private Wants, Public Means: An Economic Analysis of the Desirable Scope of Government*, New York, Basic Books

Tullock, G, A Seldon and G Grady (2000), *Government, Whose Obedient Servant?: A Primer in Public Choice*, London, Institute of Economic Affairs

Tully, J (1993), *An Approach to Political Philosophy: Locke in Context*, Cambridge, Cambridge University Press

Uff, J (2000), *The Southall Rail Accident Report*, Suffolk, HSE Books

UNICEF (2007), *The State of the World's Children 2007*

UNISON (2001), *Public Services, Private Finance: Affordability, Accountability and the Two-Tier Workforce*, London

Veljanovski, C (1988), *Selling the State: Privatisation in Britain*, London, Weidenfeld and Nicholson

—— (1991), 'The regulation game', in Veljanovski (1991), pp 3-28

Veljanovski, C (ed) (1991), *Regulators and the Market: An Assessment of the Growth of Regulation in the UK*, London, Institute of Economic Affairs

Vickers, J and G Yarrow (1988), *Privatization: An Economic Analysis*, London and Cambridge (Mass), MIT Press

Vincent, A (1994), *Theories of the State*, Oxford, Blackwell Publishers

Vincent, D (1998), *The Culture of Secrecy: Britain 1832–1998*, Oxford, Oxford University Press

Victorian Auditor-General's Office (1999), *Victoria's Government Finances 1998–99*, December

Victorian Public Accounts and Estimates Committee (2003), *Report on the Evidence Obtained Overseas in Connection with the Inquiry into Private Sector Investment in Public Infrastructure*, November

—— (2006), *Report on Private Investment in Public Infrastructure*, 71st report to Parliament, October, Government Printer for the State of Victoria

Walsh, K (1995), *Public Services and Market Mechanisms: Competition, Contracting and the New Public Management*, London, Macmillan Press

Weber, M (1947), *The Theory of Social and Economic Organisation*, New York, Free Press

Webster, RJ (1992), 'Water treatment plant tenders', September 23, New South Wales Parliament Hansard

Weinstein, S and D Hall (2001), *The California Electricity Crisis: Overview and International Lessons*, Public Services International Research Unit, London, University of Greenwich

Weller, P and G Davis (1996), *New Ideas, Better Government*, Sydney, Allen & Unwin

West, E (1979), 'Adam Smith's economics of politics', in O'Driscoll (1979)

Whitfield, D (1992), *The Welfare State: Privatisation, Deregulation, Commercialisation of Public Services ~ Alternative Strategies of the 1990s*, London, Pluto Press

Wolmar, C (2005), *On the Wrong Line*, London, Aurum Press

Zafirovski, M (2001), 'Administration and society: beyond public choice', *Public Administration*, 79(3): 665–88.

INDEX